Nicia,

Thanks for the
kindness
and all the
smiles of
the night.

Always,

BEFORE THE PICTURE FADES

The True Story of Love, Legacy and Unforeseen Triumph

STEPHEN W. HOAG, Ph.D.

Inspiring Voices

Inspiring Voices books may be ordered through booksellers or by contacting:

Inspiring Voices
1663 Liberty Drive
Bloomington, IN 47403
www.inspiringvoices.com
844-686-9605

Because of the dynamic nature of the Internet, any web addresses or links contained in this book may have changed since publication and may no longer be valid. The views expressed in this work are solely those of the author and do not necessarily reflect the views of the publisher, and the publisher hereby disclaims any responsibility for them.

Any people depicted in stock imagery provided by Getty Images are models, and such images are being used for illustrative purposes only. Certain stock imagery © Getty Images.

ISBN: 978-1-4624-1333-1 (sc)
ISBN: 978-1-4624-1334-8 (hc)
ISBN: 978-1-4624-1335-5 (e)

Library of Congress Control Number: 2021911277

Print information available on the last page.

Inspiring Voices rev. date: 06/30/2021

Contents

Acknowledgements

The two and a half years of writing "BEFORE THE PICTURE FADES ... The True Tale of Love, Legacy and Unforeseen Triumph" is the confluence of a lifetime of observations and influences and learning moments. To the many incredible people I admired and tried in vain to emulate on the athletic field as a child, may these pages do justice to all you are in character, talent, leadership, and perseverance.

The hundreds of group and individual interviews conducted for this book have provided endless anecdotes and sought-after facts that provided a richness of context for this historical story that has application to schools and school districts across the country.

My sincere appreciation to those who spent so many hours with me dramatically articulating the events depicted in this book, including, but not limited to, Rick Angelone, David Biega, Andy Borelli, John Carvalho, Bobby Corazinni, Cozette Corbett, Jill Dechello, Joseph DeDomenico, Papo Diaz, Charles DiCenzo, Regal Dorsey, Thomas Falcigno, Al Ferreira, John Gawlak, Tarn Granucci, Mel Horowitz. John Hrehowsik, Jim Karl, Tony Marotta, John Namnoum, Michael Nesti, Barry O'Brien, Cole Proctor, Mike Puig, William Quigley, Robert Riggio, Ralph Riley, Frederick Schipke, Jim Silvestri, John Skubel, Brian Stranieri, Fran Stupakevich, Robert Szymaszek, Henry Wachtelhausen, Thomas Wachtelhausen, and Don Warzocha.

For each member of the 1985 Lyman Hall High School football team who combined to create a miracle, you have my love and most profound appreciation.

The number of people who unknowingly touched this piece is endless. To the Wallingford citizenry, Lyman Hall High

School alumni, teachers, coaches, and family who supported and encouraged the research necessary to complete this writing from concept to the fullest manifestation of its intended purpose, you have my endless appreciation.

Special thanks to the tremendously talented Tony Falcone for creating the amazing cover image, Guymark Studios for the photography, and the forever inspiration, "The ONE," the magnificent Denise.

Prologue

In life, that period between birth and death, there are moments where the untainted daydream, so preposterous and implausible, may only be spoken in a whisper. Otherwise, it will vanish like a puff of smoke upon the wind.

This historical tale describes a period from the birth of a secondary school in 1916 through the subsequent 70 years when the decisions of men of good character and educational talent did all that was possible to reach one outcome but henceforth created the circumstances for the most miraculous antithetical moment in school history.

"Before the Picture Fades" is written from the eyes of, within the heart of, and sculptured by the thoughts of someone who along ago embraced Lyman Hall High School with a love usually reserved for singular persons in one's life or institutions worthy of limitless devotion.

"Before the Picture Fades" is the factual story of Lyman Hall High School athletics and the school and community's commitment to develop and sustain annual championship-level basketball teams. With the best of initial intentions, basketball became all that school administrators, faculty, and students could have envisioned. However, with the clearing of obstacles and impediments to that end, the sport of football was diminished, discontinued, and all but vanished from the landscape of high school athletic traditionalism.

After seven decades of gradual gridiron torment, almost at the very moment in time when Lyman Hall High School almost lost its coach, with the fewest number of football aspirants in school records, a miraculous season unfolded. In keeping with all that had transpired to football over VII decennium, the 1985 football season brimmed with challenges that could never have been foreseen.

As many legends of LHHS lore have passed from this life and members of the 1985 football team have also died, it was incumbent to tell this tale of trial and triumph before no one is left to paint the story that began in 1916.

This narrative's facts emanate from historical reportage, including documents, letters, scrapbooks, yearbooks, newspaper articles, and documented conversations and discourse, extrapolated from over 200 interviews of varying numbers of participants and personal chronicle (diary) entries that date back to 1962.

For expedience, the following acronyms and abbreviations are used throughout the book, Lyman Hall High School (LHHS), Wallingford Junior Football League (WJFL), Housatonic League (Housy), and Connecticut Interscholastic Athletic Conference (C.I.A.C.).

Chapter 1

Painting the Background of Dreams

In many respects, this tale is a delicate painting with its final picture a construct of pigment, color affixed to a firm matrix. Although the hues and shades of images are not applied with the traditional brush, sponge, or knives, the final work is no less a work of art.

The artists of this portrait are many, some who spread deep washes of historical context to the mosaic of what this picture would eventually become, while others applied dramatic droplets of love and humor.

In the metaphorical painting of the 1985 football season, it is easy to wax poetic, leading the painter to use a technique of the Renaissance that the Italians called "sfumato," suggesting an atmospheric or dreamy-like depiction. When the final painting was uncovered, it was hard to believe any of it really happened, but it did.

From the first stroke of the brush to the last, each touch combined to form a torrential amalgamation of unrivaled drama. Indeed, the telling of this legend, with all of its ruminative storylines, must be told before the colors fade.

The genesis of this tale begins with my wind-spun thoughts as a young boy, forever inquisitive, "too dammed curious," as my Aunt Fan once put it. I recall asking questions about most any topic to my neighborhood friends, their parents, my teachers, and total strangers. This annoyed my mother to no end. The only person I would never pose a question to was my father, an imposing man with a quick temper and a scary glare.

My earliest recollections of life are not of school-related experiences or shared holidays with family that didn't happen very often anyway. Rather, they are of a very young boy's need for heroic figures who might fill his thoughts in the alone moments. Whether it was at bedtime, just before sleep set in, walking alone to and from elementary school, or just gazing up into the sky while perched in an apple tree or swinging on a neighbor's swing ... the restless thoughts of boyhood would not be denied.

Raised on a small, cul-de-sac of 10 houses, Backes Court was a non-descript little street of no more than a few hundred yards long. The homes were essentially cookie-cutter row homes of post-World War II vintage. However, Backes Court had one redeeming feature. It overlooked Doolittle Park, a sea of bright green grass. From my backyard, I could see the fringe of the park, and it filled my imagination.

In August of 1956, I took my first solitary *sneak-away* to Doolittle, although I knew not the name of that large field at the time. It was in the simple boredom of the backyard; I dared to break out, not asking permission from my mother, ... just a blatant wandering off. Walking through the nearby woods that served as the edge of our street, I was curious about the sound of muffled voices and some noises that were foreign to me. They seemed to call to me to come hither.

Once through the few hundred yards of trees, tall grass, and a winding water brook, I stood at the precipice of a large clearing where the grass was a brilliant green. Men were running about in a large open field, but who they were and what made them run was confusing to the little red-haired boy with freckles galore. Looking about, all at once, I was scared. I had found a whole new world, with strange structures and again, big people running around, clapping hands, speaking loudly. The countless questions that filled my head made me want to go further onto the green grass. But what was this place? Who were these larger men? Why were they here? Why did they wear the same clothing? All at once, all the little boy queries without answers made me afraid, and I ran back through the wooded area towards my backyard.

Stepping through the edge of the woods, I saw my mother seated on the back porch with one of our neighbors. They were enjoying a cup of tea and an animated conversation, so I approached our backyard in relative stealth. Upon reaching their seated place at the back stoop, mom gave me a quick little smile but did not ask me where I had been. I opened the screen door and headed for my bedroom, where I sat on the edge of my bed, looked out the window, and remembered all that I had seen and heard. After that jaunt through the woods, I wanted to ask my mother so many questions about what I had discovered, but that would probably have revealed a transgression in my wandering off, so even at that young age, I learned the protective benefits of keeping things to myself. When mom went into the house to answer the phone, I quickly asked our neighbor, seated on the porch, "What is that big yard on the other side of the woods"? Humoring my insatiable inquisitory manner, she told me that it was called DOOLITTLE PARK.

All that evening, my thoughts centered on all that I had seen and heard. I knew I had to learn more about Doolittle Park, and consequently, I became preoccupied with this wonderland that I had found.

From this moment on, nary a day passed, regardless of season or day of the week that I didn't find my way to Doolittle Park. For the remainder of August ... as soon as my father left for work, I would dress quickly, forgo the bowled breakfast of milk and boxed cereal, and find my way to Doolittle Park. I remember one of the first times I found the courage to walk across its greenery boldly. In the early morning, with the dampness of dew on the ground, there were no voices or people playing games, just two men working near a circular white building.

I wanted to run on the grass of the field as those big men did when first I found Doolittle. As I stepped out onto the grass, there was a softness to the ground below my feet, like walking on my bed. The cushiony feel of the grass under my shoes made me feel I could bounce up and down. Taking some rapid steps onto the emerald surface, I began to run with no destination in mind, feeling as though I might fly if I flapped my arms. Looking about, I realized I was all alone in this place, a feeling I would often experience in my life, sometimes coupled with deep longing and other times with great reflection and sentiment.

When the greenery and bloom of the summer days were replaced with a turning to the earth tone colors of autumn, children returned for another school year. Simpson School was my elementary school, just a walk along Simpson Avenue and a turn to the right onto East Center Street. My mother walked with me that first day of school, but I was walking alone to and from school before the week's end. Additionally, I walked home for lunch, a quick peanut butter sandwich, and then back to Simpson School. Along the sidewalks of Simpson Avenue, my occasional glances through the houses on one side (the west side of the street) afforded me new views of Doolittle Park as I saw a small wooden bridge over the stream that ran through the park.

In those first few days of September, I tried to sneak away to Doolittle after coming home from school, but mom required me to change out of my school clothes and join her in the living room. There she provided rather demanding training in tap dancing and singing. As mom was raised in the theatre, she felt compelled to make her son a performer of sorts. She never gave up on that dream for me, right up to her death. By the time those musical demands had ended, dad was coming home from work from American Cyanamid, pulling up in the driveway in his '53 light blue Chevy with the white roof. That ended any chance of escape as dad demanded that supper be served to him by 6:00 pm.

I missed my daily jaunts to Doolittle Park, and even at my young age, I was devising a plot to avoid the musical instruction and get back to Doolittle. Lying in bed at night, I would daydream about what I would find at my park since the summer ended.

I decided to hatch a little plot. The plan was schoolboy simple enough. As I walked home after the end of my school day, I would <u>not</u> go directly home. Instead, about halfway down Simpson Avenue, I would turn down the little hill that I learned was Wall Street. There I saw the other side of Doolittle Park.

Making my way through the grassy area where there were swings and a teeter-totter, I spotted a white cement block building that I had seen from the clearing near Backes Court. Leaping over the small brook that twisted through the park, I ran to the building, hearing voices.

Doolittle Park looked so different from this vantage point. I was instantly deluged with questions. Every image that reached my eyes, I wanted to run to and discover its purpose and meaning. In those first moments, drinking in all that I saw and heard, I wished I had a companion to share all that I was seeing. I wondered if I was the only boy ever to behold all this wonderment. If I ever had been curious before in my young life, my curiosity was now overflowing.

Two large white wood structures in the shape of the letter "H" had been erected since summertime. They were facing each other with ample space in between. The open area between the "H's" seemed to be separated by white lines that went all the way down the open space.

Most eye-catching before me were these big men, wearing black things, like hats, covering their heads. Each man was wearing a white shirt with stripes on their sleeves, but the most compelling of all was that each person had a number on the front and back of his shirt. As I ran to the place where all the numbered men gathered together, one of them brushed by me from behind and knocked me over. He wore #30 and helped me up, asking me, "Are you, all right kid"? In the coming days and weeks, I would learn that his name was Ted. Looking at me through the front of his head covering, I drew back in fear. He ran over to the other men with numbers on their shirts.

I cautiously walked behind everyone, trying not to be noticed. After all, there were no other kids my age there, just these men with numbers with two older men speaking loudly to them. I kept thinking, "Who were these men? What were they doing"?

Just then, the older man who was wearing pants that ended at the knee with a black jacket with tan leather sleeves began to yell something, with the fervor of our neighbor Mr. Dunhill who would scream at me to "Get the hell out of his yard."

With that roar in words that I did not understand, the men with numbers moved. One group of them was standing shoulder to shoulder facing one way, and another group was lined up right in front of them like they were about to dance together. The older man barked out something, and the two groups of men instantly bent over. Each man immediately placed one hand on the ground. That looked **really** uncomfortable to me. "What could they be doing"?

The older man standing behind the two groups barked out some inaudible word that sounded like a loud cough, and the two groups smashed into each other. There was some grunting with a crackling sound as one man gave a weird-looking ball to another man who ran right into the colliding men. One of the extra men who was not banging into the others walked back to me and suggested I get a little farther away. He wore #10. He was smaller than the other men, and as I was apt to do, I asked him, "What was going on"?

He explained that this was *football* practice and seemed surprised that I didn't know anything about football. He kept his eyes on what was going on with the men who kept banging into each other while speaking quietly to me. I asked him a question, maybe two, about this game, called football, but he was trying to pay attention to the action and didn't answer me. Just then, the old man who was in charge yelled out, "Gannon, get in there at right halfback." Hmmm, I just learned that #10 was a man named Gannon, and he was about to do something called "right halfback."

Standing in one spot for some measure of time, almost mesmerized by the action before me, the sunshine was fading away. Whatever time it was, and I had no way of knowing, I felt

I had better find my way home before I got into real trouble. Making my way down the long field with the white stripes, I walked under the wooden thing, shaped like the letter "H." Then through the tall grass and trees whose leaves were of many colors and finally taking careful steps on the stones sticking up in the brook, I climbed the little wooded hill to the edge of Backes Court. Running through the backyards of the Lee and Williams families, I made it to the screen door before dad got home.

Entering our tiny red house into the kitchen, mom was at the oven making supper and listening to the Philco, our radio. We didn't own a television as yet. She didn't say a word to me then, but later that night, while saying goodnight to my brother and me, she sat on the corner of my bed and asked where I had been after school. I youthfully said, "I saw some numbers and some game called football."

Mom looked puzzled and asked, "You didn't come home from school until five o'clock, because you saw some **numbers**"?

"Yes," I self-assuredly responded, "Oh ... and I saw a right halfback too".

Mom quietly quizzed further, "So tell me about where you were and what you saw"?

I felt good about being able to share all I had experienced, even if it might have consequences. I described what I saw at Doolittle Park. I explained that there was a group of large men. They all had a weird smell and were scary with hard black coverings on their heads. Each of them had big shoulders that looked lumpy to me. Getting excited with this opportunity to tell my story, I carried on by explaining that they all wore tan pants with laces in front, but their pants only went to their knees.

Chapter 2

Beginning of a Lifetime Love

Mom smiled, almost laughing, and explained that "those men" were probably football players, and their outfits were called uniforms. Said mom, "Football players wear helmets and pads under the shirts, all to protect them from getting hurt. Those football players are probably from Lyman Hall High School".

That was the first time I ever heard the two words, "Lyman Hall."

She told me that the Lyman Hall team played football against other high schools on Saturdays, sometimes at Doolittle and sometimes at the other schools. I was fascinated by all this new information, and I couldn't wait to return to Doolittle.

Mom warned me not to make a habit of being late coming home from school, but ... she didn't say not to go to Doolittle Park to see the football players with helmets. After she turned out the lights, I remember laying there staring at the ceiling, thinking of what mom called a "football TEAM."

The next day sitting on the steps in front of Simpson School, waiting for the teachers to open the front door (school rules required all students to wait on the stairs), I told a girl sitting next to me about football at Doolittle Park. I probably sounded silly to her or anyone else who heard me, but those "football players" in their uniforms were all-consuming throughout the school day.

From that day forward, I couldn't wait for my teacher to say the words, "Line up for dismissal." Standing in line before the large wooden door with all the other pupils (our teachers of that time, called us pupils), the wait seemed interminable until that school's bell rang throughout Simpson School. As soon as I reached the door, I rapidly walked to the school's front door, down the cement stairs, then a sprint in my leather oxford shoes to Doolittle Park. There, out of breath, I leaped the creek's stones to the field with the white stripes and "H's."

Each afternoon, Monday through Friday, Doolittle Park was my destination after school, and the Lyman Hall football team the recipient of my full attention. I memorized every number, listening closely for the players' names, spoken by two older men who were in charge.

I was tiny and easily escaped everyone's notice except the older man who was in charge, and he was called "coach" by the players. As the weeks passed, I found out his name was "Mr. Schipke," although I had difficulty pronouncing that name at first. He often shot a smile my way and told me to move back or get behind him. He did a whole lot of yelling at the players, but he was nice to me. With each passing day, I was more and more fascinated by the goings-on and came to view some of the players with great admiration. Almost from the beginning, I found myself wanting to wear a numbered shirt and a black helmet.

Eavesdropping on player conversations, I often got bumped around or knocked over, but I kept going back for more, sticking my face where it didn't belong. I learned that a "huddle" is where the players gathered together in a little group, and one player would call "a play." I was confused at first because I thought the number someone called out as a play in the huddle meant the number of the player who would get the ball. I had so much to learn about this game of football.

As I was eager to be around the Lyman Hall players and their huddles, I absorbed some things quickly, such as the titles for some players such as fullback, quarterback, and left and right halfbacks. How they all fit together was a puzzlement. In the huddle, one player would say, "34 on two," or "36 on one". Usually, the person who called the plays was known as the quarterback, but sometimes, Mr. Schipke would call the play out from behind the huddle. Number 50 was in the middle of the line of football players with one hand down on the ground. He (#50) would touch the ball first by quickly pushing the ball back between his legs to the quarterback who gave the ball to someone else. I watched closely every day, but I was confused. What each player did and why they did it made me want to raise my hand as we did in school when we had a question (or wanted to go to the boys' room). Confusing or not, I was becoming enthralled with football and began looking forward to a time when I could play football.

As a young boy, I thought "games" were supposed to be fun. People playing a game should smile, laugh and be happy. But, this game, called football, I didn't see many of the players smiling, and no one laughed, except those who were standing around waiting for a turn at practice. Everything and everybody was so serious, but I couldn't get enough of it.

I always stayed at the practices until it started to get dark. I didn't want to miss anything. I picked up one of the footballs that weren't being played with, looking at it in my hands. I couldn't hold it with one hand, let alone throw it as some players did as my hand was too small. When one of the players practiced kicking the ball, I sometimes went and got the ball because the player kicking it didn't kick it to the other players that were supposed to catch it. It felt special to be asked to do something for one of the players or the coach.

Practices were so much fun for me. I could not understand why the players didn't seem to be having any fun. I thought that maybe it was because they had to wear the hard black helmet and those half-pants. The other thing about their clothes that was strange to me was they all wore black boots with thick white nails on the bottom. I couldn't figure that out at all, but they all wore the boots, and sometimes they would reach under their boots and pull the mud and grass from the nails. There was so much to know about football. I loved going to the practices, but I hadn't seen anything that looked like a "game," at least not yet.

Chapter 3

My First Football Game

Saturday and Sunday were a time when dad was usually home, and he always had me doing work around the house, washing his car, scrubbing the kitchen floor, or raking after he cut the grass; so, I could not escape to Doolittle Park. Then one Saturday in October, Dad had to work overtime at the factory. He wasn't happy about it, but he wasn't the happiest of dads anyway. On the other hand, I was overjoyed.

As soon as he left the driveway, I ran to Doolittle. Coming out from the clearing, I saw before me the big men whom I thought were Lyman Hall's players. I wasn't sure because they were in blue shirts with white stripes on the sleeves and white numbers. They looked so different, but the black helmets made me certain that this was my Lyman Hall team. When they practiced, they were always in white shirts with blue, or maybe it was black numbers. However, what was most eye-catching at first sight was that there was another team on the field with red helmets, white shirts, and red numbers. I ran as fast as I could to the closest "H." People were standing all around the field, speaking loudly, and they all looked happy.

As it turned out, this would be the first football game I ever saw. I couldn't go on the field as I did at the practices, so I stood on the side of the field where the Lyman Hall football players were all standing. I learned that that location on the field was called a "sideline" when Mr. Schipke harshly told #19 to "get back on the sideline."

I didn't understand too much about the game, but one

of the Lyman Hall fellas on the team explained to me at a practice that to win the game, you had to score touchdowns. This meant running past the white line where the big "H" was standing.

For personal accuracy, I must add that during a practice, Mr. Schipke had the team line up in front of the "H" he called a "goalpost," but I thought he said "**GOLD**post." Some third-graders made fun of me during recess one day when they heard me say "goldpost" in a conversation with a classmate. I defended my use of the term, convinced that Mr. Schipke said gold post, not goalpost. To this day, gold post still seems like a better name to me.

That first game was a fantastic memory for me. Unfortunately, the team with the red helmets were making touchdowns, while Lyman Hall was only able to run for one touchdown near the end of the game. I never stood in one place too long, moving up and down the Lyman Hall sideline, getting as close to the players on the field as possible.

Right behind the Lyman Hall sideline was a bunch of girls whom all wore short blue skirts and white shoes. They were acting happy all through the game, yelling the same words together. Even when the other team scored, they kept being very happy. I looked back over my shoulder at the cheerleaders quite a bit during the game, and I noticed many of the Lyman Hall players were looking at them as well. It was just another puzzling thing about football.

Try as they might, Lyman Hall couldn't get to the goalpost more than once. The game looked much different from the afternoon practices I had watched. The "red-helmet" team looked to be very angry as they pushed my blue-shirted Lyman Hall team backward and often to the ground. I found myself cheering like those girls who were jumping up and down with the white shoes. Suddenly, the game ended, and there was quiet. My Lyman Hall team had lost. Each team went their separate ways, and I found myself walking alone aimlessly around the field that only minutes before was the constant banging and grunting of the game. All was so quiet now as I walked around the mushy playing field.

As I made my way home, mom was at the cellar door, picking up little stones from the garden she kept at the back of the house. She asked me to sit down, and we talked. I told her all about the football game I had seen. I felt like crying, mom knew it, but I didn't understand why. Dad didn't permit crying in our house, so the urge to cry was somewhat foreign to me. She explained that it was all right to cry once in a while; just don't let your father see you. Mom went on to explain that sometimes watching your team lose makes you feel that way because you feel bad for them. It didn't make much sense to me.

She asked me about all that I had seen. I told her about the team with the red helmets and how they were meanly ramming into the Lyman Hall players. Mom then told me that when she was a girl at Fitchburg High School in Massachusetts, she never missed a football game, and she felt sad too when they lost to Leominster. I went on to describe the girls with the white shoes, and mom told me that they were called cheerleaders. She asked me, "were they pretty"? Feeling a little awkward with that question, I responded with a typical exit line, "...I don't know". Mom then explained that our babysitter, Gail, who comes over to watch my brother and me from time to time, had been a cheerleader.

Mom told me to go clean off my shoes and wash my hands before supper. I was glad that she let me tell her all about the football game, but I was still filled with thoughts of the game and trying to figure out why my Lyman Hall players couldn't have put the ball past the "H" for some touchdowns. Although thoroughly joyful and mesmerized by the week of going to football practices and seeing the men with numbers, the uncomfortable feeling of watching Lyman Hall lose made me so sad (and always would).

As the weeks passed and the chill became cold, I continued my daily vigil to Doolittle Park in the fall of 1956 until the practices and games were no more. My Lyman Hall team did not win a game that year, which confused me because I didn't know how winning felt. The discomfort of losing did not diminish my adoration for the football players of Lyman Hall.

Following a summer of racing to see the games of the

Wallingford Twilight League at Doolittle Park in 1957, my excitement for the return of the Lyman Hall football team to my park was uncontrollable.

What I did not know, but discovered some many weeks later, during the summer, was that I would never see my Lyman Hall football team at Doolittle Park ever again. Watching a Wallingford Twilight League baseball game, behind one of the team benches, I heard two baseball players talking about the new football field at the new Lyman Hall High School.

The shock brought forth instant hurt and sadness that I fought to hold back. Instantly, I ran all the way home, choosing not to enter my house. Instead, I crossed Ward Street Extension and climbed the crabapple tree in front of the Backes factory. There I sat with my back to my house and sobbed uncontrollably. Nothing had ever hurt so much. It was my first real heartbreak, but it would not be the last time Lyman Hall would break my heart.

Throughout the ages, the wisest of people have tried to define "love." In current times, the word is thrown about like confetti on New Year's Eve for all types of circumstances and in an endless variety of human relationships. When one sifts it all down, one might come to a handful of extrapolated truisms. When one loves, it seems impossible to live without that person or entity. The desire to love another, life activity or thing, requires the individual who loves to learn all that there is to learn about the object of that love and, to be sure, it is an unquenchable desire. Even when separated from the object of one's love, love is expressed in deep longing, anxiety, and pain. When one loves, truly loves, no matter the disappointments and self-inflicted hurts made possible by the defenseless heart, the love continues.

In the writing of this book, my love is laid bare. No, not for football or any other sport as I could live without them, but for the school that bought forth dreams, hopes, heroes, and heroines. This, then, is a tale of love with all of its exquisite manifestations, culminating in a miracle.

Let us begin this story of Wallingford educational lore with the creation of the town's exclusive secondary school, Lyman Hall High School.

Chapter 4

A School is Born

When a high school is built, it is the result of many hundreds of hours of community discussion and hundreds of thousands, if not millions of dollars of public funds. Hence, there is a very personal buy-in from the citizenry. Whether the school is a replacement for a building that has long since seen better days or is a new creation to provide for additional students or program offerings, a new high school is of great importance to a town/city.

With the construction of each new school regardless of the locale, size, and geographic area served, the citizenry generally wishes for "their school" to be a source of public pride, reflecting the very best their community has to offer. Wallingford, Connecticut, was no different in that regard. A New England town of pre-Revolutionary origins, it began mainly as an ideal place for farming with its fertile grounds and ample rain fall. The Town of Wallingford welcomed a variety of religious faiths and houses of worship. As with most municipalities across America, churches were the original locations where public education was first delivered.

The Town of Wallingford created its first secondary school (high school) in 1874. The school was named Central High School and remained under that title until the Board of Visitors, an early version of what we now know as the Board of Education, officially changed it to Wallingford High School in 1891. Candidly, residents were calling it Wallingford High School long before the official name change.

Located at the corner of North Main Street and Christian Street, the structure had the look of a modest 19th-century mansion with most of the 18 rooms the size of traditional bedrooms. Students enrolled at the school with the understanding that they must provide their own transportation, which for most meant walking. Students from neighboring communities were permitted to enroll at no cost, again providing they had transportation (the 4-legged type). It is important to note that there were no requirements that all children must attend school, or were there any age or grade requirements for leaving school.

The Town of Wallingford was experiencing the Industrial Revolution's impact in the latter stages of the 19th century. The train station that still operates today was opened in 1871, spurring opportunities for manufacturing and the growth of commerce, particularly along the Center Street-Main Street axis. With job growth came a modest explosion in the population resulting in the near-capacity enrollment in Central/Wallingford High School. A new school had to be built with a design that would serve more than just a secondary school population. With aging and limited purpose structures in Wallingford, such as the Opera House, Armory, and the churches, Wallingford required a building that had the capacity to serve local organizations for various purposes, from entertainment to political gatherings.

It took three years to complete the blueprints and final construction of the new high school. In March 1914, ground was broken for the new high school on South Main Street. Polled in the churches and homes of Wallingford, the collective voice of the town's people was heard, naming the new high school after Wallingford's most famous son Lyman Hall, a signer of the Declaration of Independence.

WALLINGFORD'S DR. LYMAN HALL

Lyman Hall was born in Wallingford, Connecticut, on April 12, 1724, of Puritan stock. He graduated from Yale College in 1747 in a class of 28 members as a divinity student, eventually joining his uncle, Reverend Samuel Hall, in his Wallingford ministry.

Upon graduation from Yale, Lyman Hall began his studies in medicine at Yale. In 1751, Hall married Mary Osborne and moved to Dorchester, South Carolina. Living there only nine months, Hall and his wife purchased land in Midway, Georgia, which was right next to the Midway Meeting House. Hall's affinity for oratory and his divinity training made him a popular political figure in this community almost immediately. Within a year of his arrival, the Midway Meeting House was renamed the parish of St. John with Hall the central figure in its conversion. On March 21st, 1775, the people of St. John's parish sent him to Philadelphia as the only seated delegate from Georgia in the historic Continental Congress. In August 1776, he signed the Declaration of Independence. Lyman Hall died October 19, 1790, at the age of 66.

THURSDAY, OCTOBER 19, 1916 - "LYMAN HALL DAY"

On October 19, 1916, at 6:00 am, Wallingford's citizens were awoken by a flurry of fireworks, the shrill of factory whistles, and the ringing of church bells as this was the Dedication Day for Lyman Hall High School. A national crowd of over 10,000 came to Wallingford proper, representing the largest crowd to ever see a parade in Wallingford, to dedicate Lyman Hall High School.

The first event of the day began at 8:00 am with the playing of the first football game in Lyman Hall High School history at Doolittle Park against Branford High School, a 7-0 loss for the new Wallingford High School. After waiting for the arrival of Connecticut Governor, Marcus H. Holcomb, where a 17-gun salute greeted him, the Dedication Day Parade stepped off at 10:30 am from Church Street, onto Center Street, then to South Elm Street where the boulder, commemorating Lyman Hall's birth place was honored with the placement of flowers. By noon, the parade traveled back from Elm Street to Ward

Street to South Main Street to lay the cornerstone of the new high school.

The parade included four marching units, 14 floats, representing numerous organizations and historical themes, including the Cheyenne Council of the Daughters of Pocahontas, the Flags of 1770, the Spirit of 1776, Betsy Ross Float of the Wallingford Grange, Declaration of Independence float, Connecticut Indian Encampment Float, and the Revolutionary War Float (with all participants attired in actual Revolutionary War uniforms), and 16 cars carrying the dignitaries from Connecticut and the State of Georgia.

Dedication Day was designed as a full day and night tribute to Wallingford's own Dr. Lyman Hall, drawing the largest assemblage ever witnessed in the history of Wallingford, Connecticut. The events of that day-long celebration included the Children's Choir of 400 students, a Wallingford choral group that sang "My Own United States," accompanied by the Navy Militia Band (the official U.S. Navy Band).

The formal laying of the Corner Stone took place at precisely 2:00 pm as the new school was encircled entirely by citizens and guests. As part of the ceremony, each citizen was asked to place a hand on the building as the Reverend Arthur P. Greenleaf delivered the invocation. The keynote address was delivered by the Honorable Lucien L. Knight. One of the most dynamic orators in the nation, Knight, traveled from Georgia to present this rousing address. A noted newspaper journalist, historian, and constitutional expert thrilled the crowd with his booming voice and oratorical elegance.

St. George's Inn served a 5-course dinner to all patrons for $1.00 each as the Oakdale Tavern entertained Wallingford's most distinguished citizens who were hosting honored guests from all over the country. The Wallingford Opera House, operated by George Wilkinson, provided all-night entertainment.

Thus began the life and legacy of Lyman Hall High School.

Chapter 5

Lyman Hall Demands a Great Principal

Prior to the building of Lyman Hall High School, Central High School was Wallingford's secondary school, located on the grounds currently occupied by Moses Y. Beach Elementary School. Central High School was administered by local townspeople, under the House of Burgesses' authority, Wallingford's governing body.

Late in the year 1886, the Town of Burgesses assigned the job of principal of Central High School to Kuoene Alonzo Webster, the former Postmaster of Wallingford.

As the excitement grew in the community for Wallingford's high school building on Main Street, great thought was in play by the town's decision-makers to match the state-of-the-art facility with a well-prepared, future-thinking principal. The town's House of Burgesses hired a seasoned educator with a sparkling statewide reputation, J. W. Kratzer, to oversee the administration of the new high school and all of the schools in Wallingford. Hence, Kratzer was the first superintendent of schools of Wallingford, hired in June of 1915.

J. W. Kratzer, who had previously served in various capacities in the town of East Hartford, including Superintendent of Schools, was a successful businessman who had been elected to various local offices. He welcomed the opportunity to come to Wallingford to provide leadership in preparation for opening the town's new secondary school.

Upon his hire, Kratzer immediately set upon the task of finding a qualified person for the position of principal, but little time remained before the opening of school for the fall of 1916.

It is important to remember that in the early 20th century, there were few, if any, colleges/universities that specifically trained education administrators and teachers. So much of the personnel who served as teachers and administrators for the Wallingford schools were recruited from the many local churches and the well-educated of the lay population.

Kratzer, embracing the scope and challenges of supervising all schools in Wallingford, wanted an exceptional person to lead Wallingford's "flagship" school, one of high moral character and proven organizational skills. Kratzer had planned to delegate a bounty of responsibilities to this new principal, including the design of courses and faculty hiring. Additionally, the contemporary design of the interior facilities provided many accommodations for innovative classes. Kratzer knew he needed an exceptional principal to lead Lyman Hall, who would maximize every student, teacher, and facility potentiality. He embarked on a lengthy outreach throughout Connecticut to find that forward-thinking, assiduous educator.

With construction moving ahead on schedule for a September 1916 opening of Lyman Hall High School, Kratzer had little time to conduct what he felt was a thorough enough search for a principal. Left with few options, Kratzer assumed the duties of the principal with no intention of retaining those responsibilities very long.

NEW SCHOOL AND NEW POTENTIAL

There was a distinctive exclusivity to the Lyman Hall High School building that few other secondary schools in Connecticut could match. There was the brilliant auditorium that included balcony seating with chairs adorned with a meticulously painted school logo. Separate entrances, one for boys and one for girls, were carefully chiseled into the granite blocks above the north (boys) and south (girls) entrances. The building's front facade was highlighted by eight majestic pillars that framed the three red front large doors. The 30-foot-wide staircase led to a broad courtyard that reached the sidewalk of South Main Street.

The new school had specifically designed science labs, classrooms for manual arts, homemaking, and music, requiring teachers with unique subject area expertise. The "generalist" teacher of the early 20th century who could teach a variety of subjects, general grade-level mathematics, language arts, and science would not meet the needs of a new Lyman Hall curricula that was anticipated to take advantage of these state-of-the-art facilities and the added specialized subjects in mathematics and science such as Algebra, Geometry, Biology, and Chemistry.

The front doors opened directly to the lower of the two rectangle floors of the school's classrooms that wrapped around the balconied auditorium. The floors were of grey painted metal that generated a unique sound from students' passing in their leather-soled shoes. Some male students had metal cleats on the back edge of their heels to protect the heel of the shoe from wearing down. This provided an intermittent clicking sound to the already echoing sound of student voices passing through the halls. The lower western part of the building was the gymnasium.

FINDING EARLY

During the first school year of LHHS's existence, 1916-17, part of Kratzer's regular schedule was to interview candidates for the position of principal. The aspirants included members of the LHHS faculty, two members of the local clergy, and several Wallingford citizens. As there were no state certification standards for school administrators or teachers as there are now, almost anyone could apply for the job.

In March of 2017, Superintendent and the first LHHS principal, J.W. Kratzer, interviewed Robert H. Early for the position of principal. Early, an elegant man, had a strong teaching background, having served as a teacher and an administrator with several schools in and outside of Wallingford, but what Kratzer found most compelling about Early was his unbridled enthusiasm.

In Kratzer's interviews of candidates for the principal position, he found that most of the applicants assumed a rather conventional demeanor for persons engaged in education, to wit, carefully stated responses to his questions, stating traditional approaches to teaching, discipline, and scheduling. To Kratzer's delight, Robert Early was charming and demonstrated a fresh approach regarding the manner in which a school could be run.

As with each interview, Kratzer escorted Early on a tour of the school facilities. Early marveled at the design of the building and the special classrooms for science and the vocational arts. Early was thoughtful in mapping out a forward-thinking approach for Lyman Hall High School and its students in his interview. Early shared his thoughts on the need for student excitement for learning and activities. Kratzer knew immediately he had the right person for the job.

Robert H. Early was hired and assumed the duties of principal of Lyman Hall High School on July 1, 1918.

There was a natural buzz about the new school, especially after the Dedication Day ceremony on October 19, 2016, which drew over 10,000 people from all over the state and nation. Early was the ultimate ambassador for his high school. He spent the most significant part of his weekends working on behalf of the school. He gave tours of the school to church groups and tried to attend more than his church on Sundays, promoting school goodwill. There were 14 houses of worship in Wallingford in 1918, and he made it a point to visit them all.

Chapter 6

The Early Era

The superintendent of the Wallingford schools, J.W. Kratzer, gave Robert H. Early a relatively free hand to design a plan for Lyman Hall High School's development and manage the new high school daily. Early was an educator of great vision, and despite the routine duties of running a school, the new principal had determined specific priorities for his school, students, and teachers.

Early's teaching background was predominantly in the language arts, but he had taught social studies, science, and mathematics like most teachers of the time. Therefore, Early had more than a fundamental grasp of subject content areas across the curricula. This background would serve him and the school well in years to come as Mr. Early, without hesitation, would fill in for almost any teacher who was out ill. Essentially, Early willingly became the "go-to" substitute teacher of his time. Over the years, Mr. Early demonstrated his love for his students and school in many ways, but he never shied away from any endeavor that engaged him directly with the students of LHHS.

As the teaching staff was all new to Early, he needed to get acquainted with each teacher as quickly as possible. As most of the Lyman Hall High School teachers lived in Wallingford at that time, Early was able to get in touch with most of them, inviting them to come to his office and discuss his ideas for the school and each teacher's possible responsibilities that Early was changing.

In those first meetings with individual teachers, Early explained his plan to begin crafting a group of after-school activities (currently referred to as extra-curricular) that would be designed to give each student multiple opportunities for self-expression and encouragement.

Early made it a point to learn of each teacher's hobbies and interests. He asked each member of the teaching staff to find ways to use their unique talents and skills to better serve the school's students beyond the subjects they taught during the 8:00 am – 3:00 pm school day. There would be no additional compensation for teachers to create and lead the after-school clubs and activities. However, Early made it clear to all staff that he expected every teacher to embrace his mandate to create a wide variety of after-school clubs, and the school records show they were successful in these endeavors.

Early hired nine new teachers for the start of the 2018-19 school year. Early was quick to see the potentialities of the new building, but finding teachers with expertise in the elective courses of the time that matched the facilities was a difficult challenge. Latin and French were the two foreign language courses brought forward from the Central High School days, but finding persons with sufficient backgrounds in those subjects, let alone whether they had the skills to teach, was a whole different matter. The same dilemma faced Early in finding teachers for his manual arts courses in machining, carpentry, and electricity. For those courses, Early contacted local manufacturers to find teachers, selling them on the idea that these courses would prepare current students for jobs in our Wallingford industries. The principal wanted artisans, but finding those who wanted to teach the skills that each knew was a unique combination to find.

Chapter 7

Early Reveals his Vision

A week before the start of school in September of 1918, Early convened a meeting for all teachers in the auditorium. At that meeting, some teachers were more than a little surprised to learn that they had been given different teaching assignments. As many of the teachers taught classes across traditional subject areas, Early wanted teachers to teach in no more than two subject areas so that each teacher could focus solely on specific subjects. Therefore, language arts teachers only taught grade-level classes in that area but may have also been assigned to teach a social studies class. Early designated more veteran, experienced teachers to freshmen and sophomore classes as much as possible to ensure that younger students received a firm basic knowledge and could read and do basic math.

AUDITORIUM PROGRAMS ... DRIVING STUDENT INTEREST & INVOLVEMENT

Principal Early had a wonderful vision of what he wanted his school to become. It centered around creating an excited student body who loved getting to school each day and were in no rush to leave due to the quality after-school activities. He appreciated the investment his teachers would have to make to bring his ideas to fruition. Although he was kind with an even temperment … he was not a patient man.

He needed a mechanism to communicate with all students, driving the priorities and planting the seeds of interest and enthusiasm. For this, Early planned Auditorium Programs.

Taking full advantage of the beautiful auditorium, Mr. Early introduced to his teachers his plan for "Auditorium Programs" for the entire student body. Teachers were encouraged to suggest possible topics and speakers for these school-wide programs, but through the auditorium programs, Early planned to guide the student body's focus and influence student support for the changes he planned to bring about in the years to come for the school.

One of the issues that Early would address in the auditorium presentations was building a music program at LHHS. Although Lyman Hall had an incredible auditorium and music training rooms in and around the cafeteria, the school had no structured music courses. Both the Glee Club and the orchestra were voluntary after-school activities with no faculty member to lead these organizations. Early reached out to church choral directors to serve as advisors to these music activities in his first few years. Auditorium assemblies with a music-related topic were included in the annual schedule of programs in the hope that a music teacher with a broad knowledge of instrumental and vocal expertise could be found in the years ahead.

Early hired the first full-time music teacher in 1922, but that person left teaching after two years. Three more music teachers came and went, then later in the last year of Mr. Early's tenure as principal in 1939, Lyman Hall finally found a true director of music for all instrumental and choral groups as Richard A. Otto was appointed to the position.

Each auditorium program was designed to meet specific purposes, heightening student awareness, knowledge, and enthusiasm. During Mr. Early's first three years as principal, assembly programs included a Belgium ambassador, an opera singer, and a civil war veteran. During the 1918-19 school year, five assemblies were scheduled for all students. This number of auditorium programs would grow to as many as a dozen in 1929. Each year at least one program would have a LHHS sports flavor, and as the basketball team gained statewide prominence, auditorium programs would allow Wallingford citizens to attend in standing room areas as all the French doors would be opened.

ENTHUSIASM FOR LEARNING - CLUBS

At that first group teacher meeting, Robert Early outlined how he wanted to develop "student appreciation for education." He stressed the importance of generating enthusiasm in everything that would be done at Lyman Hall High School, explaining that the students should have more out-of-classroom school activities. Early laid out his most aggressive plan, using quotes from the classics. His wry smile put people at ease, and he would often quote Shakespeare to emphasize a point.

To accomplish that goal, Early charged all teachers with developing after-school clubs. In 1917, the year before Robert Early became principal, Lyman Hall High School had only four clubs, three varsity sports that won a collective seven games, and only the senior class had organizational meetings. There was no yearbook perse, or school newspaper, although there was a "Senior Review" that included the names and commentary on the graduating seniors. The principal strongly suggested creating some specific clubs, acknowledging that developing student interest in something other than getting through school and graduating would take time. During that first faculty meeting, Mr. Early introduced the first four student organizations and the teachers who would serve as advisors. The first group included the Debating Club, The Junior College Club, The Daubers, and the Booster Club.

By 1924, there were 13 clubs, including the fascinating "Tresses Club," a surreptitious organization where you had to be nominated for membership. Teachers and students could nominate someone for consideration within the student body. In essence, female students and a few males were nominated solely on the basis of their "hair." It wasn't just the length, style, or color of one's hair. Rather, it was a matter of a student being recognized for having hair that was unforgettable. As with most decades, hair styles could encumber a wide variety of expressions, but the 1920s ushered in a wild flapper period that included fizzy curls, sculptured waves, and the Bohemian look. With no stated dress code that addressed hair at Lyman Hall, girls attended school with a plethora of coiffeurial expressions. Although the Tresses Club disappeared 11 years later, its peculiar nature brought the club great attention in the school. The Tresses Club, created by two faculty members, had no subject area relationship, but it brought excitement to the student body, and that's precisely what Early wanted.

THE STUDENT DEMOCRATIC PROCESS

Imbedded in Principal Early's plan to generate a maximal student involvement in all aspects of Lyman Hall High School was to convince the students of the importance of being active in clubs and activities. He realized that some organizations would have a narrow focus like the Radio Club, Philatelic Club, and Short Hand Club, while others like the Glee Club, plays, sports, dances, and cheerleaders would have broader appeal with subsequent participation. To bring added awareness and recognition to the LHHS organizations while emphasizing student leadership, Early directed his teachers, who served as club advisors, to include defined student leadership positions. All clubs were required to have democratically elected officers.

To that end, many of the student roles in sports and clubs were elected by general elections of the student body. All members of the Cheerleaders (females and males) and the Managers of the football, basketball, and baseball teams were all elected by some form of general election. In future years the Athletic Association (A.A.), created in 1921, and the Student Council, created in 1927, both formed by Mr. Early, would serve as the elective body for many student leadership positions.

Almost from the outset of Early's time as principal, the

captains of the three varsity sports teams were elected by school general elections. Naturally, only members of the teams were eligible. Principal Early recognized that a "lively school mood" (as Early put it) could be significantly enhanced by school athletic teams if all students felt a sense of participation even though there were only a relatively few students on each team.

Moreover, Early and legendary coach Langdon Fernald encouraged the sports teams' members to do far more than just play athletics. The athletes were encouraged to audition for roles in class plays, seek class office and attend all large school events such as concerts, dances, and plays. Early believed that if the members of the sports teams were engaged in all aspects of the school, the general student body and teachers would feel more compelled to attend the games. To Early, the sports teams must be "school activities," not just athletic demonstrations. One of Principal Early's special joys was seeing the gymnasium filled for basketball games. During his years as principal, 1918-1939, the LHHS gym was packed almost for every game. Early's strategies for student involvement in Lyman Hall, basketball games, and plays were events that students and many townspeople would not dare miss.

THE CHRONICLE

With Early's background in the language arts, especially with his penchant for the classics, he was taken aback by the lack of a school newspaper and annual yearbook. In his meetings with those teachers who taught the language arts subjects, reading, writing, and penmanship, he queried them on what efforts had been or should be made to encourage writing and reading.

Early led the effort to create a semester written school newspaper and yearbook that he assigned the name, THE CHRONICLE. He encouraged every teacher to engage their students in some manifestation of literary expression. School news was of particular focus in every issue of The Chronicle that included classroom humor, student relationships, sports, auditorium programs, school organization, and alumni updates. Teachers were asked to encourage students to write fictional pieces, poetry, and national news commentary/editorials as part of The Chronicle.

The Spring (second semester) issue of the Chronicle would include the photos of the members of the senior class and several traditional sections about the senior class, such as the class will, class prophecy, class honors, and class superlatives. To be printed in hard cover, the cost of The Chronicle would be expensive. During the term of Principal Early, no senior student was required to pay or be charged a fee for The Chronicle.

In the 1918-19 school year, four teachers were assigned to assist students in the development of The Chronicle. The hard cover yearbook envisioned by Principal Early required the financial means to pay for it. It would take a few years before LHHS would muster enough financial support for the hard cover production of the Chronicle, but Early personally took charge of securing ads and contributions to sponsor The Chronicle.

From the day he assumed the position of principal, Early was a whirlwind of energy in the community, often walking the length of Center Street on Saturday mornings, introducing himself to business owners. As he began in earnest to promote the "Chronicle," the combination of the annual yearbook and school newspaper, Early personally sold advertising. Among the many businesses that Early successfully solicited advertising from 1918-1934 were Center Street establishments, Conroys, Butler's Lingerie Shop, Shelley Brothers Headstones, W.P. Lynch Druggist, A.W. Hull Jewelers, Roudie Barber Shop & Beauty Parlor, The Wilkinson Theatre, The Wallingford Bank & Trust, Abraham Canelli's, and many doctors, dentists, and lawyers. International Silver, Factories P, L, and M each purchased ads from Mr. Early, but one of the Chronicle ads that indeed made Early smile was *"Most of the L.H. Men have their suits made at* THE TUCK SHOP."

What was also apparent to Early in his first year as

principal was meeting the expressed needs of his teachers in terms of supplies and equipment. LHHS needed the support of local business and industry for monetary contributions to pay for the many necessaries of the school as there were few local governmental funds available after the massive outlay of dollars to build and now maintain the school.

Early was the ultimate ambassador for his high school. He spent the largest part of his weekends working on behalf of the school. He gave tours of the school to church groups and tried to attend more than his own church on Sundays, promoting school goodwill.

EARLY STRESSES SPORTS

Of all the initiatives Robert H. Early brought to life as principal of Lyman Hall High School, probably nothing brought him greater glee than the triumphs of his school's athletic teams ... especially BASKETBALL.

From the beginning, it was apparent to one and all that Principal Early desired a robust athletic presence at LHHS. He was convinced that the most significant degree of widespread community and student excitement could be generated by successful high school sports teams. As with most aspects of the "hands-on" Early approach as principal, he was strident in putting in strategies to help that outcome along.

Of all the ideas he discussed at that initial faculty meeting, there was a little twinkle in his eye when he turned to the topic of sports at Lyman Hall. In that new yet compact gym, Early wanted every student to partake of athletics, albeit in direct participation or in cheering on the basketball teams and their fellow students who played the game.

As the students and teachers noted in the years ahead, the gym was the LHHS principal's (Robert H. Early) favorite late afternoon destination. Although he never viewed himself as an athlete or even a partaker in such endeavors, his passion for sports was undeniable. When his daily routine was at an end, he would usually make his way to the gym to watch an intramural game or a practice of the boys' or girls' teams.

Early's philosophy of generating high levels of enthusiasm in the school was boundless, especially in the effort to increase participation in sports. In 1921, he asked two teachers to help him create the Athletic Association (A.A.). The A.A. organization was open to all students in the school, designed to build interest in athletics, attendance at all home and away games, provide recognition for students who participated in sports, and coordinate elections of team captains, managers and cheerleaders. The Athletic Association quickly became the largest student organization at Lyman Hall, and although its focus changed over the years, it maintained its presence in the school through the decade of the 1950s.

Principal Early made it clear that he wanted winning teams, each season, each sport, each year. During his first eight years as principal, Early had one gym & exercise teacher who lasted three years, followed by one more who taught the gym classes for five years. As part of their duties, each served as the head coach (there were no assistant coaches in those years) for the three sports, but neither of those men was able to bring their teams along sufficiently to earn many wins.

Before the creation of the Housatonic Valley League in 1924, Early would contact the principals of other high schools from almost anywhere to generate the game schedules for his football, basketball, and baseball teams. There were no buses to transport Lyman Hall teams, so Early charmed many of his fellow principals to play their arranged games in Wallingford, either in the high school or the state armory (where the current police department now resides).

When away games were scheduled, Early would secure transportation from local citizens who owned cars or trucks. Among the schools that Principal Early scheduled to play Lyman Hall were Meriden High School, Simsbury High School, Southington High School, The American School for the Deaf, Danbury High School, Newton High School (Massachusetts), Irvington High School (New York), Leavenworth High School (Waterbury), and West Hartford High School.

Chapter 8

Basketball For All

Long before the days of Title IX, instituted in 1972, that established equitable sports opportunities for girls and boys, Early insisted that there be a girls' basketball team and girls' intramurals in basketball. In his second year as principal, Early reached out to other high school principals from the towns around Wallingford to set up a five-game schedule for the girls' basketball team.

Mrs. Lillian Williams, a teacher at Lyman Hall who had played a little basketball in college, agreed to coach the girls' teams in 1923. Early urged the students to support the girls' teams as they did the boys' teams and the crowds for the girls' games were usually quite good and raucous. The rules were somewhat different from that of the boys as the girls played with two guards, two forwards, and two centers, one of which was called a "running center." Forwards played only offense, and guards played only defense. Only forwards were permitted to shoot the ball. A player was limited to only three dribbles, and it was a foul to hold the ball for more than three seconds.

Intramural basketball for girls and boys was another Early designed activity, conducted by pitting teams from each of the four classes in a school-wide tournament that drew many students to the games that were held immediately after the school day if the varsity did not have a practice or home game. Games were planned as 30-minute running time contests, so many teams got to play in a single afternoon. Rules for intramural play were relaxed so that games would flow more efficiently rather than the rules pertaining to dribbling and shooting.

NO SCHOOL COLORS, NO SCHOOL MASCOT

When Lyman Hall High School opened its doors in September of 1916, there were few traditions that were carried forward from Central High School. One of the most interesting of the practices was that each year, the senior class would determine the "COLORS" for the school year and their class. Heretofore, there were no standard school colors that most other high schools had long ago adopted.

Yearly colors had a broad range of combinations. Senior class officers would usually propose two-color combinations in the spring before their senior year and then utilize those colors in school activities in their senior year.

Principal Early, who had his hand in almost everything from the purchase of textbooks to selling Chronicle (yearbook/ school newspaper) advertising to leading cheers at basketball games, did not feel it necessary to establish school colors or establish a school mascot. He left the issue of school colors alone, ... that is ... until fate and a glib valley newspaper sports writer took a hand.

Early had a very limited budget and realized it would take some years to replace these non-LHHS uniforms, but he had an idea. In the next few years, Principal Early would engage the public not to "pay for uniforms" but to produce the uniforms themselves from scratch.

CREATING THE SPIRIT

From his college background, Principal Early knew the excitement that was created when students led the cheers at games, but Lyman Hall High School needed not only "Yell

Leaders" (Early's nickname for cheerleaders), but he needed to have cheers, and there weren't any. At a meeting of a handful of teachers in his office in October 1920, Early asked the group to write a handful of school cheers. They used college cheers as a model to follow and wrote some basic "yells" with many "rah's" and rhyming words.

One of the problems was that Lyman Hall had no school colors or mascot, so they couldn't use a standard cheer such as ..." For the Black and White, for the Black and White, we'll fight, fight, fight." Parenthetically, most of Lyman Hall's uniforms, other than baseball, <u>were</u> a navy blue that appeared more black than blue until 1927. Up to and beyond 1927, the newspaper accounts of LHHS athletic squads referred to the teams as the "Hallites." That moniker was almost impossible to find words to match in rhyme and equally difficult to gain a visual picture. Case in point, "What does a Hallite look like"?

With the cheers written, but with no cheerleaders as yet, the next step for Early was to have one of the teachers teach the cheers to the entire student body. To that end, the purpose of the January 1919 assembly was to teach the student body all the cheers for the basketball games. This assembly had a dual purpose ... one, to create interest for cheerleading, and two, to get all the students to know all the "yells."

As the high school had no band at that time and at least two of the cheers had a musical foundation, one of the teachers who played the piano led those cheers. For the better part of the 1920s, a piano was brought into the gymnasium and set up on the eastern wall of the gym for home games. As the boy's basketball teams began to collect one great season after another, beginning in 1927, the demand for seats at the games (often standing room) was such that the piano had to be removed in place of more seats.

THE EARLY IMPRINT

In Robert H. Early's 21 years as principal, he had a dramatic impact on all that was to be Lyman Hall High School. Untethered by much in the way of local, state, and federal education mandates and regulations, save for budget restrictions, Early moved to improve Lyman Hall High School at every turn.

Since assuming the principalship of LHHS in 2018, Robert Early worked to build his "family of teachers," as he called them. For the fall of 1924, Early hired seven teachers; four were replacement teachers for persons who left Lyman Hall. With each year, the faculty grew younger, and enrollment increased. The priorities that Early put in place for his high school were generating the enthusiasm for education as he had hoped. Class Honor Rolls had nearly doubled from 1919 to 1924. Student activities dramatically increased in the 1920s and included a broad range of new functions, with some becoming long-standing traditions. Class rings were introduced as a ceremonial junior class activity that included a dance in the gymnasium.

By 1922, all four classes elected officers, and each class held an annual themed dance with the juniors and seniors, both hosting a formal promenade. Through Mr. Early's goodwill efforts in the community, beautiful silver candelabra, punch bowls, and tea-service were created for Lyman Hall High School by the R. Wallace & Son's Silversmiths for these formal events. During the first half of the 20th century, Wallace would design tiaras for promenade queens, trophies for LHHS athletic championship teams, and provide fine metals to local jewelers to make individual jewelry pieces for student recognition.

Class plays, manual arts competitive events, and school-wide creative writing contests created a thoroughly engaged student body. Despite the lack of success of the pre-1926 varsity athletic teams, Early continued to do all he could to promote the school's sports teams.

NO LHHS UNIFORMS

As Early began his tenure as principal in the summer of 1918, he was informed by one of the teachers that the school's athletic teams lacked a Lyman Hall "school uniform." With so many tasks to address in his first few months of service, the issue of school athletic uniforms scarcely received much attention by Early. However, in an inspection of school storage areas, Early came upon a paddle-locked storage area at the back of the cafeteria. There he discovered wooden crates that would be generally used for transporting produce from local farms. Each crate was stuffed with musty-smelling garments. Folded and stacked, they resembled scratchy wool horse blankets, but these were team athletic uniforms, but not Lyman Hall uniforms per se. Sticking together from moisture and mold, each piece of clothing had to be peeled away from the uniform piece below.

As Early unpacked what appeared to be the basketball uniforms, he saw the disparity of different lettering and use of color from one uniform shirt to the next, but most of all, he noted that the tank top basketball shirts were dissimilar. Some were heavy dark grey with a white band around the middle. A few were black or navy blue with a white band across the middle of the shirt. On the white band was an elaborate Old English "W" (presumably for Wallingford) sewn on the front with two smaller letter "B's" on either side of the "W" (probably meaning BasketBall). Despite the heavy material of the uniforms, there were rips and previous repair stitching on most items.

In another crate, labeled "football," there were thick tan canvas football pants with cardboard slabs sewn into the thigh and hip area. The jerseys were nothing more than heavy wool, black long sleeve sweaters with no numbers or logo of any kind. Some of the shirts had sleeves with horizontal stripes from the shoulder to the forearm area. As with the basketball shirts, the sweaters were not all alike as some had no stripes. Again, the aroma of mold and mildew pervaded the uniforms that suggested that they had been used long before there was a Lyman Hall High School.

With a new school, there were many demands placed on the limited funds that were available. There were new textbooks to buy with new courses, and the school's new library required that a vast array of classics and reference materials be purchased. Early included sports uniforms in every funding request to the superintendent since 1919, but Kratzer could not find the funds in his education budget to pay for such a request, so the old black and grey Central High School uniforms had to suffice for at least one more year ... and then another year ... and another.

In 1924, Dr. John Lund became superintendent of the Wallingford schools. Early asked that new athletic uniforms be purchased from the new Wallingford head of education, and again he was turned down. Principal Early finally decided to take this challenge to the citizens of Wallingford.

Each year, Robert H. Early would personally contact the various merchants on Central and Main Streets, requesting sponsors/ads to pay for the hard-cover Lyman Hall High School yearbook, The Chronicle. As he visited each shop on his walks on Saturday, he developed relationships with store owners and their employees. Many of the merchants were in the clothing business with expert tailors and seamstresses in their employ.

Such as my family heritage, tailors were of multi-generational lineage. Making a man's suit or a women's dress from "scratch" with nothing more than the customer's vision of what the garment would be was referred to in the fashion terminology of the early 20th century as "bespoke." Bespoke was the term tailors used to describe individually patterned and crafted men's clothing, analogous to women's haute couture. Along Wallingford's Center Street and Main Street were several men's and women's clothing stores, with each of them providing bespoke clothing. It would not be economically feasible for these stores to pre-make clothing, except as a sample of what each store could create, which was usually wrapped around a mannequin in the front window of the store.

In the 1920s, Early developed relationships that led to advertising in the Chronicle with The Tuck Shop, Wolf Waist Shop, Van's, Butler's Lingerie Shop, Tafeen's Specialty Shop J.J. Prior Tailor, just to name a few. As the need for Lyman Hall High School uniforms became a matter of sustained cleanliness as well as team identification, Early put together a cadre' of local seamstresses from these stores who agree to work together to design and then create basketball uniforms from scratch for the boys and girls. Early deemed that the basketball team had the greatest need as they played so many games, requiring a quick turn-around in terms of cleaning. Additionally, the wool/flannel fabric was not conducive to indoor play, where the gym heat was exacerbated by the metal walls, especially with a full gymnasium of people.

During the 1925-26 school year, the three Wallingford seamstresses team came up with several ideas, and each created their design. One had the letters L-H-H-S sewn on in a diagonal pattern, while another had two white bands around the chest with yellowish gold L-H in old English letters sewn between the bands. These sample uniform jerseys were actually used by the basketball team, further adding to the mishmash of the uniforms, which were NOT uniform.

The team photo of the 1925 basketball team shows the 14-member team wearing five different jerseys. Notable in all of the teams' photos in the first ten years of the high school was the presence of "black" as the uniform color. Observers in the past argued that it was a navy blue, but there was no consensus as to the actual intended color of the thick fabric. As the black faded from years of use, some believed that the uniform's color was grey, but it was black that dominated the garments. It wasn't until 1927-28 that Lyman Hall High School finally found a color that would define it and came about under the most bizarre circumstances.

Chapter 9

Birth of the Housatonic Valley Athletic League

Prior to 1924, high school principals or their surrogates would communicate with each other to create athletic team schedules. Given the logical restrictions due to lack of transportation, most games were between schools of close geographic locations. Such was the case for Central High School of Wallingford that played its basketball games at the state armory, presently the location of the Wallingford Police Department. Baseball and football contests were staged at either Doolittle Park or Simpson Field.

When Lyman Hall High School opened in 1916, games were scheduled with the high schools from Meriden, Branford, Southington, Bristol, and a few private schools in the New Haven area. Beginning in 1920, Early initiated talks with other high school principals in the hope that an athletic conference of nearby schools could be formed, eliminating the annual time-consuming task of scheduling games with each school. Additionally, Early wanted to include girls' basketball in the discussion of any new league, but he found that a non-starter with his fellow principals.

One of the most damaging factors in the relationships between schools in terms of competitive sport was the inevitable in-game squabbles, inconsistent officiating, and the last-minute scheduling changes. What seemed like minor or petty problems manifested into long-standing feuds between schools. Meriden High School and Lyman Hall had more than a few problems over those early years, which caused the severing of communications for years at a time. One recurring reason for discontent was the gentleman's agreement that the home team would secure the game officials. With no regional governing board of sports officials, the application and interpretation of the rules of the games were a matter of the game official's experience as a former player or fan. A teacher or town citizen of the hosting school would often be asked to serve as an umpire or referee, depending on the sport. This alone would invariably result in calls of "favoritism" by the visiting coach or spectators with subsequent screaming matches between adults and some fisticuffs.

After years of patch-work scheduling, Mr. Early received a call from the principal of Shelton High School in September of 1924 inviting him to a meeting of principals from high schools that were mostly south of New Haven. The meeting to be held in Shelton would take Early over an hour to drive the 20-mile distance.

Principal Robert H. Early attended an organizational meeting of secondary school principals from Branford, Derby, Milford, Seymour, Shelton, Stratford, and Lyman Hall of Wallingford, who were interested in joining together to form a new league. The day-long meeting opened with a discussion of the participants' shared frustration relative to the many aspects of high school sports, especially in the area of scheduling games.

The first four hours focused on the major concerns that all principals shared, leading to the writing of a constitution that would govern the three major sports, football, basketball, and baseball. Track and field and girls' sports would be left to the individual schools to schedule games.

It was unanimously agreed that the primary aim of this league would be to promote clean sport, friendly relationships between rival schools, and to codify uniform and fair rules of eligibility. While there was debate for each of the three sports, basketball received the most prolonged discussion.

Of the rules agreed to on this day, as specified in the

Constitution of the Housatonic Valley League, here are just a few of the REGULATIONS, mostly pertaining to basketball:

- All member schools of the Housatonic Valley League must offer football, basketball, and baseball so that a regular annual schedule of games will be established, whereas each league member high school will play all schools in the league. This specific league provision would lead to some significant problems for Lyman Hall High School in the years ahead.
- All matters pertaining to the league shall be decided by a conference of the principals of the member schools of the Housatonic Valley League.
- All games will be played unless the visiting team notifies the home team before 12 o'clock that weather conditions do not permit traveling.
- Basketball – All games shall begin at 8 o'clock. The visiting team is entitled to the floor by 7:45 o'clock.
- The referee shall choose the ball to be played in the game.
- Postponed games must be played within the following two weeks by agreement of the two principals involved.

This next provision of the Housatonic Valley League addressed the issue of participation and the importance of "everyone plays." There was no junior varsity as it came to be known many years later, just first-team and second-team players. Here is how the new league planned to address participation: The games were to be played in quarters with the first-team and second-team alternating quarters. The first team quarters will be ten minutes, and the second team will have eight-minute quarters. Separate scores will be kept for first-team contests and second-team games.

The constitution articulated that it shall be a point of HONOR among the principals and coaches to see that no first string player is ever played on the second team.

On **Wednesday, September 17, 1924**, the great Housatonic Valley League was born and with it the most outstanding high school athletic league in state history, highlighted by the 1985-86 school year.

Chapter 10

Early Gets his Man - Langdon D. Fernald

Of all the plans and hopes that Robert Early put in place in his first seven years as principal, probably the most disappointing was the lack of athletic team success. Class intramurals and the girls' basketball teams brought some degree of solace for Early, but the football, basketball, and baseball teams, at best, hovered around mediocrity.

With the turn of the new year in 1926, Principal Early's aggressive recruiting to fill long-standing critical teaching positions started to bear fruit. Among the nine new staff members hired for the next school year were English teacher Ruth Boardman of Wakefield, Massachusetts, who was brought aboard to take over as faculty advisor to the Chronicle, and within a few years, had increased participation to more than 50 students.

In Margaret Purdon, Early hired the teacher who would revamp the commercial and business-related subjects while establishing employment opportunities for students upon graduation. Leland Slater of Coxsackie, New York, was added to the faculty to head the science department as Doris Rayner became the school's music teacher. In the middle of all of the teaching additions who started in 1926, no one could dispute the one person who made the most immediate and dramatic impact on Lyman Hall High School.

The end of the 1925-26 school year brought an opening

of the teaching position for gym & exercise and coach for all seasons. Early had learned of the impending opening back in February and immediately put on a "full-court" recruiting press of his own to find the man who could raise the fortunes of his LHHS athletic teams. After contacting colleges throughout New England, the University of New Hampshire had a graduate from the class of 1924 who had a resume that seemed to meet everything Early was looking for in a do-it-all teacher coach.

On April 21, 1926, Langdon D. Fernald came to Wallingford for an interview with Robert Early. A tall, handsome man with his dashing fresh manner, and dazzling smile, Early immediately recognized that Fernald would be able to encourage many male students, previously uninterested in participating in athletics, to join the three seasonal sports of football basketball, and baseball. In the first few meetings with Fernald, Early explained his goals for sports at Lyman Hall, a winning expectation that delighted the energetic Fernald.

A native of Laconia, New Hampshire, "Lang" was the University of New Hampshire's, President of the Class of 1924 and three-sport athletic performer. He was Vice President of the UNH Student Council, a member of the prestigious Senior Skulls Society, Chairman of the Sophomore Hop Committee, a member of Alpha Tau Omega fraternity, and the President of the Casque Casket (the Inter-Fraternal Order).

This all-around student leader at UNH was a standout on the basketball team for three years, leading his teams in scoring, purportedly the best "long-range shooter" in recent school history. The captain and right fielder of the baseball team, "Lang," led his team in hitting with a .389 average. Earning his B.A. degree in Liberal Arts in 1924, Fernald took a year to determine what he wanted to do for his life's work. When he was contacted by the athletic office of the University of New Hampshire that an opening for a teacher and coach was available in someplace called Wallingford, Connecticut, he was intrigued by the opportunity.

In May of 1926, Langdon Dewey Fernald was hired by principal Robert H. Early to be the school's gym teacher. With the coming of Coach Fernald, the markedly unsuccessful Lyman Hall athletics period under successive gym teachers/ coaches, Lawrence Nixon (1916-17 to 1920-21) and Elliot Langer (1921-22 to 1925-26) came to a close.

Early clearly outlined to Fernald that in addition to his teaching all the male students in gym & exercise, Fernald would be responsible for coaching all three major sports and the occasional Spring-time multiple-school meets in track & field that would feature the best athletes in the school.

With Coach Fernald now in place, Lyman Hall High School was positioned for its first "Golden Age" of basketball, a historical period when the victories and championships would roll through Wallingford, but it all would lead to the demise of football, almost forever.

Chapter 11

Coach Fernald Lights the Lights

From his earliest days, the teaching and coaching skills of Langdon Fernald were undeniable as the former University of New Hampshire standout rapidly brought his football, basketball, and baseball teams to great success, as Principal Robert Early had predicted at Fernald's hiring. However, as with most high school team sports at the time, all the best athletes in the school played all three sports. Coach Fernald saw every male student in the school in his gym classes and, therefore, encouraged any and all with any promise to try out for his teams. Fernald understood that many of his boys had to work before and after school to support their families. This factor above all limited Fernald's team rosters, but no matter the number of boys on the teams, Coach Fernald's teams were more than a match for their opponents, especially in basketball.

Fernald was usually soft-spoken yet stern and demanding in dealing out his instruction. He commanded one's attention and respect without humor or wasted words. One of Fernald's strengths as a teacher/coach was his ability to demonstrate exactly what he wanted of his students.

In September of 1926, Coach Langdon D. Fernald began his career in education at Lyman Hall High School. On Friday, September 10, 1916, Fernald greets 27 aspirants for his first LHHS football team. Soon-to-be team captain Regal Dorsey remembers the first meeting, "Coach (Fernald) was a tall man, bigger than any of us. He looked at each of us in the eye, shook every man's hand, and told us the rules he expected us to follow. The one thing he emphasized was that no one could miss practice".

Practices began the following Monday, and Coach Fernald soon realized that despite half a dozen returning players from 1925, the members of the team knew little about the game of football. One of the linemen on the team who happened to be the President of the senior class, Henry Wachtelhausen had this to say about their new coach, "None of us said a word or made a sound during practice. Coach Fernald taught every man what to do at his position. He would show you what he wanted done, and he expected you to do it. Coach repeated the same things at every practice especially blocking and tackling. Coach would line up in front of every player on the team and expected you to tackle him when he said hike. When we practiced plays, he would always be on the other side and I had to block him on every play. He knocked my helmet off many times as I tried to block him. Coach was big and strong, and all of our linemen had to block him".

Dorsey, who played quarterback and called the plays, told the story, "Coach Fernald never talked about football during the school day. I would see him in gym class and try to ask him a question because I had so much to memorize for our first game of the year against Seymour, but he told me to keep my mind on my school work during the day. I was the smallest man on the team, but coach showed me how to pass the football, dropkick, and call the plays in the huddle. Practice was always hard for us because we practiced against Coach Fernald. We didn't know if we would win many games, but we always played hard as coach taught us".

In 1926 as in the football of the 21st century, the game required many varied techniques. Without team practice equipment, Fernald himself would often be the object of "tackling or blocking practice." Unlike the predominant style of offense of the day that focused on running plays with a heavy dose of line plunges and the occasional run around end, Fernald brought the pass to Lyman Hall. Throughout his tenure as the coach of football, 1926-1937, his teams never utilized more than ten different plays, all of which were called by the quarterback during the game.

Fernald's career at LHHS started with fanfare and flourishes as his first football squad in 1926 won the Housatonic Valley League Championship. This campaign marked the first non-losing (where losses exceeded victories) season in school history.

To be sure, Fernald's first foray in coaching high school football was star-crossed. A staunch disciplinarian, he worked his team of 27 players to daily exhaustion at Doolittle Park, teaching a sport that the participants had never seen, much less played. With no blocking or tackling bags, all practices were a matter of live, full-contact work, where Fernald, as the only coach, would often play in the scrimmages without a helmet or padding. Captain quarterback Regal Dorsey, a 5-5, 130 pounder who also played as a linebacker in Fernald's gap-8 defense, said of their games, "Mr. Fernald taught us every little thing, and there were no substitutes unless you got knocked out or you broke something. I called the plays in the huddle, but the only time coach talked to me was at halftime or when someone belted me out of bounds near our bench".

During the first football season with Coach Fernald at the helm, Principal Early took an acute interest in the new coach with his first team. At 4:00 pm on most days, Mr. Early would walk from the school's Main Street location, taking a right onto Center Street and then right along Elm Street to Doolittle Park where the team "rehearsed" as Early was fond of saying.

Keeping a distance from the football practicing, Mr. Early stood quietly, rarely talking to anyone. The members of the team would notice the presence of their principal, another example of how Early wrapped himself up in the goings-on of his school.

Right guard and class president, Henry Wachtelhausen, would sometimes be called into the principal's office as he passed by Early, who stood in his doorway as the students passed between classes. Henry recalled, "Mr. Early had a thing about winning for Lyman Hall. He would say to me, "Henry, you are a taller chap, so you have to get in a low position and direct your thrust to his knees, ... always the knees".

According to Wachtelhausen, "Mr. Early wanted everything we did at Lyman Hall High School to have a successful result. Whether it was the debate team, the Daubers (the arts and crafts group), or Shorthand Club, he wanted his school and students to come out on top. A very distinguished man, Mr. Early was forever promoting student participation in all activities. Mr. Early would walk the hallways between classes and was able to call out most students by name and remind them to be at the football game".

As with most first-year coaches in any era, there is a bolt of enthusiasm when a new coach comes on the scene, particularly Fernald, who was tall and handsome. Langdon Fernald seemed to tower over his team at practices and on the sidelines during games. Always dressed in a tie, he often donned a zip-up waist jacket when he wasn't in a sport coat. The fall of 1926 brought a fresh approach to football as Fernald would bring to the basketball team.

After a winless season in 1925, Coach Fernald was asked by Principal Early to "charge up their hearts." In that phrase from a handwritten memo from Robert Early to Fernald on September 14, 1926, Mr. Early was referring to not only the football team but the students of the school.

Chapter 12

Early & Fernald,
"A Dynamic Duo"

The maelstrom of enthusiasm that marked Robert H. Early's administration of Lyman Hall High School as its principal required a broader scope of faculty participation in student activities after the contractual school day. Langdon Fernald, with his incredible energy and youthful enthusiasm, began to feel the weight of his responsibilities relatively early in his career, serving as the only coach of all three sports, football, basketball, and baseball; coordinating school-wide intramurals, and organizing occasional track and field meets (four to five a year) as a heavy yoke to bear.

There was one more anvil that was forever attached to the weight, Fernald was highly competitive, and the drive to win is not a burden that can easily be put down. Every coach wants his or her teams to win, but few, then as now, know the balanced formula by which "winning" can be achieved over the long haul. Having talented student-athletes on any roster is undoubtedly a cherished priority. However, a careful review of Lyman Hall High School history shows that athletic teams in a wide variety of sports often came up short of a championship, albeit league or state, despite rosters that had a sprinkling of talent or a squad replete with athletic talent.

Early supported his coach and teams in many ways, assuming responsibilities and functions that impacted the trajectory of winning. Mr. Early was the chief architect of the annual basketball schedule, soliciting the foremost winning teams in Connecticut to play his Wallingford high school. Early and Fernald were of a single mind that playing the best teams possible would make the Lyman Hall teams better for the annual quest of league and state titles. Early scheduled small colleges, private schools, and a few Connecticut basketball powerhouses that had student populations three times the size of Lyman Hall High School, such as New Britain, Wilby (Waterbury), and Stamford. If Early could find the school on the Connecticut map, he would fit them into the schedule.

While the football team played a six/seven-game schedule throughout most of the 1920s, even with the creation of the Housatonic Valley League in 1924, the LHHS basketball teams were playing as many as 20 games per season. Some games were postponed or canceled during those years due to harsh winter weather and influenza outbreak, which decimated team rosters into the 1950s. The most prominent victim of the flu in LHHS lore was Hall of Famer Patrick Sullivan, the best performer on any team on which he played. Anticipating to sign a professional baseball contract after graduation with the Chicago Cubs, Sullivan died of influenza on April 29, 1924, less than two months before his graduation from LHHS. A plaque was erected by the class of 1924 on the occasion of Patrick's death and is affixed to the wall inside the school.

With an acute focus on the teaching of the details of athletic techniques, germane to each sport to the time required for away game travel, Fernald was far ahead of his time in that late 20th century buzz phrase, "Time Management." For Fernald, the coaching of all three major sports, to managing school-wide intramurals, recruiting athletes from each team for the track and field meets … and lest we forget, teaching all gym and exercise classes for boys was a constant time augmentation, even for the typhoon of energy that was Langdon Fernald.

Chapter 13

The 1926 Football Season

The last Championship for 58 Years

Mr. Early encouraged faculty and students to travel down to Seymour for the first game of the season, over an hour drive by automobile or truck. Coach Fernald packed many of his players in his orange-painted, wood paneled 1924 Ford Model T Station Wagon. Other team members loaded up in their fellow students' cars as a caravan of nine vehicles made their way to Seymour High School. The sizable contingent from Wallingford trekked along the endless back roads to the valley town to witness Coach Fernald and his reconstituted LHHS team come away with a 7-0 victory, only the second opening of season win since 1920.

After a 90-minute drive to Stratford High School, the "Hallites" (as they were sometimes referred to since the school had no official mascot) found a way to win their second league contest in a row. Left halfback Bill Buckley, last year's captain, carried the ball on two long runs up the middle, resulting in the only touchdown of the day for LHHS. Dorsey's extra point kick was true, and Lyman Hall carried a 7-0 lead into the final period. In that quarter, both starting guards, Henry Wachtelhausen and Harold Kast, were forced from the game with injuries as Stratford put together a successful series of plays, leading to a touchdown. Lining up for the extra point attempt, Charles Frauham broke through to block the kick, preserving the 7-6 victory for Lyman Hall.

Old-time rival Branford came to Doolittle Park for game

three for a Friday afternoon tilt with Lyman Hall. With Wachtelhausen and Kast unable to play and their line positions filled with first-year men, the Wallingfordites were unable to mount much scoring. Going into the fourth quarter, the score was 0-0, even though both teams moved the football up and down the field. At the beginning of the final period, Branford broke through with a 32-yard run for a touchdown and, after kicking the extra point, held a 7-0 advantage. A leg injury forced halfback Bob Butler to the sidelines. Coach Fernald replaced Butler with center Charles Frauham. Bill Buckley took a handoff from quarterback Dorsey and threw a pass to Frauham and the fleet "future Hall of Famer" dashed to paydirt. With time running out, less than ten seconds remaining in the game, Dorsey dropkicked the extra point as the Housatonic Valley League game ended in a 7-7 tie.

Wonder of wonders, Lyman Hall's football team had two wins and one tie, heading into the fourth game of the season, the best start to a season since the school opened.

Week four brought an odd turn of events for the Wallingford team. Playing at home, LHHS had a goodly crowd in attendance, but one of the appointed referees failed to show up for the game. This meant that only one referee would officiate the game. The Shelton coach sternly objected to having only one official, suggesting that Lyman Hall forfeit the game to his team since it was the home school's responsibility to secure game referees. After a lengthy discussion, it was decided to proceed with the contest, utilizing one referee.

Early in the game, LHHS began a play on the right side of the field, near the Lyman Hall bench. Quarterback Regal Dorsey threw a pass to Charles Frauham for a touchdown, but the referee standing on the opposite side of the field, near the Shelton bench, was heard to blow his whistle, signaling an off-side penalty on LHHS. He casually allowed play to continue, so Dorsey lined up his team after the touchdown and drop-kicked the extra point.

A heated discussion between the sole game official and the Shelton coach resulted. Not communicating with Coach Fernald, the referee decided to take the touchdown and extra point away from LHHS. The Wallingford faithful jeered the referee over his delayed ruling as LHHS onlookers began to crowd the sideline.

From this point on in the game, every official's whistle and non-call brought heated taunts and boos from the crowd, suggesting that he was not able to do his job without prejudice. The game's outcome was yet another 0-0 tie as Lyman Hall continued their no-loss season.

On Friday, November 5, 1926, many Lyman Hall students piled into cars, some attaching themselves to the roofs of the vehicles for a ride to Milford High School. A newly kindled enthusiasm marked the Wallingford contingent's excitement for football. The Hallites ran out to a two touchdown lead as Dorsey's play-calling mixed passes to fullback Walter Volhardt and the running of right halfback Bob Butler. Misfortune frowned on Lyman Hall as Butler (in the future, he would become the renowned Wallingford physician, Dr. Robert Butler), was rushed to Milford Hospital with a fractured collarbone. Left guard Harold Kast was inserted into the backfield to take Butler's halfback position. Despite the Butler's injury, the Lyman Hall gridmen held their ground and came away with a 12-6 victory.

With one game remaining on the league slate, Fernald's charges were in reach of a Housatonic Valley League title. A local newspaper, "the Wallingford Times," included a story about the upstart Lyman Hall High School football team that would need one more win or tie to clinch the championship.

On Friday, November 13, 1926, the streets of the Town of Wallingford were a bit damp from an early morning rain that lasted until after 8:00 am. As the final game of the 1926 football season approached, Mr. Fernald saw some of his team in gym classes that morning. As he welcomed them to the gymnasium, he noted their relaxed demeanor, devoid of any predictable nervousness before such a big game.

As the final game of the football season was scheduled for

the afternoon of a weekday, most citizens would not be able to attend until after their workday had concluded, but there still was considerable foot traffic along Center and Main Streets of people hurrying along to the site of the game. Principal Early had dismissed school a half hour early so that the student body could walk down to Elm Street for the critical final game of the season. The entire football team, dressed in their game attire of shoulder pads, canvas pants, and the old dark jerseys, walked with Coach Fernald and their fellow students to Doolittle Park.

As the team and throng of Lyman Hall students approached the corner of South Elm and Wallace Street, the Derby team, donning their dark red jerseys, could already be seen limbering up on the Doolittle football field. The Lyman Hall team headed for their sideline, where they changed into their spiked high-top football shoes.

The playing conditions this day were far less than desirable for any out of doors activity, let alone football. As the LHHS team practiced on the Doolittle Park field each day, the playing area field was almost completely worn and devoid of grass, especially inside both 20-yard lines. The previous evening's precipitation combined with the dirt surface formed a considerable layer of "Wallingford mud." Additionally, there was a considerable wind blowing across Doolittle.

Without any stands and bleachers near the football field, the Wallingford faithful found spots to stand along the Lyman Hall side's perimeter. There were no ropes or barriers, so people crowded around the home team's bench and sideline, mixing with the players. This experience was all new for everyone. No one from the Wallingford citizenry had ever been a part of an important Lyman Hall High School football game. It was all new and exciting, just as Mr. Early hoped it would be with the hiring of Langdon Fernald.

With both teams warming up in front of their respective benches, it was clear to see that the Derby team was much larger in size than the Wallingford boys. At 3:30 pm captain, Regal Dorsey went to the center of the field for the coin toss. Derby won the flip and received the opening kickoff. Right away, slippery conditions caused the powerful Derby runners to fall while taking handoffs as the Lyman Hall students cheered with every play.

The first half action was marred by the slippery and windy conditions, as both teams went to the half-time break covered in mud, with neither team able to pierce the other's goal line. Quarterback Dorsey attempted only two passes, both of which were unsuccessful in the teeth of the strong gusts. On the flip side, the LHHS defense was staunch and thwarted the constant "up-the-middle" pounding as lineman Ray Audette asserted himself time after time, once engendering a swinging punch from a Derby player, only to have Ray shrug it off without a called penalty.

Derby emerged from halftime to offer a solid defense that Lyman Hall could hardly dent. The black high-top football shoes that both teams wore were covered in mud. With every running step, clomps of mud took flight, covering the legs and pants of the combatants. The third quarter was played between the 40-yard lines as neither team could consistently move the ball towards the opponent's goal line.

The offense of the era, the single wing, was employed by both Derby and Lyman Hall. However, Coach Fernald employed a "Box" formation. Both of the teams ran their plays, starting with the center snapping the ball through his legs back to the fullback or one of the halfbacks. In one of Coach Fernald's first personnel moves in organizing the '26 team, he placed one of his best athletes at center, junior Charles Frauham. This move surprised the other members of the team, who recognized Frauham as probably the finest all-around athlete in the school.

Frauham was a skilled basketball player and undoubtedly the best baseball man. While the Derby center was having difficulty snapping the ball back to his backfield mates, miss-snapping many center passes back, Frauham's passes through his legs were on target throughout the game. It was the backs, Bill Buckley and Walt Vollhardt, who mishandled or fumbled the ball in the wet conditions in the second half. To make matters worse, the football itself was caked in mud, making it more challenging for both centers to snap it back to their backfield teammates.

Late in the fourth quarter, Buckley broke loose for a 24-yard run to the 12-yard line of Derby. Lyman Hall was finally moving the pigskin down the field as the LHHS students roared. There was joyous anticipation in the chilly air for a Wallingford victory if only the 0-0 tie could be broken with a score. The referee told both teams that there was less than one minute remaining as Dorsey called a play to fullback Vollhardt who ran to the four-yard line. With four seconds remaining in the game, Dorsey called for and attempted a drop-kick of 15 yards that the strong winds embraced, blowing the football off-course as the game ended in a 0-0 tie, yet giving Lyman Hall the 1926 Housatonic Valley League Championship.

Regal Dorsey commented some years later, "We might have been able to run in for a touchdown, but I thought we would run out of time, so I told Charlie (Fauham) to send 'er back to me for a last-second dropkick. I thought I had it. It was a short one, but the wind caught it, and that was it".

The LHHS students came on the field, tramping through the mud to get to their team, who were all covered from head to toe with thick mud. The students did not realize that their team had achieved a landmark championship. They were just so very proud of their fellow students.

The game had been so brutally fought, and it had gotten so dark and cold on this cloudy November late afternoon that the Derby team and fans quietly left the field at game's end, loading their cars to take them back to the Valley. The Lyman Hall teamed walked back to the school as many of their fellow students and some parents covered the team members in blankets and overcoats.

There was little cheering or banter on the walk back to Elm Street, as the team members wanted to take off their uniforms, shower, and get warm again. Principal Early, elated with his student's performance on the gridiron, walked with the team, talked with Coach Fernald and promised his first-year coach that there would be a celebration fitting the boys' achievement. Mr. Early made one memorable comment to the coach, who noted its utterance many times in years to come, ***"Langdon, my boy, don't forget that basketball begins next week."***

Chapter 14

Learning to Win, Learning to Celebrate

Principal Early had developed many relationships with local townspeople, specifically business owners and industry leaders. He had solicited advertisements for the Chronicle (yearbook/school newspaper), transportation for LHHS students to games and supplies for his teachers, but now, as his LHHS football team captured the first championship in any sport since the school opened in 1916, he made a special request of the Wallace Silver Company. Early wanted a unique trophy that could be positioned prominently in the school to commemorate the football championship. In amazingly short order, the silversmiths of Wallace made a magnificent sterling silver trophy of ten inches high depicting a ten-inch long football with hand engraving.

Mr. Early, Coach Fernald, and the football team members met after Thanksgiving to plan a most special assembly program. The team members were told to keep everything about this assembly very hush-hush by Early. Surreptitiously, plans went ahead, and not even the faculty were told of the assembly until two days prior to the event.

On Friday, December 10, 1926, this auditorium program was inserted into the already full-year schedule of (10) assemblies. In an extended 90-minute slice of the school day (most other auditorium programs were just a single class period) would honor the 1926 Housatonic Valley League Champions. For

Early and Fernald, this was a golden opportunity to further promote football and all athletics at Lyman Hall.

Dramatically, the team was seated on the stage with the act curtain closed as the student body entered the auditorium. As the curtain was drawn back to open the event, the students and citizens in attendance, many of whom stood in the open French doorways on either side of the auditorium, broke out in thunderous applause and random cheers that would last ten minutes. As Mr. Early stood behind a podium to the left of the stage, he made no effort to curtail the rhythmic clapping from one and all.

Coach Fernald began the festivities with a brief few comments about the "Great Game of Football" and the Father of Football, Walter Camp, a native of New Britain, Connecticut, who died in March of 1925. Then senior members of the team read anecdotes from the life of Mr. Camp as team captain, Regal Dorsey, handed a check for $25.00 to a representative of Yale University for the newly created Camp Memorial Fund. Each member of the team contributed to this donation.

Then Mr. Early bestowed Lyman Hall letters to each member of the team. The letters were a felt material. Each man on the team received an "L" and an "H" that could be sewn on a white sweater.

The final moments of the program were Mr. Early presenting the Wallace Silversmith-designed championship trophy to Captain Regal Dorsey that brought everyone in the auditorium to their feet with deafening clapping and cheers.

Mr. Early closed the assembly stating that he wanted all students to be at all the basketball games and telling one and all that he expected Lyman Hall to be basketball champions. Little did he know then how prophetic his words would be. With Early's love for basketball and Fernald's talent and drive, the dawn of the "Three Golden Era's Basketball" was born. Each would come at the expense of football at Lyman Hall High School, but Early's will be done.

Chapter 15

The Golden Eras of Basketball

Every public high school in America would like to point to a period of time in the school's history when the students, faculty, and citizens of the town enjoyed the excitement of enjoying a degree of dominance in a specific sport. Indeed, some high schools have been wildly successful in a single sport for what seems like an endless number of years without lull or interruption.

In the one hundred plus year history of Lyman Hall High School, there have been three Golden Eras of basketball. Although the great performers' and coaches' names are different in each era, there were noticeable similarities in each. First, there was sustained winning as one always felt the Orangemen and Trojans (beginning in 1957) would win each game. Second, the crowds packed in to see the LHHS teams play, home and away. Third, the student body was energized by the teams of each era. The student body connected to the members of the team. The players of each Golden Era were deeply emersed in the school's organizations, and activities, other than athletics and honor students filled the rosters of the teams.

There are many reasons why this string of years might be so successful for an individual school, including having an inspiring, highly devoted coach(es), a supportive school district and administration, an embracing community, and the confluence of a steady flow of talented student-athletes.

For the vast majority of schools, there are moments in time when circumstances come together, and a championship is realized, but sustaining a long run of victorious (championship) seasons is a rare occurrence.

In the epoch of the 20th century, when it was common practice for a single physical education (gym) teacher to be held responsible to coach all sports in a secondary school, it was virtually impossible to sustain consecutive years of championship-baring seasons in one or more sports. The benefit of the solitary coach is that he would develop relationships with every student who had exemplary athletic skills. This led to the best athletes in a school playing every sport. It was common in the first half of the 20th century to see the same names appearing on the football, basketball, and baseball teams. There was little or no specialization by a coach or student.

As Lyman Hall High School Hall of Fame honoree Regal Dorsey (class of 1927) once explained, "The high school teams were almost an extension of the games you played with your friends when you were not in school. You played pick-games in backyards, parks, in the streets with your buddies, all year round. When you got to high school, you just kept playing together, and you played every sport".

Before there was a Little League, Biddy Basketball, and all the other adult-driven organized youth sports in Wallingford, children played outside games with a ball, a bat, a peach basket, and any other object that would serve their desire to compete in a game.

Of all the games boys played in Wallingford since the turn of the 20th century, basketball was the game of choice. You could make your own ball, and if it didn't bounce, you ran with it, but you still could shoot to the basket.

The kids of Wallingford grew up comfortable and enjoying basketball in whatever manifestation it took. With an inside basketball court at the state armory and the sparkling gymnasium at the brand-spanking new Lyman Hall High

School opening in 1916, there was a new enthusiasm for the game of basketball.

The hiring of Langdon D. Fernald in 1926 sparked the FIRST GOLDEN ERA of basketball at Lyman Hall High School from 1927-1940. The tone set by then principal Robert H. Early set a high bar. For him and his new coach, Fernald, success was winning championships. Coach Fernald and his cavalcade of basketball stars, Charles Inguaggiato, Roger Offen, Charles Frauham, Fred Schipke, Charles Kelly, Stanley Naszcniec, Ken Spellacy, John "Blackie" Riccitelli, and so many others were the dominant basketball school in the Housatonic Valley League during that golden time.

The SECOND GOLDEN ERA of basketball at LHHS from 1943-1959 was engineered when Fred Schipke became the coach in 1943. While Coach Schipke never had a winning season as the football team's head coach, Fred never had a losing season in basketball, capturing five Housatonic League titles and two State Championships.

The THIRD GOLDEN ERA of basketball at LHHS from 1960-1968 came during the early coaching career of Roger McMahon. That period of time included seven consecutive seasons of total sell-outs and the record-setting performances of all-time greats Jim Potter, Mel Horowitz, Alban Chrisman, and Fran Stupakevich. During that era, Lyman Hall won five Housatonic League Championships.

Basketball at Lyman Hall High School was surely gold during these three eras of 42 seasons with incredible players, massive crowds, breath-taking significant victories, and 553 wins. For LHHS football during that same period of time, including the twelve years when LHHS refused to field a team, the football teams had 52 wins, 120 losses, 19 ties with no winning seasons since 1932.

Chapter 16

Football Exacts Its First Toll ... On Basketball

The 1926 Housatonic Valley League championship in football in Langdon Fernald's first year of teaching and coaching at Lyman Hall was more than what Principal Early had dared to hope. Since its first year of operations in 1916, football never generated a winning season, let alone an undefeated league champion. Early hoped that the basketball team would enjoy similar success under Fernald in 1926, and that's precisely what he got, except for one crucial factor, INJURIES. For LHHS basketball, the injuries did not occur while playing basketball but during the football season. At the expense of being repetitive, the school's best athletes played every sport, which meant playing competitive sport throughout the school year for the school's best student-athletes. The time-honored expression that "injuries are part of the game" seems to be an inaccurate or limited statement without the follow-up question, "What sport"?

Although basketball was Principal Early's pride and joy, he loved any activity where LHHS students succeeded and celebrated every little victory, such as the LHHS student who won a typing contest sponsored by Laurel College in 1934 or the winning debate team of 1935. Every success, no matter the venue, mattered to Mr. Early, but basketball, victories/titles in that sport burned a pipeline to Early's heart of hearts.

Under Fernald, Lyman Hall athletic teams played to their

optimum talent level almost all the time. Fernald proved he could do a lot with even marginal talent in both football and basketball. However, the saga of debilitating injuries suffered by multi-talented athletes during the football season that subsequentially limited all that the basketball teams might have accomplished was not something Early chose to overlook during the first "Golden Era" of LHHS basketball.

In the first and ONLY Housatonic Valley League championship in 1926 and last, until 1974, Early and the entire school community received extended exhilaration.

Unfortunately, Principal Early received something more from the 1926 football title, ... the first evidence that football injuries spilled over into basketball season.

The only returning starter on the basketball team from the 1924-25 season (the year before Fernald took over the reins of the team) was Charles Frauham. A strapping well-defined junior, Frauham was the starting center on the 1926 football team but was inserted into the backfield halfway through the season due to injuries to other players. He instantly made his mark as a ball carrier, passer, and pass catcher, saving the Hallites' bacon with a dazzling catch to preserve a 7-7 tie with rival Branford.

Frauham was the second-leading scorer for the basketball team as a sophomore in 1924-25, and Fernald looked forward to coaching the versatile athlete in his first season as head of the basketball team. In the next to last game of the football season, Frauham was injured in a 12-6 victory over Milford High School. He refused to leave the game, and despite the injury to his right shoulder, he played on, helping the Hallites to victory.

In the last game of the year that would determine the league champion, Frauham insisted on playing despite the painful shoulder malady. Charles played the entire contest against Derby, further damaging his shoulder. The following week as basketball practice began, Frauham could not raise his right arm, and consequently, he was unable to begin the basketball season in the starting lineup.

Chapter 17

Fernald's First Basketball Season

It could be argued that the 1926 football championship, with all of the fanfare it received in the school and community, spring-boarded the basketball team's success that followed in the 1926-27 season. However, the combination of the charismatic Fernald, a basketball maven in Principal, Robert Early, and a growing dynamism in the student body generated by Early and a mercurial young faculty set the stage for the start of one of the most incredible eras in LHHS history.

With only one returning regular player from the 1925-26 season in Charles Frauham, Coach Fernald had to construct his first team, literally from the floor up, but it didn't help Fernald's cause that Frauham had to miss the first five games due to a football injury. Additionally, Bill Buckley, Fernald's best candidate for a big man in the lineup at 6'1", was also unavailable for much of the first half of the season as the burley halfback had gotten banged up in the Derby football game. These two injuries did not escape principal Early's notice as the first caution light that football was having a negative impact on the basketball team at Lyman Hall.

Despite the absence of Frauham and Buckley (two future LHHS Hall of Fame honorees), the Hallites won their first seven games, mainly on the shoulders of a new brand of defense introduced by Fernald.

In the eighth game of the season, Branford and LHHS were

tied for first place in the Housatonic Valley League, with both teams undefeated. Mr. Early could not have been happier. Senior class President Henry Wachtelhausen remembers, "Mr. Early was perched outside of his office and telling everyone who passed him the hallway, "We'll see you at the game tonight."

The high-scoring Branford team would be challenged by the upstart Hallites and their bruising defense. Lyman Hall brought its stalling, sometimes brutal style of play to the distress of the Branford team and coach. Coach Fernald and the Branford coach protested numerous foul calls as the game deteriorated into a physical, back and forth game with players from both schools often knocked to the floor as the crowd cheered wildly and often groaned.

The game played before a packed gymnasium was bereft with one foul call after another as five players fouled out. Both coaches protested foul calls made by referees, but all that resulted was a long, protracted game. Branford held the lead at halftime at 14-10, but the Hallites could not close the gap in the second half as the Hornets notched a 28-19 victory and went on to the 1927 Housatonic Valley League Championship. LHHS would end Fernald's first season with a 12-2 record and a second-place finish in the league.

FERNALD AND DEFENSE

As Fernald was as a collegiate player, Coach Fernald was a fanatic when it came to defense.

When Dr. James Naismith wrote the first five rules of basketball in 1891, rule #5 stated something to the effect, ... There shall be no physical contact between players. He did not have Coach Fernald's teams in mind. While most high school teams maneuvered to get their players, shots close to the basket, Coach Fernald worked his teams tirelessly to limit, often harshly, the movements of opponents on the court and then had his players pass and hold the ball for long stretches of time before taking a shot at the basket.

The 1923-24 and 1924-25 Housatonic Valley League

champion was Branford High School. The well-coached Branford squad had fine players, and this set the stage for many hard-fought games and established a hardwood rivalry that would last until the 1960s.

The first game of the season was an eye-opener for the Housatonic Valley League. Against an experienced Stratford team, the LHHS contingent unleashed a style of defense that limited Stratford to only 12 points for the game in a 23-12 victory as three Hallite starters fouled out. To prove this defensive effort was no fluke, Lyman Hall played Derby in the second tilt and held the red-clad valley high school to only two baskets. The rest of the Derby points came on foul shots for an 18-9 win. The Wallingford "5" was vying for the 1926-27 league title when they met Branford at its shoreline court. The LHHS team battled but could not stop the skilled Branford shooters, losing 28-19.

Fernald's first team with its exciting brand of basketball filled the LHHS gymnasium for every home game, but beyond wetting the palate of the students and citizenry, Fernald was now driven to win Housatonic Valley League Championships. A loftier goal, ... to win a state championship, would become a goal of passion for Early, Fernald, Lyman Hall's students, and the basketball frenzied Wallingford citizens.

Chapter 18

The First Golden Era of Basketball

1927-1940

After the quick rise of the basketball team in the 1926-27 season, which saw the Wallingford team off and running with a 10-win season (10-6 overall record) and a second-place finish in the Housatonic Valley League, there was anticipation for the start of the 1927-28 campaign.

The Hallites faced one of the many demanding schedules they would encounter during 1927-1940. Outstanding teams awaited them on the Early composed schedule, outside of the seven-school Housatonic Valley League, but Fernald would have them ready. The 1927 gridiron captain, the fleet Roland Perkins suffered from injuries sustained in the Shelton football game and again was forced to leave the Derby game with a painful shoulder issue. This reoccurring damage to Perkins' shoulder required many days of rest after the season, causing the basketball team to do without his services for several games. Seward Stevens missed valuable practice time at the outset of the round-ball season as he healed from football injuries.

Mr. Early lamented the loss of some projected starters of the basketball squad, but Fernald drove his younger team members to fill in admirably. The Hallites lost the first league game of the season, a 36-26 humbling at the hands of Milford, then won their next nine Housatonic Valley League games with Fernald's thumping and thudding defense. In the games to come, LHHS would limit opponents to less than 20 points scored ten times. On a night of snow and sleet and no thought of postponing the game by either school, Lyman Hall invaded Milford with the league title on the line.

Milford looked as good as they did in their first confrontation with LHHS. The far taller "Milford five" held a 15-8 lead at the half and a 17-13 bulge at the end of the third period. With three Hallite starters with three or four fouls heading into the final quarter, LHHS unleashed a blistering defense. Captain Bill Sittnick led the LHHS team back to a 24-24 tie with fifteen seconds remaining on Milford's gym clock.

Sittnick looked ready to shoot from under the basket but chose to throw a pass to Charlie Frauham outside of the keyhole. The always clutch, Frauham nailed a shot that looked to be of 15 feet or more with five seconds on the scoreboard. As Milford tried to inbounds the ball, the clock ticked zero, and the Wallingford students and rooters rushed onto the court and lifted the members of their Lyman Hall team onto their shoulders. The bedlam continued for many minutes as Lyman Hall High School captured the 1928 and their first ever Housatonic League Valley championship. The Hallites finished with a record of 16-4, losing only to state title contenders Wilby, Meriden, and the first game of the year to Milford. With the league title and ten-win season, the Wallingfordites did not receive an invitation to the Yale, Class B, CIAC State Tournament. League rival Branford High School whom LHHS defeated twice, 21-17 and 17-10, did receive a bid to the Class A Tournament. This further fueled Early's and Fernald's shared mission to push the LHHS basketball team over the top into and win the Yale Tournament.

Chapter 19

A Title with Style, 1928-29

Prior to the start of the 1928-29 school year, Principal Early and Coach Fernald reportedly had their first discussions relative to minimizing football injuries. Fernald concluded to Early that if you are going to play the game of football, there are going to be injuries, some just bruises, and some very serious. The two men decided that as a first measure, no outside-of-league football games would be played, meaning that Lyman Hall would only play six football games.

The 1928 football squad had a good share of all-around athletic talent and a tremendously gifted sophomore class. Fourteen members of the '28 football team would play for the basketball team during their years at Lyman Hall. Among the star-studded cast of both sports were Lester LaCroix, Robert Butler, Joe Sagnella, Donald Briggs, Joe Konopka, Robert Cassidy, Roger Offen and sophomores, Fred Schipke and Charles Inguaggiato. The latter three would enter the LHHS Hall of Fame in the 1980s. However, there was no sneaking up on the Housatonic Valley League in football as they might have done in 1926. The gridiron team finished with a 2-2-2 slate; however, senior basketball stalwarts Bob Butler and Bob Cassidy, hurt during the football season, were forced to miss the first four games of the basketball season.

With the start of the 1928-29 season, expectations were higher than ever that this edition of the basketball season would win another Housatonic championship and have a record that demanded their entry into the state tournament. This season marked the third year under Coach Fernald and his highly demanding defensive system. As the Crosby High School coach remarked after the fourth game of the regular season, a stunning 23-19 LHHS victory over the state powerhouse, "Playing Lyman Hall is like being a tree and getting chopped down."

Principal Early's aggressive scheduling placed several top teams on the regular-season schedule against his Orangemen for 1928-29. The acclaimed Orangemen were fast, exciting, gave no quarter, and expected none. They began the season with a romp over Choate, 43-14. Then came a powerful Middletown squad, toppling them, 22-11. In a nasty, roughly played bout, LHHS beat Meriden in Meriden, 13-11. New England power, Crosby High School, went to overtime with the boys from Wallingford as the Orangemen prevailed, 23-19.

The Wallingford high school defeated previously unbeaten Torrington 33-17 and dropped the return engagement with Wilby, 13-9 in another foul-fest. When the curtain came down on the 1928-29 regular season, LHHS held a 17-2 record but held its collective breath to see if the 1928-29 Housatonic Valley League Champions would seem worthy enough to merit inclusion into the CIAC Yale State Tournament. Due to the limited number of schools deemed "worthy" for the Yale tournament, classes A and B were combined for 1929. You have to love the Wallingford teams' quirky destiny over the long history of Lyman Hall High School.

Fernald and Early's shared belief was that Lyman Hall could not be left out of the state tournament with its record that included wins against a number of outstanding teams. This time, Lyman Hall received the bid that they so wholly earned. The Orangemen were slated in the tournament with high schools Bristol, Warren Harding of Bridgeport, Bridgeport Central, Torrington, Wilby, and Hillhouse. This state champion would represent Connecticut in a national tournament in Chicago. As it happened many times in years to come, Lyman Hall was slated to play the top-ranked team in the first round. For this year, it was Warren Harding who defeated the Orangemen, 32-22. Gaining admittance into the Yale Tournament, although disappointing in the outcome, placed the ultimate carrot one step closer to the status of "possibility."

Chapter 20

The Emergence of "Inky," 1929-30

 Perhaps in the faded pages of history, but not in the hearts and minds of those who watched the tall, handsome boy enter Lyman Hall High School in the fall of 1928, will ever forget the incredibly talented Charles "Inky" Inguaggiato. There were too few of Inguaggiato's athletic stature and fewer of those who embodied the beauty of spirit of the boy they called "Inky."

Coach Langdon Fernald discovered early in the fall of 1928 how blessed he was as a coach, when he watched this tall thin freshman, known to his classmates as "Inky," run over, around, and sometimes through his senior-laden football team in practice. Unfortunately, with the limited substitution rules of the times, Inguaggiato received few opportunities to play in a varsity game.

One cannot overstate the impact of Inguaggiato on all the sports teams. With each year, he grew in his confidence as his body filled out. His deeds are legendary, but like Mel Horowitz and Fran Stupakevich of the 1960s, people came just to see "Inky" play. His feats are the fodder of mythic heroes such as Gilgamesh and Achilles.

One such story, told by scores of Wallingford citizens over

the years, was a day in the spring of 1932. As baseball captain and shortstop, Inguaggiato hit a homerun in the first inning at Doolittle Park. There was an intra-school track meet going on in the lower quarter of Doolittle, where the skating rink was situated during the winter months. When Lyman Hall came to bat into the second inning and the lower half of the Orangemen batting order scheduled to hit, "Inky" sprinted to the track meet. There he took off his baseball jersey and ran in the 100-yard dash, winning easily over the opposition, and then returned to the baseball diamond. That day he would hit a homer and a triple, leading LHHS to victory.

Fernald first saw Inguaggiato in his gym classes and knew right away he had a "great one" for his basketball team. Regal Dorsey, class of 1927 and future Vice Principal of LHHS, remembered Inguaggiato this way, "Charlie could do anything ... I mean anything in sports, but in basketball, he was something else. He was kind of thin when I first saw him, but he could jump higher than anyone else ... and fast? He had these daddy-long-legged strides when he ran, and he ran down the court in a flash".

Inguaggiato, like Fran Stupakevich, some 35 years later, was one of those rare athletes people came to see play, no matter the sport, but in basketball, "Inky" was spectacular. With all the attention on basketball in Wallingford, Coach Fernald and the basketball doting principal of Robert Early hoped to keep "Inky" healthy, but no coach, fierce opposition defense, or injury could keep Charlie off the field or court for long.

The 1929 football season marked the first time in school history that LHHS won five games in a season but did not win the Housatonic Valley League championship. Remarkable in that season was the appearance of Charlie Inguaggiato in the Lyman Hall backfield. Right from the start, the speed-merchant "Inky" dazzled the opposition's defense with long runs, highlighted by darting moves and changes of direction. Don Briggs passes to Inguaggiato brought "ooooh's and aah's, from the Wallingford faithful, as "Inky" would often leap high to snare passes.

The football season of 1929 was a coming out party of sorts for Inguaggiato, but alas, the football injuries continued to cause consternation for both Early and Fernald. Basketball captain Don Briggs was hampered by a hip injury that slowed him up in the early going of the basketball season but recovered sufficiently to lead the Orangemen to a number of victories. Lester LaCroix, one of the leading scorers from the 1928-29 basketball team, was knocked out of the Seymour football game with a head injury (concussion) late in the season but returned to the round-ball squad for the Branford game, a 19-18 win.

In his sophomore basketball season, he and fellow sophomore Fred Schipke were the talk of the town. Many thought that this pair of sophomores, along with junior, Roger Offen might finally lead the Orangemen to the state title. The 1929-30 team included seasoned seniors Lester LaCroix, and Don "Dudey" Briggs, but Offen, Inguaggiato, and Schipke were impossible to keep out of the lineup. The Orangemen would win their third consecutive Housatonic Valley League title in 1930, and in the process, defeat Branford twice. Although the Orangemen were not selected for the State Tournament, Branford **was** chosen in the combined Class C/D part of the tournament and won the 1930 State Championship.

Chapter 21

The Pressure Builds

Lyman Hall High School's continuing dominance over the Housatonic Valley League in basketball turned up the pressure for the Orangemen to reach the pinnacle of interscholastic play, winning a state championship. The stream of quality players to Langdon Fernald's teams kept edging up the local enthusiasm for basketball. The absence of *today's* social media or newspapers with an everyday sports section didn't stop LHHS student-athletes from becoming household names.

Although Mr. Early continued to shill for the basketball team, encouraging all students to attend every game of the Orangemen, it was the town's people who were clamoring for greater access to tickets for the games. The 1930-31 season expectations were never higher, at least to this point in the Fernald years, but first, the football season had to be played.

The 1930 football squad had a roster of 36 team members, the largest in terms of the numbers of players since the school opened in 1916. The team had a solid senior class presence that included captain Joe Sagnella, future All-American, Roger Offen, and Charlie Malaguti, but the lightning bolt of the team was junior, Inguaggiato, maybe the finest football player in the league. With more than a few talented athletes on the team to vie for a league title in 1930, the emergence of sophomore Richard "Dick" Barry made the Orangemen backfield more than lethal.

The 1930 season began on a rain-soaked Doolittle Park field against Shelton. Inguaggiato broke off a long run of 43 yards in the first quarter but fumbled on the 15-yard line on his way to a sure touchdown. Barry carried the pigskin 13 times in his Orangemen debut for 85 yards, but neither he nor "Inky" could dent the Shelton goal line. The mud dripped off the uniforms of both teams as the contest ended in a 0-0 tie. Game two was another scoreless duel as Inguaggiato broke off several long rushing plays, but the Milford defense did not allow him to score. Schipke kept Lyman Hall out of trouble with his punts that splashed on the sloppy surface. For the second game in a row, the Orangemen played to a 0-0 tie, this time with Milford.

Seymour traveled to Doolittle Park for the third game of the season. Inguaggiato scored three touchdowns, and Barry had two as the Orangemen ran away from the visitors, 45-6. Lyman Hall earned their second win of the season with a 19-0 victory over Stratford as Barry, Sagnella and Schipke picked up touchdowns. After a 7-0 victory over Derby, Lyman Hall had a slight chance to tie for the Housatonic Valley League championship, but long-time rival Branford nipped the Wallingfordites, 13-6 as Inguaggiato received a brutal tackle as he attempted to run around the end in the second quarter, as cries of "Oh-No" came from the Lyman Hall faithful. "Inky" had to be carried back to the LHHS bench and did not return to the game. The final 3-1-2 record gave the Orangemen a second-place tie in the league, but attention quickly shifted to the basketball court where the team would be young but loaded with basketball prowess.

Chapter 22

4ᵗʰ Straight Housatonic Title, 1930-31

The Lyman Hall High School basketball schedule could not have been much more challenging as Principal Early loaded the weeks of the season with every talent-laden team he could arrange. Coach Fernald did not object, except that the season began against teams that allowed older students to play.

Scrimmages or practice games were burdensome for schools due to travel and securing game officials, so any game scheduled against any team was included in each school's final record.

With Inguaggiato still out with a football malady, the Orangemen opened the season against Stone Business School (a two-year college). Roger Offen was a tower of strength on the backboards against the taller college team, with Charlie Malaguti leading LHHS in scoring as the Orangemen prevailed, 27-12. Booth Preparatory School was next as the graduate year institution defeated the Wallingfordites, 20-18, with Schipke, the leading scorer for LHHS.

State power, Wilby High School was next for Lyman Hall. Inguaggiato was back in the starting lineup and immediately made his presence felt in a 14-12 victory in a defensive fracas in Waterbury. The score was tied at 6-5 at the half as the referees seemed to just let the players play, rough or not. Two more non-league victories followed as the Orangemen tore into the Housatonic opposition. The Wallingford school went undefeated in the league and then faced Wilby one more time in the final game of the season.

With both teams remembering the confrontation early in the season, the Orangemen led the game throughout, leading 22-20 with little more than a minute remaining in the game. Wilby tied the game and forced an overtime period. In a brawling extra stanza, Wilby pulled away with four foul shots, 26-24.

With the annual reconfiguring of the classes, the selection panel put all of the best class B schools in with those of Class A for the 1931 state "Yale" tournament. Despite Lyman Hall's sterling undefeated league record with out-of-league victories against quality teams, the Orangemen were seated last in the eight-team tournament that infuriated Principal Early. Predictably, Lyman Hall opened the state tournament pitted against top-rated, undefeated, defending champion Naugatuck High School.

As Lyman Hall prepared for the herculean task of playing Naugatuck, a tall-lanky team that towered over the Orangemen, Fernald was faced with one more challenge. His best player, Charlie Inguaggiato, had reinjured a hip in the final Wilby game, the same one that was banged up in football, forcing the super athlete to the Orangemen bench.

Fernald's stifling defense limited Naugatuck to few shots, but Naugy led at halftime, 14-7. In the third quarter, Lyman Hall completely outplayed top-rated Naugatuck, fighting back to knot the score at 16. From that point on, Naugatuck scored in close, time and again, pulling away for a 28-18 victory. Fred Schipke led the Orangemen in scoring with seven points.

Fred recalled the game in a conversation some years later and commented, "We were a good team, but Charlie was our leader. Without him, it was almost impossible to beat that Naugatuck team". Naugatuck went on to defeat Bridgeport Central in the championship game, 27-23.

Chapter 23

Legend of the Lantern

When teacher, coach, and future principal Langdon Fernald arrived at LHHS in September 1926, Lyman Hall athletics' fortunes (particularly basketball) immediately ascended to incredible heights. Beginning in his second year as coach of basketball, his teams won six consecutive Housatonic League Championships, 1927-28 to 1932-33. By the beginning of the 1930s, all home basketball games were standing room only, made all the more unique by the gym's asymmetrical design with baskets flatly affixed to the north and south walls.

However, there was a problem for Wallingford citizens. As they loved their LHHS basketball teams, traveling to away games was challenging. Lyman Hall played away contests in Milford, Stratford, Derby, Seymour, Waterbury, Newtown, Bridgeport, New Haven, just to name a few. State highways such as I-91 and I-84 did not exist. There were no Global Positioning System (GPS) units to guide one's path, and the only communications technology available was the telephone, and it wasn't a "mobile device."

The people of Wallingford figuratively lived and died on the outcomes of the Lyman Hall basketball games. LHHS basketball was Wallingford's team.

When the team was playing an away game, Wallingford citizens, not to mention the current students, would call the police department and the principal of the school at his home to inquire about the score of each game.

Robert Hunter Early was principal of the school from 1918

until his death in 1939 was an enthusiastic fan of the LHHS team and asked that Coach Fernald call him if at all possible at the conclusion of every away basketball game. In the 1930s, Mr. Early had become somewhat annoyed by the seemingly endless telephone calls to his home inquiring about the results of the night's away basketball game. The Wallingford citizenry literally hung on the outcome of every game, home and away.

The most challenging part of the basketball season relative to game communications/results was the state basketball tournament. In the early years of the state tournament, only ten high schools were selected for three classes (S, M, L). That was later changed in the 1940s to designation classes of A, B, C. No matter the classifications, very few schools made it into the State Tournament, and Lyman Hall was one of the few mainstays, entering the very exclusive state tournament every year from 1928-1940 under Coach Fernald.

LHHS basketball was almost a winter religion for the people of Wallingford. The citizenry waited for game results like Christmas presents. Although there were those who followed the basketball team vehicle (Coach Fernald's "woody," an orange-painted, wood paneled station wagon), there were no buses to take the team or students when it traveled to tournament locations to these games.

So the throngs of Wallingford citizens and LHHS students had to wait for game results long into the evening after the team returned or wait until morning. A number of strategies were tried, but finally, Principal Early came up with an idea. In 1931 he arranged to have a candle street lantern affixed to the front of the school. When Coach Fernald called him after a victory, Mr. Early would call someone who lived close to the school to light the candle.

Over the years, large crowds would gather on the front steps and the middle walkway of the high school on the nights of tournament games to watch for the lighting of the lantern, signaling a tournament victory. One of the largest reported crowds gathered in 1937 as approximately 200 persons huddled for hours to see if the lantern would burn on the occasion of the State Final game at the Payne Whitney

Gymnasium against Branford School. Alas, the Orangemen lost in the State, Class B Finals for the second year in a row to Branford, and the lantern remained dark.

The use of the "lantern" ended after the 1948 basketball season as Lyman Hall upset the highly favored and undefeated East Haven High School team to win the Class B State Championship.

Chapter 24

1931 Football Season

Coach Fernald felt he had such a good football team coming back for 1931 that he encouraged Principal Early to schedule a few non-conference games, which he did in adding Southington and Choate.

With three members of the backfield returning for the 1931 football season in Inguaggiato, Schipke, and Barry (all future LHHS Hall of Fame inductees), the Orangemen were good enough to win the Housatonic Valley League championship, but the injury bug took its toll on LHHS. The season opened with Shelton, a bigger bunch that also had designs on the league top spot. Lyman Hall lineman Norman Kelman busted through the Shelton forces early in the game and blocked a punt, setting up a Schipke touchdown.

In the third quarter, with LHHS hanging on to a 7-0 lead, Dick Barry took a handoff from quarterback, Inguaggiato, breaking up the middle for 21 yards. Then it was Louie Bartek's turn taking a lateral from "Inky" and racing into the endzone. The hard-fought battle ended with a 13-0 LHHS victory. The Orangemen recorded their second win of the young season with a sound 19-6 victory against Milford.

The win over Milford exacted a heavy price for Lyman Hall as tackle Jack Griffin hurt his shoulder, and quarterback Inguaggiato incurred a leg injury, forcing both to miss the next game against Southington. Without the two stalwarts, especially "Inky," the field general, Lyman Hall lost to

Southington, 14-0. With "Inky" on the mend, he chose to play in the next game against Branford in a downpour.

Coach Fernald was concerned about playing his best athlete but permitted Inguaggiato to give it a go. Even with "Inky" back calling the plays, Barry and Schipke could not get their proper footing as Branford ran away with a 12-0 win over LHHS.

Week five on the schedule saw the Orangemen travel to Derby for a league contest that had to be won if the Wallingford team had any aspirations of a league title. With just under three minutes played, Barry caught a pass from Inguaggiato and ran to the 22-yard line of the home team. From there, Fred Schipke scored LHHS's only touchdown of the game but missed the extra point. Derby responded with a six-pointer and an extra point that won the contest, 7-6 that ended the Orangemen's title hopes.

Fernald added more deception into Inguaggiato's play-calling as the Orangemen defeated a much bigger Choate team, 28-6. The final football game of the year was an unaccustomed blowout, a 33-6 win over Stratford, as Fernald played everyone on his team in the game.

Charlie Inguaggiato playing in his last Lyman Hall football game and fighting through nagging injuries, called his own number often as "Inky" scored four touchdowns. Dick Barry kicked three extra points and ran for 67 yards out of the halfback position. The Orangemen ended the campaign with a 3-1-2 won/loss/tie record.

Chapter 25

Heightened Hopes ... The 1931-32 Basketball Season

Principal Early believed that this season would finally net an Orangemen state championship. To be sure, the roster was loaded (four members became Hall of Fame honorees). The team was led by captain Fred "Dutch" Schipke, honor student, a four-sport standout, and President of the Class of 1932. The state shot put championship that he won in 1932 and all his many other athletic accolades are more remarkable given that "Dutch" lost three fingers on his right hand in a boyhood accident.

With Schipke in the starting lineup alongside seniors Bernie "Barno" Sabo and George Mansolf, junior Charlie Kelly (who would average 10.2 points per game), and the prodigious presence of Charlie Inguaggiato, the hopes of the citizenry for a historic season could not have been much higher. Early was so enthused with anticipation of the 1931-32 season that he had new orange uniforms made for the team and secured practice shirts of navy blue for each member of the squad.

The first game of the year was a blowout of Trinity Parish, 44-8, as "Inky" scored 16 markers. Stone College gave the Orangemen a tad more trouble, but the Hallites won 38-23. Game three was the contest that the team, Fernald, Early, and the Town of Wallingford, had waited for since the schedule was announced ... the matchup with state powerhouse, Wilby High School.

The game was a complete sellout in Waterbury as state rankings were at stake. The contest pitted the vaunted Orangemen defense against the much taller Wilby five. With the crowd on its feet during the entire fourth quarter, the game ended in regulation in a 26-26 tie. The overtime period was hotly played, with neither team able to score.

With just under a minute remaining in the overtime, Charlie Kelly heaved up a shot from the far corner to score the winning basket. Johnny Lacey (future United States Olympic head team trainer) was high man for the Orangemen with eleven points.

After the fire and brimstone of the Wilby game, the Orangemen were off their fast-paced game but still managed a clean victory against Middletown. Lyman Hall was only able to score nine points in the first half, but Middletown High School scored .... zero. The final score was 26-7 in favor of the undefeated Hallites.

Coach Fernald disappointed in the effort of his charges against Middletown, turned up the heat against out-of-league opponent Guilford High School as the Orangemen ran away with the game, winning 71-15. Lyman Hall ran off nine straight wins to open the season and then were stopped by Meriden as a Silver City high school player shot the ball from mid-court for a basket with 55 seconds left in the game to defeat Lyman Hall.

Now, it was back to league business as the 1931-32 team throttled all Housatonic Valley League opposition to finish with a 12-0 league record, winning Lyman Hall's fifth consecutive league title.

Since Langdon Fernald began teaching (and coaching) at Lyman Hall High School, there was a gradual increase in respect from the state's sportswriters and others of influence. Following the 1931-32 regular season that saw the Wallingfordites end with an overall record of 18-4, LHHS was slated into the Connecticut Interscholastic (C.I.A.C.) Basketball Tournament, otherwise known as the "Yale

Tournament" (because all games were played entirely on the campus of Yale University).

Although this season marked the third in six years that LHHS was chosen, there still was a relatively sour taste in the mouths of Principal Early, Coach Fernald, and many others as LHHS had captured the Housatonic Valley title for five years in a row.

The number one seed in the tournament was Hillhouse High School, as Lyman Hall was slotted as number six. The Orangemen's first-round opponent was Meriden (an out-of-league opponent) that had beaten Lyman Hall twice during the regular season.

With Inguaggiato plagued with knee and shoulder injuries, Fernald turned to Johnny Lacey, and the junior responded with a tremendous defensive effort. Charlie Kelly picked up the scoring slack as the Orangemen turned the tables on Meriden High School, winning their first game ever in State Tournament play, 32-14.

Stepping into unchartered territory for Lyman Hall playing in their first semi-final game in the Yale Tournament, the Orangemen faced second-seeded Bristol High School. The much taller team from the "Mum City" took control of the game from the onset, and with Inguaggiato's limited participation, Bristol took control and won a 41-26 victory. Top-seeded Hillhouse faced Bristol in the final with the No.1 state ranking on the line as the "Hilltoppers" won the state title, 24-20 over Bristol in Class A.

The aftermath of the 1931-32 season was a combination of moderate celebration and a head-shaking lament. The question on everyone's lips was, "How would LHHS have fared with a healthy Charlie Inguaggiato"? Still in all, the Orangemen won their fifth consecutive Housatonic Valley League Championship, and there were some quality players returning for 1932-33 if only they all could stay healthy.

Coach Fernald's 1932-33 basketball Orangemen completed their sixth undefeated Housatonic Valley League season, finishing 16-3 with all three losses coming against out-of-league foes. Lyman Hall defeated tournament-bound teams

Crosby, Middletown, and Rockville in the regular season, losing twice to Meriden and once to Middletown.

The Orangemen were rewarded for their outstanding season by being slated in the Yale Tournament in the combined (with B schools) A division classification. In the first round, Lyman Hall High School was defeated by Bridgeport Central High School, 35-29. The Orangemen battled to the end, knotting the score three times in the second half. John Lacey and Charlie Kelly received well-deserved kudos by sports writers earning honorable mention to the All-Tournament team. With the stirring 1933 season in the books, there was still great expressed frustration from all who followed Lyman Hall High School basketball, especially Mr. Early, all wondering what it would take to get the Orangemen to a state championship. There was much more basketball talent coming along, but would it be enough to finally achieve what was cherished by Early and Fernald.

Chapter 26

State Tournament, Not Enough

In recent years, approximately 1990 to the present, local secondary school basketball teams and their followers are often celebratory when their team wins at least 40% of their games, qualifying them for the annual CIAC tournament. This is a far cry from the level of excellence a high school basketball team would have to achieve even to be considered for slating in the state tournament in the early years of the "Yale Tournament," beginning in 1922.

In those early years of the state tournament, a school made it into the bracket for each division based solely on "reputation," a subjective judgment call by the sportswriters and other "persons of influence" (the selection panel) who reviewed the list of Connecticut secondary schools and their season records, and with not much more than the "eye-test" determined the eight schools per division who were judged the best for that year. If the selection panel reviewed a division (based on school enrollment) and determined that only a few schools were tournament-worthy, those schools might get bumped up to the higher division.

As with all schools in Connecticut, all you could do was hope that your regular season was viewed as something special in the eyes of a selection panel member(s). For principal Early, just getting into the "Yale Tournament" was not enough, as he stated many times. With Early scheduling as many top-shelf teams as possible for the regular season along with the six league schools that were played twice, he and Coach Fernald hoped their challenging schedule and the amazing win/loss record would get Lyman Hall recognized as a "tournament-worthy" team each year. Unfortunately, Lyman Hall was left out more than a few times. For Early and Fernald, the "brass ring" was to win a state championship. With each year since 1927, the pressure increased to reach that hallowed place of state basketball achievement.

Fernald proved to be a great motivator and a skilled tactical coach, but the number of high-level athletes at Lyman Hall High School or most other schools was not infinite, so the Orangemen could not afford to lose those exceptional student-athletes to injury, if at all possible. Fernald stated publicly that his teams in 1930-31 and 1931-32 might have been good enough to win the state title as they were "shelves-full" with superb athletes.

As the LHHS football teams struggled through a 1-4-1 record and in 1933 and 2-6 slate in 1934, it was an easy switch to flip for the intense attention to basketball. Early and the student body seemed to take for granted that their Orangemen would win the league championship in basketball, but more was desired in terms of a state title.

With each appearance in the "Yale Tournament," there was growing anxiety for the Orangemen to win their way to the finals ... and win the championship. The 1933-34 team turned out to be a cold bucket of water on the Orangemen faithful as the LHHS round ball contingent had their first non-winning season under Fernald, a 10-10 final record, notwithstanding a senior-laden team.

The 1934-35 school year began with Fernald scouring his gym classes for additional football team members as the '34 squad jumped from 28 members in 1933 to 36 in 1934. Regardless of the number of participants, the Orangemen football team had losing seasons, and injuries to key athletes continued to haunt the basketball-crazed supporters.

Tommy Kavanaugh, the center and leading scorer for the basketball team in 1933, decided to come out for the football team in this his senior year. He immediately became one of the top three players on the team. During the Branford game, he sustained a leg injury that ended his football season. Kavanaugh was unable to play for the basketball team until late in the season as the Orangemen tumbled to a 7-11 record with no league championship or tournament berth. The grumblings of both Mr. Early and Coach Fernald were becoming louder that football was indeed taking its toll on the fortunes of the basketball squad. It cannot be overstated how important LHHS basketball was to Wallingford and its citizenry.

Chapter 27

Reaching the Finals, 1936

Coach Fernald had a squad of 35 men for the 1935 fall grid season. Unfortunately, almost immediately, key members of the team were battered and could not continue to play, including basketball captain David Barry, and basketball teammates, William LaCroix and Harry "Peanuts" Bartholomew. The numbers of injured mounted for the '35 football team as the Orangemen finished the season at 1-5.

Of the football related injuries that impacted the basketball team directly were those of Dave Barry, who missed the first four games on the court, then came back for two contests, then reinjured the same shoulder. Basketball starters LaCroix and Bartholomew missed time during the basketball season due to football sustained injuries.

Despite these missing starters, Fernald had his basketball team ready to compete and win during the 1935-36 season. The rough and ready Orangemen came in second in the Housatonic Valley League with only two losses, both to Branford. The season was chocked full of quality teams for LHHS to face as the Orangemen ended the regular season with a 12-6 slate. To everyone's delight, that record was enough for the selection committee to include Lyman Hall into the Class B Yale Tournament.

Because of the injuries to his starters, Fernald had played as many as eleven different players during the season, and by the start of the state tournament, they were all ready to contribute. In the first round, the Orangemen downed Hartford Public High School 31-22. Manchester Trade School was next for the Wallingfordites as the Orangemen frustrated the far taller Silk City five, gaining a 40-36 victory.

Now, for the first time in school history, Lyman Hall High School would play for a state championship. Although Bartholomew was nursing injuries, Fernald's charges would face Branford High School for the third time in the 1935-36 year ... this time in the state finals. The game was a brutal affair with numerous fouls called in the first half, but Branford, with its accurate long-range shooting, prevailed, 29-19 to capture the 1936 Class B title.

Chapter 28

The Last Football Season, 1936

Far too lightly stated, the "bangs and bruises" exacted on some basketball team members (1936 Class B Runners-up) from their performance on the 1935 Orangemen football team were impossible to ignore. Fernald had done all that he could to enlarge his football team, seeking to find new players capable of playing the physically demanding sport of football. Alas, those 3-sport athletes found their way into every lineup for every varsity sport they joined. It was the way of the times, just as the long-standing practice of the gym teacher serving as head coach for every sport.

Lyman Hall High School basketball was standing on the very precipice of a state championship. Step by step, since Langdon Fernald joined the faculty in 1926, the fortunes of the LHHS basketball team climbed. By 1931 Fernald was recognized as one of the elite coaches in Connecticut schoolboy basketball, and Wallingford was producing a relatively steady stream of quality basketball talent.

Surrounding it all were the frenzied people of Wallingford who made their way to the home and away basketball games and demonstrated their enthusiastic support by crowding around the lantern in front of the school on the evenings of away games, waiting in the cold for the candle to be lit.

Before Wallingford got to the round ball season, the football team took center stage. The 1936 football team of Langdon

Fernald dropped from 35 members in 1935 to a squad of 20 men, with few senior members. Led by captain Joe Kristan, the boys battled in every game but were hardly competitive in this ... which turned out to be the last football season until 1949.

Lyman Hall was shut out in its first three games and scored only two touchdowns for the season, finishing the season with a 1-4 record. Their last six-pointer of the year was sufficient to net their only win of the season, a 6-0 win over Stratford. Basketball Captain Bill LaCroix was banged up in the Derby game but insisted on playing in the final contest against Stratford. Both LaCroix and Silvio Sala would be slow to return to the basketball team, but return they most certainly did.

The varsity sport of football at Lyman Hall in 1936 was being criticized from administration to faculty to the townspeople. There was much to cast negative comments about relative to the sport at Lyman Hall ... a drop in team participation from 1935 to 1936; ... only two victories in the last two seasons; ... and the rash of injuries incurred by basketball players during their football participation.

From all accounts, in the brief window of days between the end of the 1936 football season and the start of basketball, the discussions on the future of football at Lyman Hall High School between Mr. Early and Coach Fernald began in earnest.

One can only guesstimate how those talks rolled out in November of 1936, but we know from the records that the decision was swift and final. As the second half of the school year began at LHHS in January 1937 Principal, Robert H. Early communicated with the member schools of the Housatonic Valley League (principals) to announce that Lyman Hall would no longer "field a football team for varsity competition in the league." That announcement set off a relative firestorm of reactions with league principals.

The Housatonic Valley League bylaws required that each member school participates in football, basketball, and baseball. Track and Field was optional as it overlapped with baseball. In essence, many of the member principals believed that the Wallingford Public Schools, Lyman Hall High School, violated league rules' basic requirements. Stratford and Milford were the most outspoken in objection to the Lyman Hall decision, suggesting that Lyman Hall resign from the league or be removed by the other league members.

It is important to remember the cache' that Lyman Hall had developed in the Housatonic Valley League and the state, specifically in basketball, since the league was created in 1924. Despite the recent losing seasons in football, LHHS was annually a competitive team that was well-coached (by Fernald). The basketball teams of Lyman Hall had dominated the league since 1927 with six consecutive titles, 1927-28 to 1932-33. The supposition of some within the league was that Lyman Hall wanted to enjoy its basketball dominance in the league but was unwilling to deal with being in the lower half of the standings in football each year.

Early had been one of the founding principals of the league and was one of the architects of the league bylaws and rules. Fernald was a visible standard-bearer for the Housatonic Valley League with early and continuous success. The league principals did not want to lose those two leaders, but with hopefully new member schools coming into the league in coming years, they didn't want the Housatonic to be seen as wishy-washy on the rules.

Mr. Early cited as the chief reason for dropping football the low number of players in 1936, so a compromise was proposed by the principal of Shelton High School. He suggested that Lyman Hall take a year off from league play in 1937 and "replenish the numbers out for football" and come back into the league in 1938.

Early and Fernald would not consider the compromise. They both wanted an end to football at LHHS and risked being removed from the Housatonic Valley League as the principals had every right to do so. To the point, Early called the league's bluff (if it was a bluff). Thus, football as a varsity sport at Lyman Hall High School came to an end with the 1936 season.

The Housatonic Valley League principals would continue

to apply pressure to the Wallingford Public Schools to rejoin the league in football, year after year, but Early and Fernald were steadfast in their opposition to football at LHHS.

In 1944 Frederick Schipke replaced Fernald as gym teacher and the all-sport coach. With all the continued success of Lyman Hall High School basketball, Coach Schipke wanted no return of football, so the sport lay buried in the metaphorical dirt of Doolittle Park until greater pressures were brought to bear in 1949.

Chapter 29

Back to the Basketball Finals, 1936-37

With new teams on the regular-season slate in 1936-37, the Orangemen welcomed East Haven High School for the first time. The Yellowjackets would become a bonafide rival in the decades to come. Additionally, the schedule included contests against Woodrow Wilson High School of Middletown, Watertown, and New Britain Trade School.

The season began with several close games, some difficult losses. However, in the midst of getting the seasoned veterans of LaCroix and Bartholomew healthy again to take their places in the starting lineup, an enigmatic sophomore of incredible basketball style and competitive fire emerged one John, "Blackie" Riccitelli.

In the absence of his main scoring threats, LaCroix and Bartholomew, Fernald's charges opened the season with a loss to Trinity Parish, 24-8. The second game of 1936-37 was the first-ever encounter with East Haven High School, a 24-17 victory over the Easties. After Woodrow Wilson High School soundly defeated the Orangemen, 35-20, Fernald had had enough of the team's inconsistent play and shook up his lineup. He inserted junior Richard "Red" Talbot and sophomore John "Blackie" Riccitelli into his lineup.

With the new blood, the Orangemen immediately started winning, stringing together nine victories in a row. The game that defined the 1936-37 team was the contest against New

Britain Trade School as a total of 53 personal fouls were called in the lengthy "slug-fest" as the Wallingford "5" won, 51-39.

The Orangemen battled in every game, but in the end, losses to Milford and Branford, two teams they defeated the first time around, made Lyman Hall the second-place team in the league, with Branford winning the Housatonic Valley League title. Finishing with a regular-season record of 16-6, Lyman Hall was chosen for the State Class B tournament at Yale.

In the first round, The Orangemen knocked off traditional league foe Derby, 29-22, to gain the semi-final round, defeating Woodrow Wilson High School of Middletown, 34-26, with Bill LaCroix leading the team in scoring with 16 points. Lyman Hall was back in the finals, and once again, the opponent was Branford, who split two games with LHHS during the regular season. This time around, the Orangemen were no match for Branford, who led from the start, overwhelming the LHHS team, 38-17.

For the first time, there were All-State teams for each division. Captain Bill LaCroix was the first Lyman Hall High School player ever selected to an All-State first team in Class B. Pete Kelly and "Peanuts" Bartholomew received honorable mention on the All-State rolls.

Chapter 30

"Blackie" Leads Orangemen in 1937-38

Pivoting off an 18-7 season in 1936-37 and with no concern of football injuries with the removal of football as a varsity sport from Lyman Hall in 1936, there was a heightened focus on basketball. Fernald had a talented team led by underclassmen who cut their teeth on the varsity level the previous season.

The Orangemen were knocking on the door of a state championship after two straight trips to the Class B finals. Robert Early, principal, crowed proudly about his school's basketball achievements and openly predicted that the state title was "just around the corner." So confident of LHHS's roundball team's near future, Early had new uniforms made for the Orangemen for the 1937-38 season. Stepping into the world of men's vestment, bordering on the frippery, Mr. Early, with input from Coach Fernald and other faculty members, designed a dark or burnt orange uniform. The words "Lyman Hall" were embroidered in script across the chest in black with solid block numerals in black under the script writing. The team wore black sneakers and orange knee pads, except for "Blackie" Riccitelli, who claimed that knee pads slowed him down.

A junior, Riccitelli was chosen captain of the 1937-38 team. He was tagged with the nickname "Blackie" by family and friends who saw him return from his summer and part-time job, shoveling coal at Wallingford's steel mill. His face often covered in soot, John would often go directly to sports games from the mill with his face and hands tinged with patches of black coal dust. In his early youth, the nickname remained with him for a lifetime and became one of the terms of endearment for a man so iconic in Wallingford and the Housatonic League.

"Blackie" was as gregarious on the court as off. Blessed with size and speed, he was a brilliant all-time athlete whose competitive fire was often a point of contention for opposing players. A non-traditional performer, Riccitelli is credited with being the first player in the Housatonic Valley League to shed the time-honored "two-handed set shot" in favor of the "one-handed push shot" that was launched with his right knee bent to his waist.

Several quality league teams marked the basketball season, a few of which defeated the Orangemen for the first time since the league began in 1924. The state tournament selection committee had become far more liberal this season, so despite the mediocre 11-7 regular season of Lyman Hall, the Orangemen were selected to the Yale Tournament. On March 8, 1938, the LHHS season ended in the first round of the Class B Tournament with a 34-29 loss to Plainville High School, a school that would exact some painful moments for Lyman Hall in the years to come. League rival Branford High School captured the 1938 State Class B Championship with a 37-17 beating of Windsor as Principal Early, and Coach Fernald would have to wait yet another year for their cherished prize. There was more than "hope" for that long-held dream as Riccitelli would return after his 14.8 scoring average in 1938, along with tall, talented sophomores Frank Nasczniec, Stanley Naszcniec, and Ralph Spellacy.

Chapter 31

1938-39, LHHS Finally had the Team ...

On October 20, 1938, Miss Barbara Lincoln, the Director of Sage Allen Department Store in Hartford, addressed the student body in an assembly program in the auditorium where she stressed the importance of mastering all academic subjects, particularly emphasizing penmanship, spelling, and arithmetic, and the necessity of maintaining a neat, attractive personal appearance. Following her comments with polite applause at its end, Principal Early addressed the assembly. He introduced a few new members of the student body who had transferred to Lyman Hall from other schools, including one Roger McMahon, a transfer from Meriden High School. McMahon would go on to a notable coaching career at LHHS in the years to come.

At the end of Mr. Early's few minutes at the podium, he encouraged all students to support their basketball team in the coming season. He ended his brief comments with the words, "... this could be our year". With so many returning stalwart starters, Early was convinced 1939 would bring a state title to Wallingford.

The third fall without football withered, as do the fallen leaves before winter. Throughout the months once reserved for football, the sounds of snapping bouncing basketballs filled the gymnasium. Coach Fernald, now free from the challenges of coaching football, coordinated boys' and girls' intramurals. In between intramural games, varsity basketball team hopefuls waited in their stocking feet to come on the court to shoot a foul shot or two; or let loose with one of those new fangled, one-handed set shots.

There was an excitement about the 1938-39 basketball team. The talk about the team was everywhere. Spontaneous "Orangemen Yells" broke out almost daily at the Sugar Bowl (the after-school place to be for students) on 150 Center Street. Mr. Early wanted basketball to ignite a genuine enthusiasm for his school. His fondest hopes were more than realized as people all over Wallingford were caught up in the basketball fervor of Lyman Hall High School.

Early saw to that, and Fernald knew he had a "special" squad. Even with 13 members of last year's team in tow, 22 new candidates for the slim varsity and junior varsity team openings attended week-long tryouts. Coach Fernald had coached both the varsity and junior varsity teams since he came to Lyman Hall in 1926 and felt that this was a necessary arrangement in order to develop all his players. The many league titles won under Coach Fernald speak to the effectiveness of his dual coaching plan.

The November (Thanksgiving) assembly program was mostly about basketball. Each member of the junior and varsity teams was introduced to repetitive "Orangemen Yells," and even team manager Morris Gelblum received an ovation.

The season began on December 2, 1938, as LHHS defeated Berlin, 39-24. An important fact regarding the depth of Lyman Hall's talent and Fernald's coaching of the junior varsity team was that his sub-varsity squad had held eight opponents to less than ten points for the game. Whether varsity or junior varsity, Fernald taught a ball-hawking, nasty brand of basketball. The junior varsity would complete the season 17-0, averaging 31 points on offense and allowing only 10.5 points per game to any and all opponents.

The 1938-39 team was Mr. Early's every basketball dream. The flashy attired Orangemen were handsome, chiseled young men who were popular in the school, involved in many non-athletic clubs and activities, and generally fine academic students. Fernald was coaching a juggernaut. The crowds were over-flowing home and away, and although Early didn't attend many away games, he waited patiently by the phone when the boys were playing at an opponent's gym. In 1938-39 every call to Early from Fernald led to the "lighting of the lantern" until the evening of Tuesday, February 21, 1939.

On this cold night, the Orangemen would shoot even colder. Heading into this second encounter with Branford, the orange-clad forces from Lyman Hall had dominated all opponents, running out to 18 consecutive victories with no defeats. John Riccitelli (#11) led the Housatonic Valley League in scoring, averaging 16.3 points per game. Branford High School, the first school that Lyman Hall ever played in any sport (football) on October 19, 1916, was the successful antagonist on this night. Although the Orangemen defense was stern, going into this contest, allowing an average of 19.8 points per game, it was their usually prolific basket-scoring machine that averaged 39.3 per game that was less than normal.

On this night, the referees watched a game that was marred by hard collisions all over the floor, but few fouls were called. The game officials just seemed to let the two teams play, no matter the contact between players. The Branford defense assigned a man to guard Riccitelli throughout the game and harshly move "Blackie" away from the ball. The fiery "Blackie" got into a jawing session with the Branford player who hounded him throughout, but few fouls were called.

With the game never varying much from a one-point lead for either team, "Blackie" found a completely open Ken Spellacy (#8) under the basket with less than a minute to play. Two Branford defenders upended the shooting Spellacy as the ball rolled off the rim. With no foul called on the play, Coach Fernald rose from his seat on the bench to protest the lack of a call, but the referees ignored Spellacy, who was lying face down on the court, and Fernald, voiced his displeasure, but the extreme action continued. Moments later, with Branford dribbling the ball in a stalling tactic of sorts, the Orangemen saw their winning streak end as Branford prevailed in a heart-breaker, 26-25.

The Orangemen were once again Housatonic Valley League champions as they headed into the State Class B Tournament with the best record in school history at 19-1. Despite its outstanding record, the selection committee placed Lyman Hall down the bracket that pitted the Orangemen against East Hartford High School in the first round. With all that LHHS had accomplished in the 1938-1939 season, the Orangemen went down to defeat in this first-round game to an East Hartford squad that would win the 1939 State Class B Championship, a resounding 48-33 triumph over Manchester Trade School.

Mr. Early and Coach Fernald were equal parts disappointment and frustration. For both of them and Wallingford, they would have to wait at least another year for a chance at the brass ring.

Chapter 32

Robert H. Early Never Sees his Cherished Championship

Unfortunately, Robert H. Early, the principal from 1918-1939, who was the most enthusiastic advocate and supporter for LHHS student activities, especially the "apple of his eye," the basketball team, died in 1939, just weeks after the 1939 state tournament.

Early never saw his beloved "basketball boys" reach the pinnacle, both he and Coach Fernald worked so hard to attain. Mr. Early gave twenty years of devoted service to Lyman Hall High School and to the Town of Wallingford. To his faculty and students, he was a loyal friend, a thoughtful counselor, always ready to rejoice in any success, and always there to share their challenges and burdens.

In his heart, there was room for each of his children (his students). No one who ever knew him did not feel the buoyancy and warmth of his spirit. He shunned the closed door of his office to afford access to any one of his children or teachers who may need him. He made it a point to know how students were doing in each class and would often call someone by name from the hallway to his office because he learned of a good grade or marked improvement.

Mr. Early led the cheers and was always seeking ways to improve his Lyman Hall High School. Elegant and so softly sophisticated in his conversations, even a necessary rebuke brought a calm to the moment.

He loved LHHS and all who worked and learned there. He was fond of saying, "Let us be joyous in the learning." On the morning of Thursday, March 30, 1939, Robert Hunter Early passed from the hallways of Lyman Hall forever, with his truest memorial being in the lives of the students and teachers who were touched by his life.

In July 1939, Dr. William H. Curtis was hired as principal and would be leading the school when the Orangemen finally won the state title, the first state championship in school history. Curtis would serve as principal until 1943 when he would answer the call of his country as a U.S. Naval officer from 1943 to 1945.

Chapter 33

The First State Championship, 1939-40

When John "Blackie" Riccitelli walked the aisle of graduation, many thoughts that Lyman Hall had seen their last hope for a state title depart with him. Langdon Fernald now once again demonstrated just how outstanding a teacher and coach toiled in Wallingford.

The Housatonic Valley League would be challenging for the Orangemen to navigate in 1939-40 with so many players untested in varsity competition, but Fernald would have them playing his aggressive style of defense. For the first time in school history, LHHS named co-captains for this season as Stanley Naszczniec and Ken Spellacy, (#8) returning veterans for 1939, led the team.

Allowing 18.4 points per game on the season, the Lyman Hall round-ballers played one nail-biting game after another. The Orangemen reeled off 17 victories losing three games, twice to Branford and once to eventual league champion, Stratford High School, as LHHS tied for second place with East Haven and Branford.

Lyman Hall was slated into the Class B state tournament with their sterling record as Stratford was placed high in the rankings in Class A. On March 8, 1940, after wins in the first two rounds, the Orangemen found themselves in the state finals against Middletown High School. The Payne Whitney Gymnasium on the campus of Yale was the site of the state finals. Hundreds of Lyman Hall students and supporters entered the gothic building to hopefully witness a Lyman Hall state championship at long last. Before the Orangemen took the court, Coach Fernald reminded the team that Mr. Early would be with them in spirit.

The Lyman Hall team wasted no time unleashing a suffocating cloak around the Middletown shooters as the Orangemen ran out to a 12-1 lead at the end of the first quarter. Ken Spellacy (#8), who scored only one point in the semi-final victory over East Haven High School, was almost unstoppable, scoring 16 points. From there, Lyman Hall ran away from Middletown, capturing its first state championship of any type in sport, 45-18. With the victory, Lyman Hall ended the season with a 20-3 record. Housatonic Valley League champion Stratford High School was downed, 35-25 in the Class A Tournament.

With the title, the Town of Wallingford broke loose in celebration. A parade led by the Lyman Hall High School marching band under the direction of Richard A. Otto traveled along Main Street and down Center to cheering crowds. A special school-wide assembly was held as the team received a silver state championship trophy, and each member of the team presented with a gold basketball.

The town was not through with their basketball heroes as Wallingford merchants who long ago were embraced by the engaging, now deceased principal, Robert H. Early, honored the team with a banquet at the state armory. Coach Fernald was given a gold wristwatch, commemorating his long-awaited state title, and each member of the team was awarded a gold ring.

Chapter 34

World War II Years, 1941-1945

The State Championship of 1940, with its all-consuming Wallingford celebration, was a local momentary distraction for a world that was about to be upended by a global war. Before the United States entered into the war following the attack on Pearl Harbor on December 7, 1941, the congress of the United States enacted the Selective Training and Service Act of 1940 on September 16, 1940. This was the first peacetime conscription in our country's history.

This legislation required all men who had reached their twenty-first birthday but had not yet reached their thirty-sixth birthday register with the local draft board for military service. This affected several male faculty members. Once America entered World War II, the Act was expanded by amendments that made all men between the ages of 20 and 44 to be subject to military service and required all men between the ages of 18 and 64 to register.

The unprovoked attack on the United States fleet at Pearl Harbor heightened the sense of patriotism across the country, and the students of Lyman Hall High School did their level best to support the war effort. In 1942 Lyman Hall High School was recognized with a state award for collecting tons of scrap metal as part of the "War Production" program.

More profound was the significant number of Lyman Hall students who enlisted in the military's various branches even before their date of graduation. Student-athletes who a short few years, or just months ago were being written about in the newspapers for their exploits on the playing fields of Doolittle Park and the basketball courts of the Housatonic Valley League were now serving in combat in foreign lands. Of the many young men who turned in their Orangemen uniform for a uniform in one branch of the military or another, serving their country with distinction, some gave the supreme sacrifice. Those fallen Orangemen included Albert Canelli (football, class of 1934), Phil Germain (basketball, class of 1935), John Hayes (baseball, class of 1935), Bill Bartek (football, class of 1935), George Magee (basketball, class of 1940), Leonard Golub (baseball, class of 1942), Frank Pochino (baseball, class of 1942) and Harry "Peanuts" Bartholomew (football & basketball, class of 1937).

The business of education at Lyman Hall High School would continue during the war years. The many clubs and activities initiated during the years that Robert H. Early served as principal would continue under new principal Dr. William H. Curtis until he joined the navy, serving as an officer, 1943-1945. His replacement as principal during World War II was Wilmer L. Schultz.

The title "Housatonic Valley League" was officially shortened to Housatonic League at the end of the 1939-40 school year. Travel was significantly curtailed as rationing of most commodities such as gasoline meant fewer away games for schools. East Haven had joined the league in 1938, and there were charter member schools who would depart the ranks for various reasons, one of which was the lack of action taken by the league principals when Lyman Hall discontinued football in 1936.

The threshold or measurement of a school's seasonal record for securing admittance to the state basketball tournament was relaxed to some degree in the decade of the 1940s, but the brackets for each division did not exceed eight schools for several years.

Langdon Fernald continued to coach the Lyman Hall basketball and baseball teams through the baseball season of 1943. Lyman Hall won the Housatonic League title in 1943, Fernald's last coaching season, with an abbreviated schedule of games due to travel limitations.

With the end of the 1943 school year, Langdon Fernald, extraordinary teacher, and coach called an end to his coaching career before embarking on a year as vice principal and then a 15-year run as principal of Lyman Hall High School. During his 17 years as an all-sport head coach, his Lyman Hall teams won eight Housatonic League basketball titles and compiled a 212-106 record. His last baseball team captured the league championship, and his first football team won the 1926 Housatonic Valley League title ... the last football championship for another 48 years.

Chapter 35

Pressure Mounts
for Football

Under principal Robert H. Early and coach Langdon Fernald, Lyman Hall became one of the winningest high schools in basketball in Connecticut. Under Early and Fernald, Wallingford did indeed become a "basketball town," and its trappings with flashy orange uniforms, school cheers written exclusively for basketball, and overflowing gymnasiums were a condition no one in Wallingford wanted ever to see changed.

To state the obvious, in the minds of many, especially Fernald and Early, football, with its annual rash of injuries to prominent basketball players while engaged in football, was negatively impacting the basketball team's pursuit of league and state championships. With the focus on basketball and the heavy burdens placed on the singular coach for all sports, convincing each other (Early and Fernald) that football had to go was a clear path for Early and Fernald.

However, many Wallingford merchants, prominent citizens, and the Housatonic member schools' principals were well-aware of the facts. To wit, following the end of World War II, Wallingford was one of the fastest-growing communities in southern Connecticut as the town was a center for manufacturing jobs and the construction of many housing developments for rent as well as purchase. Many men returning from the service relocated to Wallingford, where they could find well-paying jobs. After their discharge from the military in 1945-46, a heavy influx of men came from Pennsylvania, a hotbed for high school football. Additionally, Lyman Hall High School had been on double sessions throughout most of the 1940s, and a new Lyman Hall building was in the early discussion stage. Enrollment at Lyman Hall was growing exponentially, visa vie, there were many male students who could ..., who might ..., who should ..., play football **if** encouraged to do so.

It was one thing to argue against football with those from other communities albeit, the school principals of the league members. It was quite another when the grumblings to restart football at Lyman Hall High School came from Wallingford citizens, from factory workers and business leaders. During the years 1941-45, schools tried their best to maintain the status quo whenever possible. For Lyman Hall, with fewer teachers after so many faculty members, especially the male teachers, went off to war, some school organizations were put on hold until after the war. Some school clubs never came back after 1945. Every high school across Connecticut was experiencing these same difficulties, so there was no high pressure exerted on LHHS to either field a team or *leave* the Housatonic League, that is, until 1946, when the cauldron of pressure turned up the temperature on Lyman Hall High School.

The Housatonic League member schools would continue to pressure Wallingford Public Schools' administration following the 1940 State Championship basketball season to force Wallingford's hand to field a football team at Lyman Hall. As congenial as the meetings and conversations between principals were in the months before World War II, the league principals stressed "compliance" with LHHS principal William Curtis that the Housatonic League's bylaws stated that each member school must "fully participate" in all three varsity sports. Lyman Hall, through its principal and coach, steadfastly argued their reasons for not wanting football at LHHS.

For Fernald and Schipke making the case against restarting football was a simple one, but by war's end, community pressure, added to that of the league's schools, would be too much to overcome.

In the meantime, interscholastic sports schedules were pruned to accommodate the limitations of a country at war. During these years, Lyman Hall High School, without football, escaped the perpetual consternation of the member school principals of the Housatonic League as there were far more critical issues to address. However, the league principals never let the administration of LHHS and its new all-sport coach (as of 1943), Fred Schipke, ever forget the league rule of participation, requiring each league member to fully participate in the three major sports. There would come a time when Lyman Hall High School would have to address the issue of football, but until then, Coach Schipke was pleased that he didn't have to coach varsity football.

Chapter 36

Schipke Puts his Stamp on Lyman Hall

In September 1943, there was a new face at the helm of the sports teams at Lyman Hall High School. The truth be told, it wasn't a new face. It was the face of one of those outstanding former student-athletes who, after graduating from Arnold College, was personally chosen by Langdon D. Fernald to succeed him as gym teacher and coach at Lyman Hall.

Frederick "Dutch" Schipke was President of the class of 1932 and a 4-year high honors student at Lyman Hall. A member of the Student Council, Fred played three years of football, four years of basketball and baseball, three years of track & field, culminating in capturing the Class B shotput championship. These accomplishments are more than remarkable when one considers Fred had only the thumb and forefinger on his right hand due to a childhood accident. At Arnold College, Schipke earned Dean's List recognition, lettering in basketball and baseball. A skilled teacher, craftsman, and outdoorsman, this highly organized gentleman was the right person for the position Fernald had vacated to become an administrator at Lyman Hall High School, beginning in 1943.

As Schipke began his career at Lyman Hall, he supervised intramurals in 1943 and prepared to coach the basketball team. Schipke and Fernald were adamant in not wanting football at Lyman Hall. Obvious to all was their opposition to the sport. Publicly, both men stated the exact reasons for eliminating football that were given in 1936, "There was not enough interest in the sport in Wallingford," and "Lyman Hall had very few students of sufficient size to play football."

In private, Fred Schipke felt that the burdens of coaching football, basketball, and baseball were all too much for one person to manage, especially with teaching duties, but as with most other secondary schools in the state, a gym teacher coached the sports, one and all. At Lyman Hall, beginning in the 1930s, school dances, promenades, vocational arts demonstration events were held in the gymnasium, and the scheduling of those extensive activities required the gym teacher's direct involvement. With no outside fields directly connecting with the school building, except for the back of the school parking lot, every time the gym was used for dances or formal events, the gym was decorated from ceiling to floor. The time required for setting up the decorations took days to complete, forcing all gym classes to be moved to other locations, whether it was the parking lot, the library, or the cafeteria. This responsibility fell to the gym teacher. Heretofore, Schipke and his predecessor, Langdon Fernald, until he became assistant principal in 1943 (and principal in 1944), experienced nary an idle moment as gym teacher and all-sport coach.

For the students of Lyman Hall, there was an assortment of challenges in daily life during the years of 1941-1945. The school was forced to go on double sessions, primarily due to limited teaching staff. More students than ever needed to work before and after school, supporting their families with so many adults now serving in the military. During those five years, 14 Lyman Hall faculty members would temporarily leave teaching for military service, including Dr. Richard A. Otto, who was building the music programs of Lyman Hall into a nationally recognized performing groups and the newly appointed principal, Dr. William H. Curtis, who would return to Wallingford, becoming superintendent of schools from 1945 to 1959.

Fred Schipke was a disciple of Langdon Fernald and coached with the same intensity and competitive fire as his mentor. Basketball under Fernald had become a community passion, and no matter the year or the young men who donned the "orange," the people of Wallingford came out to see the boys ...WIN. The Schipke led Orangemen had winning records in the first four seasons of his remarkable tenure, with an overall record of 52-23, being selected to the State Class B Tournament each year. Like his mentor, Langdon Fernald, Schipke was building great teams that culminated in 1948.

Coach Schipke's first basketball team, 1943-44, finished with a 10-7 record and earned its way into the Class B State Tournament, winning a first-round game against Shelton before falling to league foe Branford in the quarter-final game. East Hartford would defeat Branford, 39-37, winning the 1944 State Class B Championship. Coach Schipke's first baseball team would win the 1944 Housatonic League title led by Joseph Dunn, who notched a career 12-3 pitching record, establishing a then Housatonic League record of 81 strikeouts in 63 innings in 1944. In that 1944 season, Dunn struck out 14 batters in a game against Shelton.

With the end of world war II, new families flooded into Wallingford as manufacturing jobs were aplenty. Wallingford required new schools, and Lyman Hall remained on double sessions as the first major rumblings of building a new high school, a new Lyman Hall began in earnest.

The AM and PM sessions of LHHS necessitated creating dual activities for each session, including the school newspaper, assembly programs, and sub-varsity sports teams. The demands on Mr. Schipke, as with all other faculty members, were doubled, but Coach Schipke's day was especially taxing as he had to schedule and conduct practices for AM freshmen, PM freshmen ... and then the junior varsity and varsity teams.

Chapter 37

"The Cinderella Team" 1947-48 State Champions

Basketball talent was bountiful at Lyman Hall for many years, but when the class of 1948 entered LHHS as freshmen in 1944, Fred Schipke was aware of this class's uniqueness. As Schipke once said at a reunion of the 1947-48 team, "These kids were always smiling. They loved their time in the gym. Coaching that group made every day a pleasure".

Schipke, like his predecessor Fernald, tended to stock his varsity team with juniors and seniors. Both coaches made the underclassmen "wait their turn" and earn their way into an appearance in a varsity game. Schipke didn't anoint anyone, no matter how talented a player might be. Both Fernald and Schipke would only dress players for the varsity games who they fully intended to play. "The varsity team is not to give kids experience. The varsity team is to win games," stated Schipke.

As Coach Schipke identified his roster for the 1945-46 season, one sophomore drew his attention, Gene Combs. He was six foot and solidly built for so young a player. Schipke loved his shooting style, and during foul shooting practice, Gene rarely missed a charity throw. When all of the years, practices, and games of Combs' Lyman Hall career had concluded in March of 1948, the record shows that he never missed a practice or a game for any reason. He never fouled out of a game. Coach Schipke dressed Gene Combs for the varsity basketball team during the 1944-45 season as #12 appeared in eleven games. When a sophomore, Gene Combs became a starter for the basketball team in December of 1945, he would start every game, culminating in the 1948 state title game.

Fred Schipke mandated that his team comport themselves with humbleness and dignity. Where Fernald's teams of previous years were full of fire and brashness, Schipke taught his troops to remain calm and in control, so when there were big moments in a game, they could handle the pressure without high emotions or useless actions.

The 1946-47 team was senior-laden with many talented underclassmen playing at high levels for the junior varsity team. Coach Schipke would have a special challenge in cobbling together his varsity team members for 1947-48. He began with his captain and cornerstone, Gene Combs (#12). Howard Kummer (#6), a junior, was a slender front court player who could leap to the glass with the best of them was chosen as a starter. John Carretta (#11), the tallest of the Orangemen at 6-2, a strong defender, would combine with Combs and Kummer to form one of the state's most dynamic front courts. Voted by his class as "Most Popular" (#5) was Billy Quigley, a tenacious player who brought incredible energy to this team that no one thought had a chance to even make the state tournament in 1948.

Within this incredible team was a sophomore who possessed outstanding athletic skills, coupled with a competitive spirit in Johnny Carvalho (#7). He could do anything on the basketball court, fast, sure-handed. Schipke charged his youngest player to be the team's chief ball-handler.

As his teammate senior, Gene Combs, said of Carvalho, "John had a unique shuffle and gait, like no one else, and moved like a prizefighter. John was our guard who would take the ball up the court. John was such a good shooter from the outside. He never seemed to miss from the outside. He would shoot when we needed two points to open up the defense so that he could pass the ball into the forwards and center. John was a team player all the way".

The 1947-48 season of the "Cinderella Team" began on November 27, 1947, at the LHHS gym against an out-of-league opponent, Terryville High School. From the opening tap of this game until the final whistle, it was clear that this team of two seniors, two juniors, and one sophomore had a "magic," and their fellow LHHS students loved them. As was the case in that first game against Terryville, the scoring was spread among the five. The Orangemen would open the season with seven straight wins before dropping a 41-33 decision to Milford. Three days later, LHHS would lose their second game to Shelton's Galloping Gaels, 56-50 in the Valley.

The Schipkemen looked like the prognosticators might be correct in picking the Orangemen to finish back in the Housatonic League pack. Schipke told the reporters that his team was getting better with each game. The regular season ended with LHHS logging a 15-4 record, with two of those losses coming against a veteran Shelton team, led by their Captain and top scorer, Danny Simonetti.

Selected to the Class B State bracket, the 1948 State Tournament began on February 25, 1948, at the Payne Whitney Gymnasium on the campus of Yale. LHHS was at the bottom of the bracket, being the last team to gain selection. In the first round, Lyman Hall was in against a favored Killingly High School team, led by high scoring All-Stater, Bobby Moe. The Orangemen swarmed around the shooting wiz, Moe, holding him to three buckets in the first half, but Killingly still led by six at the half. The Lyman Hall crowd experienced a harrowing moment when leading scorer Gene Combs crumpled to the deck with what turned out to be a sprained ankle. Captain Gene returned to lead the Orangemen.

The Lyman Hall five fell farther behind to Killingly in the second half, extending its lead to nine points as Moe hit four shots despite being repeatedly fouled by the Orangemen. Quigley and Carretta were making life miserable for Moe as the Schipkemen clawed back. All five starters scored in the second half, led by Howie Kummer, but it wasn't until the last minute of play that the Orangemen finally took its first lead, hanging on to overcome Killingly and Bobby Moe's 18 points for an opening-round win, 43-41. After the upset of Killingly, the newspapers began to refer to Lyman Hall as "Cinderella" and asked the farcical question, "When would Lyman Hall turn into a pumpkin"?

In the second round on March 5, 1948, the Wallingfordites were up against a highly favored Wilcox Tech team. The Indians of Meriden led throughout the first half, but the game's turning point was not a made or missed basket. Late in the second quarter, with Wilcox ahead 16-13, Wilcox's Ted Piniazek attempted to steal the ball from Johnny Carvalho. Bent low and forward in his attempt to pilfer the ball that Carvalho dribbled and protected, Piniazek was knocked out cold.

Whatever life Wilcox Tech had was suddenly lost with the Piniazek mishap. John Carretta led Lyman Hall in the first half with nine points. In the second half, the smooth moving Orangemen had a balanced scoring effort as Combs had eight, Quigley eight, Carvalho totaled four, and Kummer netted six for a 45-34 victory over the higher-ranked Wilcox Tech five. For all the perceived drama the Orangemen overcame against higher ranked opponents in the first two games, the semi-final opposite the second slated Windsor High School squad would top them all.

In basketball-wild Wallingford, even early season league games were must-attend events. When the Orangemen got to the state tournament, the caravan of cars lined up on Main Street for the ride to the Payne Whitney Gymnasium, the parade of vehicles resembled a state funeral procession. Even with a late wintry temperature of 28 degrees still upon Wallingford on March 9, 1948, students traveling to New Haven still wound down the car windows, screaming "We are Lyman Hall" and "Orangemen, Orangemen, Rah, Rah, Rah."

Windsor was the top-ranked team in Class B, sporting a 19-1 record and another herculean feat to be faced by LHHS on the way to a state title. Over 1,000 Lyman Hall fans poured through the turnstiles at the Payne Whitney to cheer for their orange-clad boys as Windsor exploded from the opening tap, patient in their offensive sets and hitting five shots from the top of the key. As always, the Wallingfordites received balanced scoring with Combs, Quigley, Kummer, and Carretta, each netting two baskets in the first half, but Windsor had few possessions without scoring. At the half, the muted Lyman Hall crowd saw their team down, 27-19.

Windsor maintained their shooting touch, extending their lead to 39-25 late into the third quarter, and looked in command of this semi-final game at the end of the third period, ahead 39-29. With the Wallingford faithful standing and yelling, the Orangemen came into the fourth quarter with a sense of urgency, not yet seen in this game.

Gene Combs heated up and hit three shots in a row as John Carretta, and Johnny Carvalho began to dominate the backboards. The Orangemen defense was frustrating Windsor in the quarter as the Lyman Hall team came roaring back. Carvalho, who was scoreless in the first half, was magnificent in the second, scoring nine points. With five minutes and change remaining in the game, Quigley received a perfect pass in a perfect spot from Carretta and scored, giving the Orangemen the lead for the first time in the game. Instantly, the Windsor coach called timeout. A made foul shot by Windsor deadlocked the score. With less than two minutes remaining. Gene Combs hit from the top of the key, and Carvalho followed with a free throw to extend the LHHS lead to three points.

A charity toss would be all Windsor would get in the final minute as Carvalho scored from the outside to seal the victory, 46-43. The high-powered Windsor team was held to a meager four points in the fourth quarter as the Orangemen scored 14. It was a remarkable comeback for the 1948 team, led by Carvalho's brilliance in the fourth quarter. The Lyman Hall students and fans stormed the edges of the court, but there was still one more tall "Everest" to scale for the state title.

The newspaper writers of the New Haven Register, and Hartford Courant, both latched on to the "Cinderella Team" moniker for the 1948 Lyman Hall basketball team, and after three upset victories against higher ranked teams, even the Wallingford fans were preparing posters to be used at the State

Championship game. Two of the posters read, "We're Keeping the Glass Slippers" and "The Pumpkin Carriage Is ORANGE."

The State Class B Finals would match Lyman Hall against Housatonic League Champion Shelton. The Galloping Gaels had defeated Lyman Hall twice during the regular season, 56-50 and 56-48.

On March 12, 1948, at the Payne Whitney Gymnasium, Shelton and Lyman Hall would tangle for the third time. The Lyman Hall team of Fred Schipke donned their shiny orange with the black trim uniforms. As predicted, both teams would play well against familiar foes with a 10-10 score at the end of the first quarter, and Lyman Hall held a 26-19 bulge at the half.

The Gaels were fierce in the third stanza, taking a 33-32 lead at the end of the quarter. The game was tied six times, but the fourth quarter belonged to Schipke's squad once again. The second half was a hotly contested brawl as Howard Kummer, and Johnny Carvalho fouled out. For their part in the battle, Shelton saw three of their starters foul out. As the game neared its end, Coach Schipke made sure that his captain, Gene Combs, had his hands on the ball as much as possible as the Orangemen outscored Shelton 15-5 in the final period to run by the favored Gaels.

There were 39 fouls whistled in the game. Combs led all scorers with 17 points, Kummer 14, Quigley eight, Carvalho five, and Carretta had three as LHHS won the first state championship for their Coach Fred Schipke, 48-38. At exactly 9:22 pm on March 12, 1948, bedlam broke out as the final second ticked off the clock as Lyman Hall High School students stormed the court.

Gene Combs was named Most Valuable Player of the 1948 C.I.A.C. Tournament and would be named to the first-team All-State Team for 1947-48. Joining Gene on the first team All-State Team was junior Howard "Howie" Kummer, who would earn that distinction for the second time in 1949.

A phone call was made back to Wallingford, and the LANTERN in front of Lyman Hall High School was lit as dozens of Wallingford residents stood in the front courtyard of the high school, waiting for that "sign" (the lit candle) to signal that the Orangemen had indeed won the state championship.

Escorted by state and Wallingford police were seven bus-loads of students and fans with an estimated 100 cars in a single file, all equipped with red flares that were shown brilliantly throughout the victorious caravan ride back Wallingford and the beginning of a town-wide celebration. An estimated 400 people assembled on the town green as the Lyman Hall High School band, led by Dr. Richard A. Otto, escorted the championship team up Center Street.

Back to the high school, one and all assembled for an open house celebration that culminated in the gymnasium as a tumultuous ovation greeted coach Fred Schipke and his team.

The afterglow of the 1948 State Championship burned long into the future. Town celebratory events were scheduled for the team that included award rings, cufflinks, and gold basketballs. The 1948 Orangemen were guests at the Ithaca College Band Concert, and the Town of Wallingford sent the team to Boston to witness the New England High School Tournament.

In every home in Wallingford was jubilation as Center Street was one big party until 3:00 am. Indeed, on March 12, 1948, the "Cinderella Team" had found its prince, the State Class B Championship.

Chapter 38

The Tipping Point ... Football Returns "We Wanted To, But We Couldn't Say No"

By the late 1940s, the Housatonic League had developed into one of the most successful interscholastic organizations in Connecticut. In recent years, the member schools had changed, with Stratford leaving in 1947 and Milford would follow in 1951. East Haven had joined the association in 1948, and with Branford, Derby, Seymour, Shelton, and Lyman Hall, there were only six league members. This number was too small by which to build annual schedules in all sports. North Haven and Cheshire would not come into the Housatonic League until the 1954-55 school year. In 1953- 54 those two schools would play their new varsity teams against league junior varsity squads.

The Housatonic League was in a state of flux as each league member was compelled to find outside of league schools to fill out their schedules in football, basketball, and baseball. The principals were candid in their meetings in stating that they had more important tasks to complete than looking for opponents for their sports teams, year after year.

To sustain the league and create stability in scheduling, the Housatonic League principals agreed to become actively engaged in recruiting other high schools from the general geographic area to join the Housatonic League. However, the sore spot (since 1936) for the Housatonic League in 1948 was Lyman Hall's persistence not to participate in football. The issue got to a boiling point at the league principal meeting in March 1948.

The Housatonic League was a model for other regions of Connecticut, seeking to create a collegial relationship between schools with mutual responsibility for the administration of athletics and the conduct of students who participate in sports. Collaboration was the Housatonic League benchmark since its inception in 1924 in many fields of high school life and interest, far beyond athletics, that included debating, school newspapers, student councils, vocational and creative arts, cheerleading, and music (band and choral). Additionally, teachers from Housatonic League schools engaged in intra-school subject area professional development.

By 1948 Housatonic League schools had appeared in 19 state basketball finals since 1924 and won eleven titles. The league had been a tremendous success, but it was the consensus of the principals that ALL schools must participate in a "comprehensive fashion."

Langdon D. Fernald, of the most successful coaches in Connecticut and the Housatonic League, became principal of Lyman Hall High School in 1944. A thoughtful man of great integrity, he saw the fragility of the arguments he had shared with the former principal, Robert Early, and now, Fred Schipke for the reasons to keep football out of Lyman Hall.

Fernald's career and notoriety as an educator in Connecticut were impeccable. He was no longer the aspiring coach who wished to insulate his basketball players from football related injuries. He was now representing all of Lyman Hall High School as a co-equal partner in the Housatonic League. Fernald's judgment relative to football would have to take a much broader view.

In future years, Fernald would serve as the Assistant Director of the Connecticut Interscholastic Athletic Conference

(C.I.A.C.), where he would craft a redesign of the state basketball tournament.

Fred Schipke had just completed his first state championship season in 1948 when the league principals met to discuss the Housatonic League's future. Shortly thereafter, Mr. Fernald met with Coach Schipke to discuss starting football in the fall of 1949. As Schipke put it, "Lang was in a tough spot, he wanted to, but he couldn't say no to the league about football. Lang and I talked about the problems with football many times. We wanted to say no. I didn't want football, but we couldn't say no. There were people in town who wanted a football team. We just had to do it".

Fernald gave Schipke little choice in the matter, although Schipke was adamant that football wasn't a good fit for Wallingford. For Fred Schipke this meant that he would have to coach a sport of which he had little interest and no desire to coach, a sentiment he would carry for the rest of his illustrious career.

Funds were immediately secured for football equipment, and plans were made to erect a football field at Doolittle Park after the conclusion of the 1949 Twilight League baseball season. Schipke's arguments against football were many, but the one point he continued to make to Fernald was that one person could not coach football all by himself. This led to a concession by Fernald to allow Schipke to find an assistant coach for football, only if one could be found in the faculty. LHHS would add an additional physical education teacher in 1950 and one more in 1951, but until then, someone in the faculty would have to be found to assist Schipke with football. Parenthetically, both of the new physical education teachers hired in 1950 and 1951 were graduates of Lyman Hall, although neither was a part of the football team for the Orangemen, but were prominent in basketball during their high school and college careers.

Chapter 39

Football Returns ... In 1949

Concurrent with the 1949 baseball season, Coach Schipke announced in his gym classes that there would be football at Lyman Hall in the fall. He encouraged many students of *girth* to play but still was reticent about the game, not wanting to see his prominent basketball players on the football team. Schipke knew he would have an outstanding basketball team for the 1949-50 season.

During the spring and summer months, Coach Schipke read up on football, focusing on the book "The Modern T Formation," written by Frank Leahy. He could take little from his basketball coaching that would help him, other than his extraordinary skills as a teacher. As new as football was for Fred Schipke, noting he played for LHHS in the early 1930s, no one could have possibly imagined how *new* it was for the students who came out for the team.

Television had just been introduced to America, and one of the first baseball games ever televised was but a few weeks before the 1949 football season. In any event, not many people had a television set. Football games might have been listened to on the radio, but how many young boys would have spent their weekend days sitting in front of a radio in 1949. Newspapers did cover some college football stories, but that was a long way from actually seeing a football game. One movie about football was shown at the Wilkinson Theatre on

Center Street in 1949, "Father was a Fullback," a comedy starring Fred MacMurray.

Indeed, Coach Schipke had his work cut out for him. Fred was able to find a teacher in the building to be his first assistant coach, A. Raymond Mahan, a social studies teacher who played football in high school. As they were both learning the game almost from scratch, early practices were a painstaking process.

From the moment Coach Schipke reluctantly accepted the responsibility to coach a third sport, football, he was most concerned about pitting his team against seasoned rough football teams. He felt that the first season of football should have a schedule of lesser opponents in order to "get their feet wet."

Principal Fernald, ever the mentor for Schipke, approached the Housatonic League schools' principals and requested that LHHS play an abbreviated schedule for football's first season. Shelton, Derby, and Milford were not included as opponents in 1949. To fill out a six-game schedule, Fernald reached out to nearby smaller high schools to arrange games for his reborn football team. The opponents would include Berlin High School, St. Mary's High School of New Haven, and league members Seymour, Stratford, and Branford.

Thirty-two boys reported for the first practice on Monday, September 5, 1949. Twenty of those football candidates were seniors. The only member of the team who had played any football prior to this experience was all-everything athlete, Johnny Carvalho who played a little football with a men's league in Wallingford. Carvalho would serve as the captain of the basketball and baseball teams, but for the first Lyman Hall High School football team since 1936, Johnny was immediately named the quarterback.

Practices were patterned after the diagrams in the Leahy book with emphasis on tackling and play memorization. As Schipke and Mahan did not have a real sense of what player might be best for each position, they decided to put all the bigger guys in the line. All the blocking for the linemen was straight ahead. In other words, "block the man in front of you." It never got any more complicated than that.

Tackling and blocking were emphasized in every practice, and more than a few members of the team got banged up in the full-force tackling drills. At the time, the technique of tackling was taught, with the first goal being ... "put your head in the runner's chest." In 1949 tackling was a head-first technique.

John Carvalho described the plays the team was taught in practice this way, ... "We had dive plays for the halfbacks and fullbacks. We had sweeps to the outside and a few passes to the ends".

After ten days of practice, Lyman Hall was set to play its first varsity game in 13 years. The "Orangemen" were dressed in black jerseys with sleeves of black and white Princeton stripes from shoulder to wrist. The pants of heavy canvas were tan. For many years well into the 1960s, each player wore what was referred to as "target socks" that were last worn by the 1985 State Championship football team on December 7, 1985. The helmets were of black leather with no facemasks.

The "limited substitution" rules were still in effect as they were in the 1930s, meaning that the starting team played both offense and defense, and only in the event of an injury did a substitute come into the game.

The first game since 1936 was played on Saturday, September 17, 1949, at Doolittle Park versus Seymour High School. To everyone's surprise, the Orangemen played a strong game on defense as Seymour was content to run the football into the line with an occasional end run. The final score, Seymour 13 – LHHS 0. In the second contest on September 24, 1949, Lyman Hall met St. Mary's High School of New Haven. In a game of six fumbles, neither team could dent the other's goal line as the affair ended with a 0-0 tie.

The third contest of the season pitted another out-of-the Housatonic League opponent for the Wallingfordites. This time the Berlin Redcoats attired all in red were ready to tangle with LHHS. This game was of special significance as quarterback Johnny Carvalho (always the competitor) decided to adlib the plays he called in the huddle. As the first two games of the abbreviated season netted zero points for Lyman Hall, quarterback Carvalho told his teammates just to do what he outlined in the huddle.

Rather than call "left halfback dive" and "fullback sweep right" as they practiced each day and ran in the first two games, Carvalho would just tell the backs or ends what to do. In essence, they played it like "touch-football." The line just blocked straight ahead anyway, so nothing changed for them. Like a touch football game, John would tell one of his ends to "go out for a pass, run to the sideline I'll throw you the ball," or something akin to, "you block the end, and I'll follow you."

When asked how Coach Schipke responded to his play-calling, avoiding the plays run in practice, Carvalho responded, "Mr. Schipke was a different coach with football than basketball. He was very laid back with football and didn't say too much to us during a game. We went out and tried to win. Basketball was very serious to him and all of us. With basketball, there was always a lot on the line".

So, on Saturday, October 1, 1949, Lyman Hall won its first football game with a 25-0 victory over Berlin, the first win since Friday, November 7, 1936, a 6-0 win again Stratford High School in Stratford.

After the Berlin win, East Haven shutout the Orangemen, 20-0. The season concluded with a 2-0 victory over long-time league foe Branford. Lyman Hall ended its first football season of somewhat of a modern era with a modest record of two wins, two losses, and one tie, but the hard times of football were about to get complicated.

Chapter 40

As Basketball Rolls On

The 1948-49 Lyman Hall basketball team tied for the Housatonic League Championship with East Haven, as Howie Kummer, the "Mr. Everything" at LHHS in his senior year, earned his second straight first-team All-State selection as the Orangemen compiled a 16-6 record. Upon graduation, Kummer held the school record for most points scored in a season with 331. LHHS was slotted #2 in the Class B Tournament but fell to Killingly in the quarter-final game.

The 1949-50 basketball squad with captain Johnny Carvalho leading the way was a league dominant squad, winning yet another Housatonic League Championship with an 11-1 record. After two wins in the State Class B Tournament, the Orangemen fell to Darien in the semi-finals.

... FOOTBALL ENTERS A LONG DARK TUNNEL

With a full Housatonic League games schedule beginning in 1950, no mercy was shown to the fledgling Lyman Hall football team. After the 2-2-1, .500 season of 1949, Fred Schipke's football teams would never again approach a winning season. From 1950-1956, the last seven years of Fred Schipke's 8-year tenure as football coach, the Orangemen were 6-35-3.

Lyman Hall High School's reputation in sports was that of a top rung team in the league, heading into the 1950s.

The Housatonic League schools had been given regular defeats at the hands of the Orangemen in basketball since the Housatonic Valley League began in 1924. As LHHS tried to find its footing in football, they were far behind in the game's nuances, positional technique, and general game management. No opponent was going to take it easy on Lyman Hall, nor should they. It could not have been easy for Coach Schipke, a proud man who knew winning on the highest levels in basketball. Lyman Hall football was so far behind the rest of the football-rich Housatonic League. It would be a slow, gradual climb from becoming competitive to victorious. For Lyman Hall football, starting from the bottom would take years ... decades.

Chapter 41

The 1953 State Championship, "Beating The Unbeatable"

After winning back-to-back Housatonic League basketball titles in 1950 and 1951, the 1952 team had a modest (to say the least) 10-10 season. The Wallingford basketball fanatics were starting to be more than a little concerned. Conversely, the football teams of 1950, 1951, and 1952 were a combined 2-16-1, and hardly anyone noticed. It was still a basketball town, and Wallingford was about to discover "King Tut's Tomb."

In a rare preseason of pessimistic prognostication of Lyman Hall basketball in Connecticut's newspapers, LHHS was declared to be an average basketball team for the 1952-53 season. They lacked size, experience, and returning scorers, but they had Head Coach Fred Schipke. A fine basketball tactician who once spent a few days with legendary college basketball coach Adolph Rupp to learn his offensive system. As Connecticut coaches far and wide discovered, Schipke's teams should never be underestimated. His ability to get the most out of his players and never shrink in the most significant moments of basketball games made the humble Schipke one of the best coaches of any era.

The 1952-53 roundball team was an interesting mix of juniors and seniors. They played a great brand of defense, and as with all Schipke teams, there was balanced scoring among his starters. Unfortunately, the Housatonic League in 1952-53 was stacked with quality teams, led by East Haven High School under coach Frank Crisafi. The Yellowjackets were thought to be invincible and were just about to begin a string of 77 consecutive wins without a loss ... after the state championship game of 1953.

During the regular season, Lyman Hall didn't record any victories of significance, losing to St. Mary's, twice to Southington, twice to Branford, and twice to undefeated Housatonic League Champion, East Haven, 47-46 at LHHS and a 67-43 blasting at the Easties gym. East Haven was ranked the number one team in Connecticut, heading into the State Class B Tournament. With a record of 11-7 in the regular season, Lyman Hall was the lowest ranked team in the Class B bracket. The Orangemen's strength was in the balanced scoring within the team. Captain Arthur "Bucky" Catapano led the scoring with a 13.6 average, followed by Walter Pluta at 11.4 points per game. Ernie Bercier had an 11.3 average, Mike Hazard 9.6 per game, and Ted Krol scored 5.6 points per game average.

Lyman Hall opened the state tournament with a decisive 60-47 win over Plainville High School. Jumping up in class, the Orangemen were matched up against the 4th ranked

Killingly High School of Danielson. The Killingly team held an eleven point lead at one point in the second half, but a ferocious comeback by the Schipkemen deadlocked the score at the end of regulation time, and the game went into overtime. With both teams holding the ball for long periods of time in the overtime stanza, Lyman Hall pulled out a 71-70 victory.

On to the Semi-finals, the Orangemen would face the 2nd ranked team in Class B, Southington High School, a team that defeated LHHS on two occasions in the regular season, 68-60 and 62-45. Schipke's zone defensive strategy worked well in denying Southington from scoring in close to the basket. The Orangemen appeared faster and quicker than at any time previously during the season, making it look easy at times for a 52-35 victory.

Defeating three higher ranked opponents in a state tournament would be cause for celebration in the streets of most other boroughs in Connecticut, but in Wallingford in 1953... in basketball ... winning championships was the only measure of success.

It would be enough to meet any other adversary in the state title game, but Lyman Hall High School, as history has shown before and since 1953, always seems to face an unbeatable foe. Waiting for the Orangemen was undefeated, state top ranked, No. 1, East Haven High School.

The Hartford Courant was clear in its prediction that East Haven will have little trouble with a seven-loss Lyman Hall team in the Class B title game.

Of all the predictions made far and wide for an easy victory by East Haven over Lyman Hall in the state title game of 1953, the most dramatic was announced by Bob Steele on his WTIC morning broadcast on the day of the game. Steele, whom most Connecticut residents woke up to, listening to his homespun humor, news, and weather forecast, were drawn to attention, as Steele uttered these words,

> *"... and in the Class B final, East Haven will have no trouble with Lyman Hall of Wallingford. If*

*Lyman Hall beats East Haven, I will go to Lyman
Hall, stand on my head, and sing "Swanee."*

The Steele guarantee was the talk of Wallingford and Lyman Hall High School, but it did emphasize the preponderance of sentiment across the state that East Haven, No.1 in Connecticut and in the top five in New England entering the final, would easily punch their ticket to the 1953 New England Championships at Boston Garden.

GAME DAY

East Haven wore their blue jerseys, so the Orangemen donned their new white uniforms, a recent home or away option so that teams would not wear the same color jerseys. The Wallingford faithful would have preferred to see their team wear their traditional shiny orange uniforms, but the long-shot Orangemen wore white on this day.

Coach Schipke carefully prepared his team to meet an opposing juggernaut that had beaten Lyman Hall twice in the regular season. Schipke planned to play each quarter like a game within the game.

Since the 1948 season, the Lyman Hall students and basketball fans had become enthusiastic poster makers. At each game, posters depicting slogans, player's names, and portions of basketball cheers were handwritten on posters. Many posters were mounted on wooden sticks to be bobbed up and down during the game. Larger cloth posters would be affixed between planks, carried by two persons and paraded in front of the stands. On this night at the Payne Whitney, the posters were in every row, down every aisle, forcing the fandom to stand through most of the game to see the action. The noise for Lyman Hall was a ceaseless cacophony of screams; cheerleader led basketball cheers through megaphones, staccato "ahhhhhh's, ooooh's, and the periodic, "c'mon ref," that started the second the Orangemen took the court. There were no bands or loud artificial piped-in music, just the pure student-generated enthusiasm that would send everyone home, hoarse.

With the opening tip, Lyman Hall raced out to a fast start and got the lead as Coach Schipke had his players hold the ball on each possession. For Lyman Hall, there was no rush to shoot the ball as the East Haven players became visibly frustrated at times. During the second quarter, with East Haven's Tony Massari leading the way, the Easties took the lead, and with three minutes left in the half, East Haven led by nine points.

The huge Lyman Hall crowd maintained its raucous cheering in the third quarter, but the Easties ended the third period with a 33-26 advantage. With poise and careful passing, Lyman Hall edged its way toward closing the point differential. Behind by three, 47-44, with a minute remaining in the game, Bucky Catapano sank two free throws to bring the Orangemen within one point. With the Payne Whitney clock ticking down under fifteen seconds, Lyman Hall gained possession. East Haven packed in their zone, not wanting to give up a shot close to the basket or commit a foul that would put Lyman Hall on the line with a chance to tie the game.

Ernie Bercier (#15) dribbled to an open spot, some 15 feet from the basket with less than 10 seconds remaining, as LHHS trailed by one solitary point.

There was a sudden hush as Bercier let fly with a one-handed set shot. The ball cleared the cords that set off a blast of ear-splitting thunder. With that Bercier basket, Lyman Hall had done the impossible, beat the unbeatable, and climbed the highest peak, a 48-47 victory, earning the 1953 State Class B Championship.

Shortly after 10 PM, Wallingford became one rousing celebration. Residents who had not gone to the game came to the high school before the parade of cars arrived back from New Haven. The "Lantern" in front of Lyman Hall High School was lit for the final time that evening.

In New Haven, a Wallingford patrol car radioed a report of the victory to Lieutenant Jack DeLucia at Headquarters in Wallingford. The police car led the long line of an estimated

200 vehicles from New Haven up State Street, North Haven, and Wallingford. The North Haven Police helped clear the way for the line of cars into Wallingford proper.

Once in Wallingford, some 600 persons piled into the small LHHS gymnasium where a victory rally took place. An enormous cheerleader's megaphone was passed from player to player who, upon the shoulders of their fellow students and fans, gave reports of the great plays which led to the momentous victory. Each player's voice was drowned out with cheers before they completed their statements.

Ernie Bercier, who sank the winning basket, said, *"I guess this proves there's no such thing as an unbeatable team."*

The celebration was only beginning as the Student Council hastily organized a Victory Dance the following week. A school-wide assembly was held in the auditorium, and indeed, Bob Steele did attend ... take the stage and sing "Swanee" while standing on his head.

The Town of Wallingford sent the team to Boston for a weekend to see the New England High School Basketball Tournament that was won by New London High School, who lost to Wilby High School in the Class A State Tournament. A banquet, open to Wallingford's citizens, was held where all team members were awarded championship jewelry.

It would be the last basketball state championship for Lyman Hall High School. The Orangemen, turned Trojans in 1957, would play for the state title in 1959, 1961, and 2008.

At this writing, Lyman Hall High School never again stood in that cherished location where only one team can emerge victorious ... in basketball, but in 1953 the basketball town of Wallingford was galvanized once again.

Chapter 42

Fred Schipke Walks Away from Football

After eight seasons of doing what he was "asked" to do by Principal Fernald, bringing football back to Lyman Hall as a varsity sport, he had had enough. Still, the highly successful basketball coach of Lyman Hall High School, Coach Schipke announced his repeated phrase, "... I've had it"! The gym or physical education teacher's age-long tradition coaching all athletic teams at a given secondary school had become a worn-out practice and a heavy burden for anyone with a young family.

Although assistant coaches were added at Lyman Hall in the 1950s, they didn't always have the background acquired through playing a given sport or previous coaching experience to lift a team to more remarkable achievement. If coaches, head or assistant, wanted to be better in teaching the sport, they had to seek out other coaches (high school or collegiate) with expertise and pick their brains. The days of coaching clinics had not yet arrived in the 1950s, and few coaches were given time off from their teaching duties or the financial means to travel to meet with other coaches. Fred Schipke had traveled great distances during the summer to fish and hunt with a few outstanding basketball coaches and talk the game he loved. For football at Lyman Hall, a coach had to learn on the job, and assistant coaches had to heavily rely on the head coach for the skills and information they needed to impart on the practice field. The only other avenue available to head football coaches in the development of football knowledge and skill was to bring in assistant coaches with some depth of understanding of football.

During Fred's years as head football Coach, A. Raymond Mahan served as his assistant (football and basketball) from 1949-1954. Mahan's career in education would continue to flourish, becoming Assistant Superintendent of Schools in 1959 and playing a unique role in Lyman Hall High School football lore in 1961. Roger McMahon became a football assistant coach in 1955 and held a similar role as the Junior Varsity basketball coach.

In 1953, Walter Schipke began as a volunteer assistant coach for the football team and thus began an association with football through 1960. Walter Schipke was a dedicated science teacher, highly organized, always eager to learn. Walt Schipke graduated from Lyman Hall in 1944. Involved in many activities at LHHS, he was a talented musician who played in the orchestra and band, where he was quartermaster. Walt Schipke had a leading role in the school production of the comedy "June Mad," where he played Dr. Wood. Walt was an LHHS cheerleader, but he did not participate in sports beyond that during his high school years.

In 1956, Fred Schipke was finally given permission by the administration to remove himself from coaching the football team. Although Mr. Schipke wanted to entirely take his hands off anything to do with football, he still would have to work with the new football coach as part of his responsibilities as Head of Physical Education that began in 1954.

Langdon Fernald, principal of LHHS, required that all the school's athletic coaches be a faculty member. This made the task of finding a new coach for football especially challenging. John Riccitelli and Roger McMahon were the two other physical education teachers with Fred Schipke. Riccitelli and McMahon briefly served as assistant football coaches early in their respective teaching careers at Lyman Hall, but neither had any interest in football. Both men, graduates of LHHS, had aspirations to one day become the head basketball coach after Fred Schipke left the position. McMahon would become an assistant basketball coach and one day take over the head coaching duties of the basketball team. Riccitelli was an assistant and future head coach of the baseball team. As Fred Schipke ended his eight years as head football coach in 1956, no physical education teacher was interested in the position.

Chapter 43

Walter Schipke Becomes 6th LHHS Coach

Fernald combed the faculty for a teacher who would be willing to take over the football team. It wasn't a pressure position as it would have been if this had been to coach basketball, or even baseball, as few expected the football team to win many games. With a total faculty of 53 (male and female) in 1956, only one teacher stepped forward as a candidate for the head football job, Walter Schipke. Principal Fernald named Walter Schipke, head football coach, in June 1957. Fernald understood this sport's challenges and "strongly encouraged" John Riccitelli to "give Walt a hand," becoming an assistant coach for one season.

Coach Walt Schipke enlisted the help of two fellow faculty members to assist him in developing a football team, Bernard Pilichowski, and Richard Fitzsimmons. With quality instruction from his teacher coaches, Walt Schipke brought structure to practices and games. Don Warzocha, a member of Fred Schipke's last football team and Walt Schipke's first team, characterized the change in coaches, "Walt and Bernie (Pilichowski) taught us the game and the skills we needed to be successful. With Fred (Schipke), things were a little laid back, whereas Walt drilled us on the skills we needed with great attention to detail. From the first day of practice with Walt, you could feel the difference".

In the fall of 1957, the students and faculty of Lyman Hall

moved from the high school building on South Main Street to the brand new Lyman Hall facility on Pond Hill Road. It was all exciting ... new building ... new coach, the first <u>official</u> school mascot (Trojans, as voted on by the senior class), and a fresh feeling about football. All that had to happen now was WIN. The athletic talent was there in the hallways to win, not just in basketball and baseball, which occurred in 1957-58, but in football. Walt Schipke molded his team, getting them to feel they could compete with any team.

Walt Schipke's first team in 1957 won three games, the first time a Lyman Hall team had achieved three victories in a season since 1931. The "Trojans" with newly adopted school colors of Blue and White still wore the black helmets.

As a footnote, ORANGE was never an official school color, and when the student body had an opportunity to vote in orange as a school color with either white or black (in 1957), the vote was decisive. There were a number of color combinations offered on the ballot, but Blue and White received more than half of the votes cast. For many alumni, it was sentimental "goodbye" for the color orange that gave Lyman Hall a color brand and symbol of so many championship and historical moments. Particularly broken-hearted was Fred Schipke, who understood its meaning to Langdon Fernald and the high school's legacy. Schipke would find a way to insert the color orange into the uniform designs in future years, but Fred never accepted the students' indifference about a color that, as he put it, "...was earned, and was part of our history".

WALT SCHIPKE, 1957 - 1960

The 1957 season was a wonderful debut for Walt Schipke. The team was led by future LHHS Hall of Famer Bill "Bull" Gannon (#32) and quarterback Bob Popovich. The Trojans made an immediate impact on their opponents in 1957, starting the season in the T-formation, winning their first game of the year against a new and future Housatonic League foe, Amity Regional High School, 22-7. As the Blue and White prepared to face the powerful Shelton Gaels, a flu epidemic wiped out all of the games for the next three weeks. After this long layoff due to the flu, the Trojans unveiled a new offense, the single-wing, and defeated the previously unbeaten East Haven Yellowjackets of Coach Frank Crisafi. For the first time in many years, a Lyman Hall football player gained state-wide recognition as Bill Gannon earned a second-team selection of the All-State team.

WINNING SOME, NOT ENOUGH ...

The 1958 football squad won three games as quarterback, and Class President Don Warzocha led the Trojans. Wearing the #10 proudly, Don Warzocha personified leadership both on and off the field. Don Curtis was a tri-captain with Warzocha as "Big Don" #75 earned first-team All-State honors and is generally regarded as one of the two best offensive tackles in school history with Ralph Riley (class of 1986).

Curtis captained the 1958-59 Lyman Hall basketball team to the State, Class B Finals in 1959. As a track team member, he was the leading scorer in 1959, never failing to place lower than second in the javelin, discus, and shotput. Undefeated in the javelin, Curtis was an All-State choice and held the javelin's state record for 14 years. Matriculating to Tufts University, "Big Don" was a four-year Dean's List recipient and a 4-year member of the football team, captaining the Jumbos in 1962.

For anyone who was part of the class of 1959, all you can do is smile broadly. The football, basketball, baseball, and track & field teams were wealthy with future LHHS HALL OF FAME inductees. Junior Mark Klausner (class of 1960) was the first team All-State end in football in 1959 and entered the Hall of Fame in 1990.

Junior Cole Proctor (class 1960), a renowned college and professional football coach, was a lineman on the 1958 football team and was inducted into the Hall of Fame in 1992. Ken Marhevka (Class of 1959) was a versatile member of the 1958 football team and was inducted into the Hall of Fame in 2007. Then ... there were Don Curtis and Don Warzocha, legendary in their own right, inseparable and distinctive in so many ways. They both were inducted into the Lyman Hall High School Hall of Fame in 1988.

In the last year (1960) of Walt Schipke's *quattuor annos* (four years) as head football coach, Kenneth Warzocha was named to the All-State first team at the center position, marking the first time in school history that a football "first team" All-State selection was chosen from LHHS in three consecutive years. This was evidence of the football building blocks that Walt Schipke had put in place. Unfortunately, despite the progress, the end would come quickly for Coach Schipke, and his coaches as two members of the Wallingford Board of Education pushed for a change at the football team's helm as the Trojans suffered through a 1-8 season in 1960.

Under Walt Schipke, the football fortunes of Lyman Hall were on the upbeat. For the first time, since football's return in 1949, the scores of games against the Housatonic's best teams were getting closer to victories. So many games in other sports, basketball, baseball, and others, claim "Moral Victories" when they play a close game (and lose) to a quality team. In football, as the best coaches on every level attest, there are no moral victories, only wins, and losses. The 1959 squad won three games for the third consecutive season under Walt Schipke, and the '59 Trojans lost less-than-a-touchdown games with East Haven and Derby while tying Shelton 0-0.

Walt Schipke and his staff were making a positive difference in LHHS football, but the tenor was the same, ... win a few, lose too many. The new Lyman Hall High School had a new football field, named after a young member of the faculty, science teacher Richard Fitzgerald, who had died soon after the LHHS on Pond Hill Road had opened. Everyone's heart was in the right place with the naming, but as most people discover, sooner or later, the naming of specific facilities, buildings, fields, and streets might best be left for when someone's connection to the aforenamed field or structure has a relationship to the object of the naming. The general feeling was that there was no person associated with football, player or coach, who merited such recognition to alumni and the citizenry. Heretofore, why not name the field after an exceptional teacher, taken before his time.

After three seasons, 1957-59, the Walt Schipke led Trojans had yet to experience a winning season. More dramatically, since football was restarted at Lyman Hall in 1949, the school had not won more games than it lost for eleven seasons. Although Walt and his coaches seemed to be making progress, circumstances in Wallingford and a new awareness of the game of football through the new media giant, "television," would help to bring an end to Walt's tenure as head football coach.

Chapter 44

TV awakens Wallingford to Football

Unlike basketball that was deeply entrenched in the Town of Wallingford's ethos and psyche, football was essentially an afterthought. The popularity, or lack thereof, of football in Wallingford, was minimal at best after its return in 1949. Small numbers of non-students and non-parents attended Lyman Hall High School football games. The varsity football rosters of the 1950s averaged 29.7 players per year. While the basketball teams were fair at best after the 1953 state title, baseball was racking up good seasons in the decade. Football had made progress under Walt Schipke, but football was far behind the rest of the Housatonic League.

With the influx of people moving into Wallingford after World War II, there was a rather dramatic increase in enrollment in the Wallingford Public Schools. New elementary schools were built, and by the early 1960s, the town had three junior high schools, feeding into Lyman Hall High School. The Town of Wallingford began to embrace youth sports in the 1950s with the growth of Little League baseball, Biddy basketball, and the YMCA playing a significant role in young people's opportunities to become athletically engaged.

However, football was largely ignored until a few events came together to force feed football into the Wallingford public psyche. Television had taken over the 1950s as the medium of choice for entertainment and news.

On December 28, 1958, the National Football League's championship game between the Baltimore Colts and the nearby New York Football Giants was played at Yankee Stadium. It was broadcast on television on NBC. For most Wallingfordites, that meant channel 4 on the dial of their television sets. This was the first nationally televised football game in history. Television sets with the rabbit ear antennas ranged from ten-inch screens that people would mount on top of their radio consoles to 24-inch screens that were stand-alone pieces of furniture.

The most popular makers of television sets in the 1950s were RCA, Philco, Teletone, Hoffman, and Westinghouse. They were the center of attention in Wallingford's living rooms, but on this cold day in December 1958, whichever family in the neighborhood had the bigger TV set, the more neighbors gathered around it. On that day, football was the most popular show in America. New York City was blacked out from watching the game, and thousands of New Yorkers, fled to Connecticut to get motel and hotel rooms to watch the game.

The popularity of football was almost instantaneous, especially in the Northeast corridor, as Chris Schenkel and Chuck Thompson announced the game on television. The game was a back-and-forth affair that went into overtime with the Colts winning, 33-27. In every home in Wallingford, families were huddled around their little television sets to watch... FOOTBALL. Men, women, and children who had no previous interest in football were now drawn to the helmets, uniforms, and constant excitement of this sport.

The impact of television had another powerful effect on the growing proverbial football interest meter in 1960. With the growth of Pop Warner Football nationally (Wallingford chose NOT to affiliate with the national Pop Warner organization in 1959), the Walt Disney company produced one of its acclaimed children's movies for television, and one of the most viewed shows of the year, "Moochie of Pop Warner Football." Aired on ABC in 1960, Moochie, one of the recurring characters of spin-offs from the Mickey Mouse Club daily television shows, featured a little boy who designs a play for his Pop Warner team, called the "skillymoochplay" and won a big game. Every family with elementary school kids always tuned into anything Disney created, and this football fantasy with child-favorite Moochie brought even more enthusiasm to youth football.

Chapter 45

Wallingford Junior Football League (WJFL), 1958

As the second half of the 1958-59 school year began and Lyman Hall basketball once again took center stage for the town's people, there was a new sports interest, and it was about to receive a great big shot in the arm.

The scores of Wallingford men returning from military service, along with many non-indigenous Wallingford veterans from all over the country who flocked to the town because of available manufacturing jobs, brought a fresh, youthful feeling to the populous. Many of these vets had played sports in high school and in the service. Where basketball was the most popular sport in Wallingford, so many of these new residents, growing up in Pennsylvania, Ohio, etc., were brought up with the game of football.

There was a common question from management to hourly workers, "Why doesn't Wallingford have leagues for boys to play football"? From casual conversations on the factory and shop floors, men learned that football was discontinued in 1936 and then started back up in 1949 at the local high school. Those that lived in Meriden and worked in Wallingford shared that their town just up the road had the Meriden Junior Football League that had been around since 1954.

There were no exclusive sporting goods stores in

Wallingford. Athletic equipment for any sport had to be bought at scrambled merchandising department stores such as W.T. Grants on Center Street, but the selection was limited. In the early 1950s in Wallingford, why would boys ask their parents for a football or a helmet? In the school yards of the town's elementary schools, the boys played basketball, kickball, and occasionally baseball/softball during recess, but football? NO! Once football began to be televised after the 1958 championship, a growing interest spawned in the youth of Wallingford. Father's and their sons started to throw a football around on the weekends, particularly during half-time of New York Giants games. Keep in mind, during the latter part of the 1950s and early 1960s, the Giants were literally the only game in town.

In the summer of 1958, Wallingford's first efforts to create "something" for boys who wanted to play football began to take form. With leadership provided by William M. Hutchinson, Mansfield A. Lyon, Donald C. Lunt, Frederick M Killam, and others, word went out for men interested in starting a youth football league. More than 20 men and women attended the organizational meetings. They reached out to the Meriden Junior Football League for assistance in putting together an organizational framework.

The Wallingford Junior Football League organized and began play in the fall of 1959 with the following rules and structure.

1. Boys between the ages of 9-13 were eligible to play, providing each weighed a minimum of 65 pounds and did not exceed 95 pounds.
2. Each boy with a birth certificate and meeting weight minimums and maximums would be assigned to a team organized by geographic location within Wallingford (or from contiguous neighborhoods).
3. There would be four teams of 25 boys each with team practice locations that generally included Westside Field, Simpson School, Yalesville (Parker Farms School), and Doolittle Park.

4. Each boy must have his own football equipment, helmets, shoulder pads, and pants (meaning the parents had to buy the equipment).

The most intriguing component of the Wallingford Junior Football League's first year was the acquisition of uniforms. The fledgling league had no operating funds or any equipment of any kind, not even footballs. A few members of the organizing group approached the management of the brand-new discount department store in Wallingford, Barkers, on Colony Road just before it opened for business. In that first meeting, they found an accommodating partner that wanted to establish a family-friendly reputation in Wallingford.

Barkers agree to provide all game jerseys for the first season with their company logo emblazoned on the front with a different color for each team. The league decided to encourage all parents of the players to buy their football equipment from Barkers. Overnight, the Barker's toy department was filled with Wilson (red) shoulder pads of a heavy card board material, tan canvas football pants with cardboard padding sewn into the thigh, and two options for helmets, the Spalding Jon Arnett model with a white plastic, one-bar facemask, and the Hutch model with a white plastic two-bar facemask.

Although most parents did buy their sons the helmet, shoulder pads, and pants at Barkers, many parents bought their son's gear in other stores or resurrected a family air loom helmet. Youth football gear was considered "toys" in the 1950's so there was minimal actual padding or protection in the equipment.

As the jersey colors for the teams were black, green, white, and red, finding youth helmets of those colors was just not possible, not in 1959, so the fathers used their various occupational skills to color the helmets. The helmets were of two basic materials, plastic and leather. The process of painting the helmets had to work on both surfaces. It was a skillful, time-intensive process by which all the helmets of a given team were spread out on the ground and spray-painted in the team's color. Then the helmets were "baked" in the oven of the boy's family stove or someone's stove, hardening the paint. Ovens in kitchens all over Wallingford were stuffed with green, black, red, and white plastic or leather shells that had to be carefully monitored in the oven, or the heat might melt the plastic or burn the leather.

The games were all staged at Doolittle Park, rain, snow, or shine on six consecutive Sundays, starting at noon. For the most part, each team was coached by the fathers of the players or men who played football in high school with plays run out of the T-formation. Each play began with the fullback and two halfbacks standing parallel in the backfield; then, each backfield mate raised his arms out so that their fingertips just touched each other. This meant that they were properly aligned to start the play, and the quarterback got under center and called a simple cadence, "Set 1-2-3". All of the teams had that basic start to all plays and cadence.

The games were an instant smash! Doolittle Park, once the playing field of Lyman Hall High School, baseball and football was now the fall home for hundreds of youth football families. They came with younger children, relatives, friends, all carrying lawn chairs, blankets, coffee, and hot chocolate thermoses. There were kids throwing footballs to one another. There were cheers and excitement, all in the spirit of the game of football.

The number of boys who registered to play in the Wallingford Junior Football League in 1960 was nearly twice the number who stood on the scale to register in that inaugural 1959 season. In the space of one year, all equipment and jerseys were provided by the league thanks to a ground-swell of enthusiasm and public embrace for the Wallingford Junior Football League.

Team sponsorships soared and began to change annually as businesses and organizations virtually competed to place their name on a WJFL team. Among the most prominent contributors were Wallace Silversmiths, Bunting & Lyons, Barkers, Ortense, Wallingford Automobile Dealers Association, Dime Savings, First Federal Savings, and Loan Association, Yankee Silversmith, Yale Motor Inn, and many other partial sponsorships. In 1960 alone, the WJFL received sponsorship donations from 72 Wallingford stores and businesses.

Starting in 1960, four teams of 25 boys (and a waiting list for each) went through a schedule of playing each team twice. Almost immediately, the names and football deeds of some WJFL players emerged from the lips of a football star-starved adult fan base. The crowds were packed around the Doolittle football field for every game, every Sunday, and the names of boys, ages 10-13, gained a name following. Some of those early league notables were Leonard Suzio, Robert Long, Bob Rigby, Thomas Wachtelhausen, Bob Mesolella, Phil Wielgosh, Barnard Barnis, Tommy Theis, and the incomparable, Fran Stupakevich.

WHY CAN'T LYMAN HALL WIN?

The repeated words coming from so many on-lookers were, "Wait till these kids get to Lyman Hall." This refrain was just beginning to take hold and would place enormous pressure on current and future LHHS coaches. One of the "fools-gold" outcomes of the Wallingford Junior Football League was that some of the teams made it look too simple.

People wondered, "Why can't the Lyman Hall team do that, meaning the scoring of touchdowns from all over the field"? Some of the league coaches began to be viewed as football experts, and some of those coaches started to believe their own accolades. What followed was ..." We need this (WJFL) coach to coach the high school team." As the Lyman Hall football teams continued to struggle to win games, the presence of the WJFL was adding unintended pressure on the LHHS coach, no matter whom he happened to be.

The collective thinking and discourse around the company lunchroom, watercooler, and in the numerous Wallingford waterholes were "Look at the talent the WJFL is sending Lyman Hall High School. When will the high school finally win in football, and who will coach the team"?

Stephen W. Hoag, Ph.D.

THE WALLINGFORD "PONIES"

The WJFL created an almost overnight sensation. Subsequently, a dramatic change in the interest level regarding football was experienced all over town. Where football at Lyman Hall had seemed to be almost invisible at times, now there was a palpable excitement as boys were coming through a football pipeline of sorts, eventually leading to Lyman Hall ... or so, people thought.

Such was the enthusiasm for football that the WJFL created a second tier for older boys, "The Wallingford Ponies." The age restrictions of the WJFL topped out at 13 years of age, generally meaning that boys would be too old to participate by the end of their 7th-grade year. The three junior high schools, Moran, Robert Early, and Dag Hammarskjold, were grades 7-9. There was no junior high school football at that time. As grade nine was not in Lyman Hall High School, there was no freshman football. All this meant was there was no place for early teenage boys to continue learning the game of football.

The Wallingford Ponies filled that gap and in a very dynamic way. The "Ponies" had an age category of 13-15 with a weight limit of 150 pounds. The "Ponies" played in the Charter Oak Conference, a statewide league that had a relatively short life span, 1962-1965 and over those years included teams from South Windsor, Meriden, Manchester, Glastonbury, Portland, Plainville, and Wallingford.

For the Wallingford Junior Football League, the "Ponies" provided a natural bridge from the ages of 9-13 WJFL to high school football. More than anything, the "Ponies" became an all-star team, loaded with the best players from the younger teams and those boys who weighed too much to be in the 9-13 league component.

The coaches were two former Lyman Hall High School football players, Jim Bilyak, (class of 1959) and Gene Fontanella (class of 1954). Together they provided a more serious approach to youth sports, ... to youth football. Every coach in the WJFL wanted their son's team to win, but at that stage of football evolution in Wallingford, few knew how to position a team to win. Unlike basketball and baseball, football is a very aggressive, physical game, and athletic talent alone is never enough to carry the day.

Whereas most practices for teams in the WJFL were primarily a matter of running a few fundamental plays over and over again with a first team and a second-team taking turns, the "Ponies" practices were two hours of full speed blocking and tackling. The fact that the "Ponies" had several outstanding athletes made the practices ever more challenging.

The Charter Oak Conference did not place restrictions on participation. In the Wallingford Junior Football League, every boy on every team must, by league rule, play at least a quarter of each game. The "Ponies" under Bilyak and Fontanella were under no such mandate. Like high school teams, the best players played, and no member of the "Ponies" was guaranteed to get into any game.

Each boy on the team fully understood that if you didn't earn your way onto the field by hard work in practice, there was a good chance that you'd never leave the team sideline. As there were only six games in the Charter Oak Conference season and one more game if a team made it to the championship game, practices were of critical importance and were never approached casually.

In 1962, the Wallingford Ponies were undefeated in the regular season. They dominated the league, made up of town teams from the greater Hartford area. The Wallingford "Ponies," loaded with outstanding youth athletes, made the game of football look far different than that of the high school team. From the huddle to the offensive formation, they looked so different. They ran with the football with amazing efficiency. No matter the town they were pitted against, the "Ponies" made it look easy.

The center piece of the 1962 Pony team was Tommy Theis, possessing a natural power running style that seemed almost impossible to stop, whether it was running the ball up the middle or outside. Early in the 1962 season, Theis had his nose broken, a common, painful, and bloody injury. The WJFL and its older level team, the "Ponies," had no cage facemasks on their helmets, just a white two-bar mask of plastic. If Tommy were to continue to play with the broken nose, some additional protection for Theis's face had to be devised.

In 1962, the Wallingford Junior Football League and their Pony team decided that all league helmets would be the same, a cost-cutting decision. The helmets were white with a dual white facemask that was molded in a slightly downward direction. Left alone, this facemask covered the chin and mouth, but little else. Tommy decided to unscrew the mask on his helmet and turn it upside down in order to protect his damaged nose. The rearranged facemask added a gladiatorial appearance to Theis, yet another element of difference to Theis's already distinctive running style.

The 1962 Wallingford "Ponies" would win the Charter Oak Conference Championship with a convincing win in the title game, played at Dillon Stadium in Hartford. The on-the-field success of the "Ponies" brought the growing football audience to the Lyman Hall football field, where the team played its home games.

One of the unique outcomes of the "Pony" experience was that Wallingford boys filled the roster, but the individual players would not necessarily attend Lyman Hall High School or play football at LHHS. Although LHHS got a share of the talent from the Pony roster in Tom Wachtelhausen, Billy Smith, AJ Namnoum, Don Roy, Tom Theis, and Bob Mesolella, just to name a few, there were others who chose to enroll at Notre Dame of West Haven, Fairfield Prep or decide not to play football at LHHS.

Chapter 46

Basketball Rolls On ... And On

Roger McMahon had taken over for Fred Schipke as Head Basketball Coach in 1959-60 as Fred remained as athletic director and golf coach. No coach could have asked for a better first season than McMahon.

The basketball Trojans were chockfull of hard-nosed players who had played on the playgrounds of Wallingford together since their early childhood. To begin, the Trojans had the best backcourt in school history. To that statement, there is no argument. Mel Horowitz and Jim Potter were the best 1-2 punch in the Housatonic League, let alone in the entire state.

Horowitz, with his slashing style and innate leadership abilities, triggered the Trojans. In this third and last golden era of basketball, the LHHS hoopsters rolled over all regular-season competition in 1959-60. Close games were rare, but each nail-biter added superb theatre to a season that was perfect ... almost.

Jim Potter led the state in scoring in 1959-60, averaging over 28 points per game, but it was the dazzling Mel Horowitz, just a junior, who brought the packed houses to their feet time and again, game after game. Mel's passing skills were unmatched in Connecticut school-boy lore, and if they kept statistics for assists as they do today, the record book would have been sealed forever after 1961.

The 1959-60 season saw the Trojans roll up an undefeated regular season. Wallingford was still a basketball town, and this juggernaut of a team captivated the citizenry, as did those of yesteryear with the likes of Charles Inguaggiato, Roger Offen, John Riccitelli, Gene Combs, Johnny Carvalho, and Ernie Bercier.

There was a magic that covered Wallingford during that year. Members of the team could not walk down Center Street without being noticed. Local restaurants would not let them pay for anything. Haircuts were free. Saturday night out with their girlfriends at the Wilkinson theatre was a free pass. Fellow Lyman Hall students crowded around their basketball heroes from the start of the school day till dismissal.

To be sure, Wallingford was basketball-crazy once again, but as it happens when a season ascends so fast and so high, there can be a dramatic and harsh tumble from grace.

Lyman Hall saw its 1959-60 season come to an abrupt and painful end when a snowstorm impacted some of the Lyman Hall players' arrival to the Payne Whitney Gymnasium for the state title game. East Haven, Housatonic League rival, whom LHHS defeated twice during the regular season, knocked the Trojans from the mount, beating the Wallingfordites, 45-36.

Cloaked in the exhilaration of the 1960 basketball season was the removal of Lyman Hall's football coach. If you want to call it that, the announcement was scarcely more than a few lines in the Wallingford Section of the Record Journal (the local newspaper). This was one of the many recurring indicators that football at Lyman Hall was a mere accessory to the basketball team.

Expectations were not nearly as high at the start of Lyman Hall's 1960-61 season as Mel was the only starter returning from the Housatonic League Champions of a year ago, but Mel, with his "winning is the only thing" approach, led a new crop of champions, largely from an undefeated Junior Varsity team from the year before. Circling Horowitz's prolific scoring and play-making were Walt Michonski, Dick Dombroski, Larry Sage, Ron Pietruski, Dick Wrinn, and Johnny Linaberry as the Trojans exploded out of the gate.

The 1960-61 season was brutal, and Mel led the Trojans to many a high-wire conclusion victory. Only Cheshire High School found an answer for defeating the Trojans as Horowitz made a last-second shot to win the game, only to have it waved off by a referee.

The 1961 Semi-Final game in the State Class B Tournament is one of the three greatest games in the history of the school. Lyman Hall faced top-ranked New Canaan, led by All-Stater Gary Liberator at the Payne Whitney Gymnasium at Yale. The back and forth battle, fought before a standing-room crowd, mainly of Wallingfordites, went down to the last minute.

The Trojans fell behind 51-50 with 13 seconds remaining. A missed foul shot by Liberator was pulled down by Dick Wrinn, who immediately passed to Mel. With the seconds ticking away, down by one, Horowitz attacked down the middle of the floor as the capacity crowd stood and screamed. With Mel looking for any teammate with an open shot, finding none, Horowitz pulled up some 25 feet from the basket and launched his shot. As the ball split the twines, the throng of Wallingford people exploded into pandemonium. They knew Mel, as he had many times before, would win the game for them. New Canaan called time out with two seconds remaining, but it would not be enough as the crowd of 1,600 plus flowed onto the court at the buzzer. LHHS had won 52-51. Mobbing Horowitz, the hundreds of Lyman Hall faithful lifted Mel over their heads, tearing at his #24 blue jersey. He had done it again and led Lyman Hall into the state finals for another battle with Plainville.

The Trojans lost in the finals, 45-36, but the state's sportswriters still named Horowitz the state tournament's Most Valuable Player, totally unprecedented in Connecticut schoolboy lore.

TIME RUNS OUT ON WALT SCHIPKE, 1960

After three years of three-win records with no winning seasons (1958-60), coupled with the local notoriety of the Wallingford Junior Football League, there was heightened interest in football ... winning football, (that is), and increasing tensions for the Trojans to finally begin to win ... in FOOTBALL. The question entering the 1960 season was, "could Lyman Hall football finally win more than it lost"?

There were 45 members of the 1960 Trojans, a good sized squad for any LHHS football team in any year with a number of quality juniors on the team, usually a sign of real potential. Unfortunately, the season did not turn out anything like the expectations of the team and its coaches. Consequently, there was a wave of harsh scrutiny from the community by way of the Wallingford Board of Education members.

The Lyman Hall football team, playing its first nine-game season, finished with a record of 1-8, and the board moved rapidly to remove the coach. Neither the principal, Langdon

Fernald, and the athletic director, Fred Schipke, were involved in the coach's dismissal, and as it turned out, neither would choose to be involved in any aspect of the selection and hiring of the next coach.

Walt Schipke and his assistants brought Lyman Hall football to an improved level of play and respectability. When asked why he thought he was not rehired following the 1960 season, Walter Schipke stated, "I guess we didn't win, ... enough".

Chapter 47

Joe Corbett, A Unique Start

With the end of the 1960-61 school year, a few issues were facing the Wallingford Public Schools. There was a teacher shortage for the next school year on the elementary, junior high school, and high school levels. Connecticut colleges were not producing the number of teachers required by the school districts of the state. The Wallingford Board of Education and superintendent, Frank Donovan, recognized that the answer to the teacher shortage needed a more aggressive teacher recruiting effort than just in Connecticut.

In the spring of 1961, Assistant Superintendent A. Raymond Mahan was dispatched to the Midwest states and the teacher preparatory colleges of Pennsylvania and Ohio to meet prospective teaching candidates personally.

While in Ohio, searching for teachers, he met with Joseph E. Corbett, an acquaintance from many years ago. Joe had recently received his master's degree from Ohio State University after earning his undergraduate degree from Morehead State University in Kentucky. Joe Corbett was born in Hartford and served in the Navy during World War II. Corbett had a basketball background as a player and coach but had not been involved with football. Mahan offered Corbett a position at Lyman Hall High School, teaching social studies. As Joe and his wife Cozette were expecting their first child, they needed some time to consider the offer since it meant relocating to Wallingford, Connecticut.

As Cozette remembers, "Joe and I talked for hours about the job, but the teaching salary was not near enough to pay for all the costs of moving, especially with the baby on the way. We decided to turn the teaching job in Wallingford down and stay in Ohio".

Joe informed Assistant Superintendent Mahan of their decision, but Mahan asked that he reconsider. With that, Mahan sweetened the deal by offering Joe an additional paid "duty" at Lyman Hall if he took the teaching job.

The additional paid "duty," as Mahan called it, was serving as the Head Coach of football at Lyman Hall High School. With the combination of salaries from the teaching position and the coaching job, Joe and Cozette reconsidered and moved to Wallingford.

The naiveté exhibited by Mahan, casually offering the head football job as an "extra duty," placed Joe Corbett in an extremely challenging position. Corbett had already gained the reputation as a quality teacher, a skill that would serve him well in the next four years as Head Coach, but he had to learn the game of football. For that, Corbett received a special gift in the person of Anthony Ruotolo.

Corbett and Ruotolo were first-year teachers at Lyman Hall in the Fall of 1961 and immediately developed a friendship that would last the rest of their lives. As Ruotolo had an extensive background in football, he was a perfect fit for Corbett as his assistant coach, who would need all of his expertise, taking over the football team.

Tony Ruotolo had been a first-team All-State selection in 1955 at Wilbur Cross High School in New Haven. He went on to play four years of football at Colgate University. Together, Corbett and Ruotolo brought a marvelous synergy of teaching talent, patience, and concern for their players' welfare.

Coach Corbett's years at Head Coach had a rocky beginning to say the least. The hiring of Corbett as head football coach was negotiated without any involvement of the athletic director, Fred Schipke or Principal, John Price.

Schipke maintained his arms-length approach to football he had espoused since he began his long tenure at Lyman Hall back in 1944.

On the first day of pre-season practice, Coach Corbett planned to give out equipment and then run their first team drills. This was less than a week before the actual start of school. Upon arrival, there was no one there to meet the new coaches at the school, unlock the storage areas, or was there even a hint as to where the football gear might be located. Mr. Corbett tried to reach Schipke by phone but was informed that he was out of state and wouldn't return for some days. Equipment distribution was delayed as Corbett was able to borrow a few footballs to get practices started.

THE CORBETT YEARS

Corbett's first team had 41 players, with some exceptional student-athletes. One of the team co-captains was quarterback, punter, and defensive back, Jim Lynch, who years later would serve as an assistant football coach under Phil Ottochian. Although the team possessed great enthusiasm, a new blue uniform jersey with white UCLA shoulder stripes, the helmets were still black (with a white stripe), the season was a series of large scores, mainly on the opponent's side of the scoreboard. After a 0-0 tie with Seymour in the season's third game, the Trojans managed their only victory of the season, a 14-8 win over Branford, finishing the year 1-7-1. The 1962 football season felt like a continuation of the previous one as the Trojans once again won but one game while losing eight.

The crowds at the Wallingford Junior Football League games in 1962, particularly those of the undefeated Wallingford Ponies, exceeded those of the high school team. While the "Ponies" were racking up the victories, the LHHS football team struggled to score touchdowns. Parents at Pony games' grumblings spoke to their shared concerns about sending their sons to LHHS if these traditional "losing ways" should continue.

After the 1962 Charter Oak Conference championship

of the Wallingford "Ponies," there was a new optimism as a handful of the "Ponies" would be beginning their high school careers as sophomores at Lyman Hall. A few would play three years of football, and few would choose not to play football at all at Lyman Hall ... a few others would play high school football, but not at Lyman Hall.

ON WISCONSIN ... "THE LOSING LAMENT"

When the new high school opened in 1957 on Pond Hill Road, there was a conscious effort to add new elements to the landscape of the school while eliminating others. The affectionately embraced moniker of the "Orangemen" was pushed to the curb, and a new school mascot was voted upon with a good portion of the voting student body casting their ballot for "Trojans" with a somewhat dubious ribald intention. Official school colors were voted upon by the student body after 31 years of school history, with blue & white as the chosen color combination with no reference to the historic "orange." This infuriated many loyal alumni.

Other new developments included the appearance of an LHHS marching band at home football games. Despite the enormous talent of LHHS musicians and many student musicians in the band each year, football games' music was rather mundane and routine. Unfortunately, no single piece of music played by the band elicited enthusiasm from the modest crowds that attended the Saturday Lyman Hall football games.

Typically, the music of any marching band of every school (high school or college) on football game day is designed to add color and excitement to the football event of the week, but the football games of Lyman Hall High School in the 1950s and 1960s were anything but exciting, to say the least. Lyman Hall never developed a fight song as most high schools had over the years. A fight song for any school is that one tune that brings the faithful to their feet soliciting periodically inserted cheers, and most importantly, it is the piece of music played every time "our team" comes onto the field, and SCORES a touchdown ... that is "A FIGHT SONG."

As Lyman Hall's marching band, primarily a national award-winning **concert** band with a few on-the-field dance steps, began to play at all home football games in 1957, the music department teachers selected a group of six songs to be played at the games. One of those tunes was "On Wisconsin," a popular song among high school marching band units. It was easy to perform in the coldest of weather, emphasizing brass and rhythmic drums. This was the song chosen by the marching band director, Harold Crump, to be played after every Lyman Hall touchdown. Mr. Crump rehearsed the band to get up "On Wisconsin" with these words, he barked out, "Let's hear it as the team comes up the field."

Yes, this was the song someone figured could be the Lyman Hall fight song, but alas, it turned out to be something entirely different. As Lyman Hall suffered through season after season with opponents scoring many touchdowns as the Blue & White scored too few, "On Wisconsin" was of little use in the band's repertoire. In the 1960s, Lyman Hall would often score a touchdown or two late in the game when the outcome was no longer in doubt, and the benches had been cleared.

Gradually, "On Wisconsin" began to be played for any touchdown either team scored, meaning that "On Wisconsin" was played by the LHHS band more for the Trojan's opponents than for Lyman Hall's football team. Whatever the intention, the outcome was that many people in the stands and even band members used the phrase ... "The loser's lament" every time "On Wisconsin" was called up for playing. This was just another negative ingredient to the fortunes or lack thereof that hovered over Lyman Hall High School football during the years of losing.

POWERFUL VOICES

The friction that surrounded the revolving sphere of Lyman Hall High School football lost some of its lubrication in 1963.

After two straight one-win seasons for Joe Corbett's charges, there was a fresh optimism with the influx of a high-profile **football** sophomore class. In generations past, there would be a similar emotion over a strong incoming basketball class of sophomores such as that of 1930, 1937, 1946, 1957, but in football? ... no such feeling over a group of incoming sophomores was ever experienced at LHHS. However, the 1963 team did have an incoming group of some renown, welcoming a sterling sophomore class that included Billy Smith, Tom Wachtelhausen, Pete Mezza, Dave Friend, and Tommy Theis.

The 1963 team, with a roster of 45 players, had speed and size, but the Trojans were stung early and often, losing their first eight games. The season would end with what turned out to be known as the "Saga of Steve Wells."

Steve Wells was a gifted athlete who excelled in baseball and football. As a sophomore in 1961, Steve started in the backfield for Lyman Hall. Life circumstances came against Steve, and he decided to enlist in the military before earning his diploma. Steve spent the 1962-63 school year in the United States Marine Corps, returning to Lyman Hall to finish his high school education in the fall of 1963. As a result of his military training, Wells returned to Lyman Hall as a much stronger and faster young man than when he left Wallingford.

Upon enrolling for his senior year, the Connecticut Interscholastic Athletic Conference (C.I.A.C.) declared Wells ineligible to play for the football team for the 1963 season. Joe Corbett and Tony Ruotolo were more than incensed over this decision as Wells had gone off to serve his country. Corbett and Ruotolo argued the decision before the CIAC Board and came away with the basic ruling that Wells had to complete one academic marking period before he would be eligible for athletic competition. This meant that Steve Wells would be eligible to play in only one football game, the last contest of the season in the traditional "Bean Pot Trophy" game against Cheshire High School on Thanksgiving Day at Cheshire.

Wells, the coaches, the '63 team, and the collective student body were energized by the drama that unfolded during Thanksgiving week with the return of Wells. No one knew for sure how Wells would perform as he hadn't played in a game in two years.

The pre-game facts leading up to the "Beanpot Game" were that Lyman Hall had scored only five touchdowns that season and was held to a touchdown or less in seven straight contests. Only one opponent had failed to score at least three touchdowns against the Trojans. Cheshire was a well-balanced team that used the pass more than most of the other teams in the Housatonic League.

So the stage was set with Lyman Hall in its usual holding place as a huge underdog. On an overcast and cold day on November 28, 1963, the Lyman Hall bus turned into Cheshire High School. Led by quarterback George DeSola (#21), the Trojan offense began to give the Rams of Cheshire a steady dose of the hard-charging Wells (#40). With roars from the Lyman Hall students in attendance every time Wells carried the ball, the Trojans were right in the game against the favored Rams, the first time the Trojans had stayed within a touchdown of an opponent since the Amity game back in September. With great performances from Rich Cassello (#72), Bob Christman (#64), and Fred Gordon (#55), the Trojans played inspired defense.

As Lyman Hall students huddled together, holding hands as the Cheshire time clock wound down, Wells broke off one more long run to seal the outcome as the Trojans beat Cheshire, 14-6. As the game clock ran out, Steve Wells ran to Joe Corbett. Wrapping his arms around his coach, they both fell into tears as the team and students in attendance surrounding Coach Corbett and Wells. That day, Wells set the school record for most rushing yards in a single game with 148 yards on 14 carries.

The afterglow of the Thanksgiving Day victory was short-lived as a few outspoken members of the community who were associated with the Wallingford Junior Football League were sewing the seeds of discontent, beginning the push for a change of the football coach at Lyman Hall once again. Although neither the athletic director nor principal did much to deflect or quell the criticism, Joe Corbett approached the 1964 season with optimism with many returning players.

Chapter 48

1964-65 School Year, One For The Ages ... Except for Football

There was great anticipation from every corner of the Wallingford citizenry with the start of the 1964-65 school year. Among the highlights of the year was a jam-packed senior class of high-performing academic students. Dr. Richard A. Otto's band and orchestra's musical talent would result in five students being selected as All-State, first chair musicians.

In this year, Lyman Hall High School would produce the first school-wide musical, "Oklahoma." Every member of the 80-student cast, 22-student stage crew, and musician in the 20-member pit orchestra was an LHHS student. There was no artificial or piped-in, pre-recorded music. It was a totally live performance. The lead role of Curly was played by three-sport athlete and LHHS Hall of Fame inductee Tom Wachtelhausen. Each performance of the show was a standing room only sell-out.

The baseball team of coach John Riccitelli completed a second place, 12-4 campaign in 1965 as power-hitting Tom Dokas drew heavy attention from professional scouts, and the San Francisco Giants signed pitcher Jack Milici.

All of this schoolwide fanfare would fill the pages of any yearbook, but unfortunately, the fall of 1964 began with the arduous fortunes of the 1964 football team. With the blazing halfback, Tom Theis, now a staple in the Trojan backfield, the season kicked off with a resounding 26-6 win over Platt High School of Meriden, one of the largest margins of victory since football was reinstituted in 1949. There was reason to look ahead after that first convincing win, but the LHHS defense became the most porous defense in the league in the next six games, giving up an average of 35 points per game while scoring an average of just three points per game during that stretch.

The football Trojans rallied in the final game of the season as Lyman Hall High School captured their second consecutive "Beanpot Trophy" in 1964 on Thanksgiving, beating Cheshire 18-14 as Tom Theis has his best day in the Blue & White.

With a final 2-7 record, Head Coach Joe Corbett faced the barbs of members of the Board of Education and a few of the persons who had helped grow the Wallingford Junior Football League. The discontent grew within the Wallingford Board of Education. Corbett had his enemies in Wallingford, but that handful of men never met with the humble Corbett to discuss the football team and his plans for the future. To be sure, he was treated with an indignity that broke his heart with no explanation given to him by anyone, including school administrators or the athletic department.

In April of 1965, Joe Corbett was officially dismissed as Head Football Coach by the Wallingford Board of Education. Mr. Corbett chose to retain his teaching position in the social studies department at Lyman Hall and continue to raise his family in Wallingford, watching his sons participate in sports at Lyman Hall. Over his career as a teacher, he was honored with yearbook dedications and the accolades of class valedictorians and class presidents in their speeches at commencement ceremonies, citing Corbett's numerous acts of kindness, leadership, and selfless dignity.

Tony Ruotolo, loyal to his friend and colleague, never coached at Lyman Hall again, although he was approached to coach by the next two head football coaches. Ruotolo would rise to become the principal of Lyman Hall High School from 1991 to 1996. Mr. Ruotolo, the inspirational teacher, and friend to so many students, served as a member of the CIAC High School Committee and the Eligibility Committee.

It is doubtful that there ever has been any coach of any sport at Lyman Hall High School more loved and admired than Joe Corbett. Devoted to his students and players, Mr. Corbett encouraged them onto matriculation into college. During his four years as Head Coach, and long after, the Corbett home was frequented by his players, who wanted to talk, share a smile, and sit with a man who would listen and understand any problem or reason for celebration.

Chapter 49

The Final Decade of Gold

While the football fortunes since 1949 were anything but a treasure chest of opulence, the basketball golden glow continued into the 1960s with one sinkhole in the middle. After Housatonic League Championships and deep runs in the state tournament in 1959, 1960, and 1961, there was a lull and just one horrible season in 1963-64 as Lyman Hall's regal basketball sunk to a 2-16 record. This was the first losing season for a Lyman Hall basketball team since 1934-35, 7-11 season that ushered in back-to-back trips to the state finals in 1936 and 1937.

The 1963-64 team included some outstanding sophomore basketball players, who did not see much game action, except for a few late game appearances after a game was all but lost. Coach McMahon relied on the time-honored policy to play his seniors. This uncharacteristic campaign seemed to be the flick of a spark that reignited the light that was to shine brightly for the next four years when the third golden era came to a halt after the 1968 season.

While the Board of Education searched for a coach to take over the football team in the winter of 1964, the basketball team led by the super-sized front court of Alban Chrisman, Tom Dokas, and Randy Taylor, coupled with the sophomore sensation, Fran Stupakevich, won the 1964-65 Housatonic League title with a 17-1 record, before falling in the second round of the state tournament to Weaver High School, 62-46.

Head basketball coach Roger McMahon was honored as the Connecticut Coach of the Year.

Emerging from the dust and debris of the 1963-64 season was the most dominant "big man" of all time in one, Alban Chrisman, who shockingly played in few games in his sophomore campaign. At 6-6 with soft hands and a humbleness of character, this outstanding team leader averaged 16.2 points per game for his career and an average of nearly 20 rebounds per game in his senior year. Chrisman was the captain of the 1964-65 and 1965-66 teams, each of which won the Housatonic League Title. In both seasons, Al earned All Housatonic League honors and second-team All-State selection in 1966.

Alban became a first-team All-American at Gannon College in Pennsylvania, establishing the Gannon record for scoring with 1,540 points. After earning his degree, Dallas Cowboys Head Coach Tom Landry contacted Alban to try out for the Cowboys, having never played football at Lyman Hall or at Gannon.

The notion of Alban Chrisman's impact on the LHHS football should he have been encouraged to play by family or the members of the athletic department speaks to the continuing negative status of the sport at Lyman Hall. Alban's own words many years hence, "There is no doubt in my mind I could have made an impact on the football team if I had played."

The incidental mention of Fran Stupakevich in this narrative now mandates a far greater portrayal.

Chapter 50

He Cometh ...
Fran Stupakevich

In the early 1960's one name above all others spiraled from the playing fields and courts of youth sports of Wallingford to the skies above. His name was Francis Stupakevich, a thinly built, blonde-headed boy whose reputation among his age contemporaries was "mythical" and to those who beheld his play, "unforgettable."

He grew up on Clifton Street in Wallingford, a stone's throw from Westside Field and Washington Street School playground, the breeding ground of so many top-flight youth basketball players. You didn't have to see him play or even have seen him walk to Boylan's Confectionery Store on South Cherry Street to know who he was. His name and reputation in Wallingford, "Stupe" or "Fran," was enough to evoke the question, "...Have you seen him"?

Whatever sport or athletic skill Fran performed, you couldn't take your eyes off of him. In Little League Baseball, he played for the Hungarian Club, a middle-of-the-pack team, where he hit routine ground balls to second base and beat them out for hits. When Fran hit one to the gaps in the outfield, if it dropped, he had a homerun. He could pitch, hit, and even catch behind the plate. Whatever field position you might put him in, he was the best. It all looked so easy for Fran ... and it was.

He played for the Barkers team in the Wallingford Junior Football League, whose team jersey color was gold (with gold helmets). It was fitting that Franny's team color was gold and that he wore #10 for Barkers. He played quarterback, and although the Barker's team was so-so in terms of player ability and team record, everyone in attendance (Sunday games of the WJFL averaged 260 persons in 1960-61, not including league players.) stopped and watched when Fran was on the field. His running style of quick bursts and changes of direction with an occasional passing play made Fran the best quarterback in the WJFL in 1962 and maybe the all-time best of any year.

At the end of the 1960 and 1961 seasons, All-Stars of the Wallingford Junior Football League played the Meriden league's All-Stars. With a lot of hype and the vision of just being able to see Wallingford's best in youth football in the same color jersey, the Meriden teams of those years drilled the Wallingford stars by lopsided scores. The Wallingford team was not equipped to play at the level of Meriden. In 1962, the WJFL All-Stars, with Fran Stupakevich under center, decisively defeated the Meriden team as Fran ran and threw for touchdowns.

With all of the flash that Stupakevich brought to baseball and football, it paled in comparison to what Frannie brought to basketball. In youth basketball from Biddy League to the travel team of the times, the Meriden Wildcats, to junior high school play, Fran's teams won every championship and never lost a game. All of the mythical stories surrounding Frannie were all true ... no one could make this stuff up.

EVERY COURT HIS STAGE

As early as twelve years old, Fran and his circle of basketball contemporaries would attend the Wallingford adult league basketball games with teams made up of stars from bygone LHHS days. Fran was often accompanied by friend, John Hrehowsik. They would sit in the stands, carrying a basketball, watching the senior men bang away at each other and, at the conclusion of the games, take to the floor.

There, without warm-up, Fran would put up a 25-foot shot. He didn't miss the first shot or the second shot as the senior teams' members turned and watched. Fran and John would look around the stands for a few boys of their age group at the senior games. Once located, John, the slick-talking salesman, who could make you believe that it was a privilege to go two-on-two with Fran and him, got you to agree to play a quick pick-up game. Making you feel that playing a little two on two was something of an honor, John never got a "no". John and Fran would always give their chosen opponents the ball first, and that was the last time Fran and John didn't have the ball.

If you were the one to guard Frannie, you were treated to something akin to trying to keep a comet in front of you as it streaked through the sky. Fran would take a first blistering step and then fly to the basket for a layup. He never gloated or gestured at his ease of scoring. Every so often in this mini-game to ten points, Fran would dribble the ball far above the free-throw line and then, placing his backside to you, would skip the ball to John with a behind-the-back bounce pass as John hit a two-handed layup.

Fran and John tried to slow their impromptu game down to extend their playing time on the court, but anytime Frannie felt like it, he would steal the ball from his opponents, then whirling about, choose one of an assortment of left and right-handed layups, and score at will. If Fran wanted, he would dribble the ball 30 feet from the basket and then take to the air for his patented two-handed jump shot.

THE STUPAKEVICH HOME

The Stupakevich home was adorned with a basketball hoop at the end of the driveway. Two floodlights lit the driveway and the basketball court on its pavement. There throughout Frannie's formative years, the game of basketball was played. Kids came from all over to play there, and no matter the weather or time of day, basketball players of the future were developed. Even with Frannie an "early to bed" child (8:30 pm), the games went on all evening with Fran or his father Jack, yelling out, "Turn the lights out when you're done."

No matter the manifestation of the basketball game, two on two, three on three, horse, etc. Fran played. The contest for real basketball players was called "contex." In this form of the game, everything was allowed. There were no fouls, at least none that anyone had the guts to acknowledge. Traveling was overlooked, and no one that took to the court would dare say, "Hey, that was a foul."

Adults from nearby drinking establishments or parents seeking the best free entertainment in Wallingford came to watch the basketball at the Stupakevich home. The basketball skills of dribbling, screening, picks, and passing were all there to see, and the boys who played didn't need an adult to direct or coach.

It was in this environment that the legend of Fran was born. Fran developed a two-handed jump shot that placed both his hands in close proximity with his thumbs together. At the apex of his jump that was considerable, the ball appeared to be shot on a string, no arch, no fancy spin. A bee-bee from his hands, his jump shots just cleared the rim and made a zipping sound as each punished the hoop and net if there was a net.

Frannie could be double-teamed, and if he didn't throw one of his creative passes, he would dribble, stop on a dime, and drill his shot, usually from 25 feet or more. There were no three-point lines in basketball in Frannie's time. It is scary to wonder what his scoring records would have been with the three-point shot.

CHRISTMAS EVE

On a Christmas Eve at his home, Fran's father approached him with a huge mixing bowl filled with hundreds of pennies. The Stupakevich's home had a backboard and hoop attached to their home at the driveway's end. It was before that basket on Clifton Street that Frannie would practice shooting, day after day, night after night. On this Christmas Eve, Fran's father brought a huge bowl with a hundred pennies and an empty mixing bowl.

Fran's father explained to him that Fran would shoot foul shots. Every foul shot Fran made, his father would put a penny into the empty bowl. If he should miss a foul shot, a penny would be taken out of the previously empty bowl and put back into the other bowl. So, it began, on a chilly Christmas Eve. One by one, Fran hit every foul shot as his father dropped penny after penny into the bowl. Some neighbors witnessed the event and lined the driveway to watch Fran shoot foul shots. On Christmas eve, what better form of entertainment. In a matter of a few hours, all the pennies were Frannie's.

Chapter 51

The DeDomenico Years

The hirings of Walt Schipke and Joe Corbett were indicative of the abject casualness by which football was viewed at Lyman Hall by the administration and the athletic department. Unlike basketball and even baseball, it would have to force itself on decision-makers' hearts for football to matter. Something monumental had to happen. There had to be a significant win against a state-ranked opponent, or the football Trojans would have to string together five, six, or more victories in a season. It was easy to point criticism and mock the football teams of Lyman Hall, and maybe someday Lyman Hall football would be a source of school and community pride ... but not yet ... not in 1965.

As a new school year neared in 1965, the Board of Education authorized a new teaching position for the mathematics or science departments. With no interest in the coaching position within the current faculty and the policy that non-teachers were not considered for coaching positions, head coach, or assistant, the position was left open until the summer months.

Finally, an experienced teacher of science who had taught at St. Mary's High School and Wilbur Cross High School submitted his application for the science and head football positions. A member of the board of education interviewed and subsequently brought Joseph DiDomenico's name to the board for approval. Once again, the Lyman Hall administration and athletic department remained silent relative to the appointment of a new coach.

Coach DeDomenico, a resident of Hamden, was the president of the class of 1951 at Hamden High School and an army medic during the Korean War. An outstanding lineman on his high school football teams and at Arnold College in Bridgeport, DeDomenico was an assistant coach at Wilbur Cross High School under head coach Horace Marone until coming to Lyman Hall.

With the late hiring, Coach DeDomenico had little time to find assistant coaches and then train them to teach his chosen offense and defense methods. Finding two new faculty members willing to serve as assistant coaches in Charles Farley and Phil Silvestro, DeDomenico went about the job of introducing a new offense and defense.

Coach DeDomenico would welcome an experienced senior class to his first team in 1965, but both the junior and sophomore team members lacked numbers and physical size. While the offenses of Walt Schipke and Joe Corbett were rather basic and straightforward, the offense of DeDomenico included some traps and misdirection plays, a hybrid of the wing-T offense, that would become popular in high school football in the years to come.

DiDomenico's first team featured a good-sized offensive line that included co-captain Ed D'Onofrio at the center, Dave Friend (6-2, 210) at guard, and Pete Mezza (6-4, 230) at tackle. The backfield were all members of the 1962 undefeated Wallingford Ponies in Bill Smith (#24), Bob Mesolella (#33), and returning leading rusher Tom Theis (#27).

The challenge for DeDomenico was finding a quarterback. For that, he looked to two-year starter Tommy Wachtelhausen, who had played end in his sophomore and junior years but never quarterback. With the same energy that Tom embraced so many varied activities at Lyman Hall High School in music, theatre, school leadership, and other sports, Tom learned the DeDomenico offense, becoming the play-caller for the 1965 Trojans.

There is a grace period early in the season with any new

football coach when the opposing coaches don't know what offense or defense the new coach might deploy against them. There was very little advanced scouting of opponents in the 1960's and no sharing of game films. Early in the 1965 season Lyman Hall defeated old nemesis Branford High School and Wachtelhausen threw the ball as well as any quarterback in recent memory, primarily to senior end, Tom Sala. The following week, DeDomenico's squad won in Seymour. For this game, Tom Theis was recognized as the first Lyman Hall recipient of the New Haven Register Player of the Week. It would be four more years before a Lyman Hall player would earn the honor when tailback Danny Weed received the award in 1969.

From that point on, the season became an uphill battle as the DeDomenico Trojans dropped five games in a row to Housatonic League foes. In the season finale, versus Cheshire in the annual Beanpot game, despite the running of Theis and the razzle-dazzle play of left-handed halfback Bob Mesolella with his throwback passes to Wachtelhausen, the game ended in an 18-18 tie.

Without sarcasm, but deep regret, the 2-6-1 record of the 1965 football Trojans, would be the high-water mark for the DeDomenico football years. The same people and others who felt it was their responsibility and niche in Wallingford to suggest that they knew exactly what to do to make Lyman Hall football a winner now began to level their attentions at Joe DeDomenico ... after only one season. Joe DeDomemico was a tough man but had a sensitive side that would cause the stings of criticism to cut deep, and unfortunately, worse times lay ahead for LHHS football ... and Coach D.

Chapter 52

Genesis of the "400 Twins"

Concurrent with the football teams of 1964-67 that were suffering through another lean stretch of seasons with only five wins in four seasons, the basketball teams were reveling in a golden period of standing room only crowds at the Lyman Hall gymnasium. The victories were plentiful, and the names and photos of LHHS players graced the newspapers daily.

In the Fall of 1964, Fran Stupakevich entered Lyman Hall High School with a basketball reputation that demanded at the very least, the curiosity of the fandom in Wallingford. In the mid-1960s, the school was teeming with high-caliber student-athletes, but as the 1964-65 school year began, no student received the pre-season buildup, like sophomore Fran Stupakevich.

Frannie would join Alban Chrisman, who was entering his junior year on the basketball team, to become known far and wide as the "400 Twins". During the 1965-66 basketball season, they would each score more than 400 points. They were a spectacular duo, a Mr. Inside (Chrisman) and a Mr. Outside (Stupakevich).

They worked so well together, a seamless synergy of passing and scoring efficiency. When Fran worked his way open beyond the top of the key (today's three-point line), his shot was deadly, but the manner in which he released the ball with an almost arc-less shot, Fran was able to transform the shot into a pass. His passes primarily to Alban made guarding Fran almost impossible for opposing teams. It cannot be over-stated that Frannie's passing was basketball theatre. He would launch full-court bounce passes or pinpoint darts in the half-court offense to a waiting teammate or find Pete Mezza, who was often neglected by the defense.

Both Chrisman and Stupakevich were outstanding athletes who could play any sport. Starters for the Housatonic League Champion baseball team in 1966, they were of the best in school lore at their respective positions, Chrisman, catcher, and Stupakevich, shortstop.

They both might have played football together but were strongly urged by family and physical education teachers not to play football. Might they have starred in football? YES! Might the Trojans have been a more successful football team, maybe earning the first winning season since 1931 with them on the team? Probably! Alas, two of the finest all-around athletes of all time never played football for Lyman Hall, and many others didn't either.

It is rare, if ever that the buildup of a young boy's athletic reputation ever lives up to the hype. The exploits of many youth players are often performed in leagues and games against marginal competition.

In Wallingford in the 1950s and 1960s, long before the proliferation of pay-for-play travel teams, a young boy burnished his athletic skills playing the game against his contemporaries on the playgrounds, backyards, and anywhere there was an open field or basketball hoop. This was the environment in which Alban Chrisman, Fran Stupakevich, and scores of others grew up in Wallingford, where you had to be good enough to stay on the court. In pick-up games, not everyone was "picked." Sometimes boys might sit for hours and wait for one opportunity to get into a pick-up game until someone got called by a mother's whistle to get home for dinner.

In these unstructured, non-adult-driven venues of basketball, a boy learned the game and the nature of competition. There were no rules regarding participation. If other boys thought you were good enough to pick for their team, you played. If not, you sat down or went home. For many boys, if you wanted to learn how to shoot, you got up near dawn, grabbed your ball, and went to the nearest playground with a hoop and practiced. It was the only way to get on a court and learn the game.

For Fran, like many others, who were good enough to be invited to play against older kids, stay on the court due to his exceptional skills and competitiveness, he was a complete player, a boxed brownie, when he arrived at Lyman Hall.

Together, Chrisman and Stupakevich would go on to light a basketball bonfire at Lyman Hall, capturing back-to-back Housatonic League championships and leading the Trojans to the most iconic home basketball victory of all time. However, before a single basketball was bounced in the fall of 1965, the football season under a new coach had to be played.

With the beginning of the 1965-66 school year, a tsunami of excitement had already been underway for the basketball team. In the midst of the 1965 football season, there was a buzz among the often sparse Lyman Hall crowds of "...wait til basketball".

In anticipation of the over-flow basketball crowds, athletic director Fred Schipke made preparations for the start of the 1965-66 basketball season. Additional portable stands were placed behind the area where team benches would be located on the eastern wall. Fred Schipke knew that this extra seating would exceed the gym's posted capacity, and the local fire chief would have to be appeased, but Fred knew all the right things to say.

THE BIGGEST GATE FOR BASKETBALL

Athletic director Fred Schipke knew how good the 1965-66 basketball team could be, especially with an exceptional returning cast and a strong bench. In early 1965 Schipke did something not done since Principal Robert Early was scheduling the top teams in the state in the 1930s to play Lyman Hall. Rather daringly, he invited Hillhouse High

School to come to Wallingford to play the Trojans early in the 1965-66 season.

Hillhouse had won three consecutive Class L (largest school category) state championships (the 1963 title, 68-65 over Wilbur Cross; the 1964 title, 64-49 over Hartford Public; and the 1965 title, 57-51 over Notre Dame High School of Bridgeport). In scheduling Hillhouse a perennial state champion, Lyman Hall challenged the royalty of Connecticut high school basketball.

The hype for the Hillhouse Academics vs. Lyman Hall Trojans began in the New Haven Register's sports pages in the fall of 1965. On Thursday, December 14, 1965, tickets went on sale at the high school one week before the game. In less than a day, by 3:00 pm, the game was a complete sell-out. Schipke negotiated with the Wallingford fire marshal to allow 125 additional standing room tickets to be sold (at the regular ticket price). Whether you were seated or standing was contingent upon how early you arrived on game day. The scalping of tickets took place in the school parking lot hours before the varsity game, but few Wallingfordites who had tickets would give up their tickets at any price for this basketball battle for the ages.

So, on December 21, 1965, at 6:45 pm, the Trojans in their fleece white warmups with navy blue shoulder stripes and trim took the court against the vaunted Hillhouse Academics. The crowd of 1,246 paid attendance packed into the Lyman Hall gymnasium. During warm-ups, the din of the Lyman Hall students' roars and the basketball faithful made it impossible for anyone to have even a mouth-to-ear conversation.

The Lyman Hall team huddled around Coach Roger McMahon before the opening tip, and there was an air of confidence in the team's faces. There were no superficial rah-rah gestures or spoken cliches. Rather, a poised and highly intense Trojan basketball team lined up as Al Chrisman took center circle for the opening game tap with the angular Hillhouse center. The home Lyman Hall crowd screaming before the game had even started were all on their feet, and some people were jumping up and down to see over the standing spectators all around them.

A singular sustained roar that hovered in the building's atmosphere was suddenly sliced open by an earsplitting explosion of high-pitched screaming as Chrisman tapped the ball to his LHHS teammates. The home team broke fast out of the gate and made open shots with Pete Mezza and Chrisman ripping down errant Hillhouse shots off the rim.

The high level of constant high-pitched screeching never diminished but often reached a stinging crescendo as Stupakevich set sail, stopped on a dime, and hit a 25-foot jump shot. The cheerleaders, never seated, spread out in front of the home bleachers, could be seen leading the cheers, but no one heard them over the incessant pro-Trojan din.

All of the home Lyman Hall basketball games had all been sellouts since the beginning of the previous season, but no Lyman Hall home game before or since December 21, 1965, has ever approached the wall to wall excitement like this game against Hillhouse.

The Trojans went into the locker room with the lead at intermission, but the cheering remained constant throughout halftime as the varsity locker room walls rattled from the noise. The Hillhouse team's pedigree shown brightly in the second half as the Academics battled throughout every minute. The duo of the "400 Twins" was just too much for Hillhouse as Alban Chrisman pulled down 16 rebounds to go along with 20 points. Stupakevich was dazzling with an assortment of drives to the basket and long-range two-handed jump shots, pouring in 29 points for Lyman Hall.

As the legendary contest neared its end, there was just no stopping the Trojans as they stunned the three-year state champion, Hillhouse Academics, 67-56, before the largest audience ever to see a Lyman Hall home basketball game.

AN ABRUPT END – THIRD GOLDEN AGE

The 1965-66 basketball team would all but breeze to the Housatonic League title and ranked No.1 in Class L heading into the state tournament. Unfortunately, the tournament schedule makers slated Wilbur Cross High School as Lyman Hall's first opponent. The Governors of Wilbur Cross proved too much for the Trojans as the Hallites lost in the first round. Cross would go on to win the 1966 State Championship with a 58-56 win over Weaver High School of Hartford.

Stupakevich returned for his senior season in 1966-67 and was all but unstoppable. After finishing his junior season, when he doled out an average of 11 assists a game and scored with a 25.3 points per game average, "Stupe" as a senior led the state in scoring with a 34 points per game average. Fran scored 51 and 50 points in two games in the season, and it appeared that the Trojans were on their way to a third consecutive Housatonic League title. In the wanning minutes of a runaway victory against Derby at the Lyman Hall gym, Stupakevich was headed for an uncontested layup at the north basket. He came down awkwardly on his knee and collapsed on the court. The cheering sold-out crowd was instantly converted into a sobbing multitude, covering their eyes as Fran Stupakevich, LHHS's greatest athlete's career, all but came to an end. Wearing a heavy metal knee brace, Fran would attempt to play in the state tournament game against Norwalk, but his knee would not hold up as the Trojans were eliminated, 85-63.

The 1967-68 season would summarily end the third golden era. Stocked with a group of seniors who were essentially back-ups in the previous year, the Trojans were picked to finish near the bottom of the Housatonic League, but in a season labeled "the impossible dream," Lyman Hall won the league title in 1968.

Chapter 53

Keeping Football Down, Soccer Begins

It is difficult to believe that football, or any sport for that matter, could be treated so inequitably, but that's precisely what happened at Lyman Hall for decade after decade with football. As the losing seasons mounted, and the head coach removed every few years (four coaching changes from 1957-1968) with little evidence of patience, organization, or leadership when it came to mapping football's future, a life-line was needed for football, if it was to survive.

All athletic teams had been the physical education teachers' responsibility since Lyman Hall High School opened in 1916, but football was slowly diminished after the initial ten years and finally starved out of existence in 1936. In 1949 football was brought back to Lyman Hall, but not with the necessary support systems to develop winning teams as basketball enjoyed.

The Wallingford Junior Football League began in 1959, but linkages between that youth endeavor and LHHS football were never created. Logically, the gym or physical education classes are a perfect place to encourage male students to join the football team, but that was not an overt strategy at Lyman Hall throughout the 1950s and much of the 1960s. It wasn't until 1968 that Lyman Hall had a physical education teacher, primarily the football coach.

The community took a positive football stance in 1959

with the WJFL and the creation of the Wallingford Ponies in 1961. The three junior high schools began to play football in 1967, which brought about a natural progression to high school football. All seemed to be on the up-tick for LHHS football, then came the fall of 1966.

In that year, Joe DeDomenico was in his second year as football coach. With little, if any, concern for football's plight, the Lyman Hall physical education teachers decided to begin a varsity soccer team. There was no advanced announcement to the student body or faculty in the spring of 1966. Instead, there was a rush of last-minute planning to start a soccer team with questionable motives on the first day of the 1966-67 school year.

Instantly, the physical education classes were all teaching soccer in the fall of '66. The physical education teachers began to recruit the best athletes in the school to play soccer. Of their many recruiting lines to students in physical education classes was, "... it will get you in shape for "basketball." Mr. DeDomenico, in a conversation from 2013, stated, "I was shocked when they instituted soccer. The only boys I saw were in my biology classes".

A complete varsity schedule of games, a home soccer field created on school grounds, uniforms, and equipment with John Riccitelli as head coach was all put together in a matter of months. Most of the very best athletes in the school were on that hastily created soccer team. A three-sport standout, Tom Falcigno remembers that fall, "Mr. D asked me to come out for the football team at the end of my sophomore year, and I was considering it. When Mr. Ric (Riccitelli), our baseball coach, asked me to play soccer, that was it. It was soccer".

There were 37 boys on that soccer team, led by Hall of Famers Steve Page and Fran Stupakevich. There were 15 members of that first soccer team who played for the Wallingford Junior Football League. In contrast, the 1966 LHHS football team had 36 players. Incidentally, the 1966 soccer team in their first year went undefeated in the regular season.

FEELING AN ADVERSE CLIMATE

DeDomenico battled more than the Housatonic League teams in 1966. With soccer now a varsity sport, Coach DeDomenico had to argue a strong case with the athletic director to hold onto what was known as the "varsity locker room" during football season. Additionally, there was a groundswell of interest in a new group within Wallingford that would soon be known as the "Friends of Lyman Hall Football." One day, this group would make a significant contribution to the development of LHHS football, but in 1966 there were members of this group who were outspoken critics of football and its coach's current status.

The start of the 1966 season began the longest winless streak in Lyman Hall High School football since the school was opened in 1916. As the marching band continued the practice of playing the "lament" at home games, even the school yearbook was starting to indirectly show its disregard for football. The yearbook included photos of the 1965 football team, rather than having all of the limited football pictures in the yearbook be of the current year's team. The 1966 team, with only nine seniors, ended the season with a 0-9 record.

The third year under Coach DeDomenico was a harsh one for the Trojans, who began the season with a 14-14 tie with Platt High School. After that first game, LHHS was shut out four times and scored a single touchdown in the four other games. Defensively, Lyman Hall allowed 33 points per game.

The 1967 football squad had only seven seniors and just 30 players on the team. Co-captain John Zocco, 160 pounds of toughness and determination, played every game at defensive end and tight end despite a severe knee injury incurred early in the season. In an example of the compassion and caring Coach DeDomenico carried for his players during these difficult months of losing, he called in football trainer Tom Altieri of the New York Jets to come to Lyman Hall and work on Zocco's knee.

The final 0-8-1 record set off a torrent of negative vibes throughout Wallingford, clamoring for DeDomenico to be gone. The Wallingford Board of Education moved swiftly after the season, dismissing DeDomenico of his football coaching duties. In the same distinguished manner as Joe Corbett, DeDomenico opted to hold on to his teaching position at Lyman Hall while becoming an assistant coach at Hamden High School.

The 25 game, non-winning streak was not a pleasant foundation for whoever was chosen as the head football coach in 1968, but there was a change-a-coming.

Chapter 54

1968 ... "A Change A-Comin"

The entire world of Lyman Hall High School football was about to be shaken to its fragile core in 1968, right in sync with the rest of America. Cue the music of Curtis Mayfield, "People get ready. There's a train a comin. You don't need no baggage. You just get on board".

The year of 1968 was one of great upheaval in our country. The Vietnam War raged almost out of the control of political decision-making. The influences of presidential candidates and our Presidents themselves since Dwight Eisenhauer, along with popular music, movies, and almost every mode of cultural expression, had kicked the sides out of our society.

In the 1960s, the Town of Wallingford became a hotbed for local rock n roll bands filled with junior and high school musical talent. The parking lot of Caplan's Market on Main Street staged summer concerts, and the Wallingford bands drew wall-to-wall crowds. The Oakdale Theatre, once the venue to see "live" Broadway shows" and name celebrities, gave way to a weekly schedule of the hottest bands in the world that included The Who, Dave Clark Five, The Loving Spoonful, Paul Revere, and the Raiders, The Byrds and so many others. Indeed, Wallingford was the place to be for the expression of what was hip in America.

The town in the 1960s was still growing, actually at a faster pace than the previous decades, when hundreds of

G.I.'s came home to settle in Wallingford. The designers of the Lyman Hall High School facility in 1955 were charged with crafting a futuristic plan for the new high school, spending considerable funds on projecting the student population needs far into the future. In fact, the architects were accurate in their data projections for the future. Unfortunately, local political power individuals on both the board of education and the town council opted for a wait-and-see approach to construction, reallocating funds for other town needs that ultimately resulted in the construction of a second Wallingford secondary school that was never discussed or part of the 1955 plan.

The new Lyman Hall High School was a state-of-the-art, deck-driven design project. The architect's original proposal included space for constructing four additional decks to be connected and built on the lands that reach the edges of the current baseball field at Dag Hammarskjold Middle School. Those supplementary decks to be built, starting in 1958, would house a minimum of 35 classrooms, lecture halls, and labs, easily accommodating an additional 500 students. This plan, subsequently APPROVED by the Wallingford Board of Education in 1955, would have met all student enrollment projections through 1975. Alas, the Board of Education opted to curtail all construction of the planned attached eastern decks of the Pond Hill Road high school in order to meet the 1956 schedule of moving the school from its Main Street location to the Pond Hill Road site.

The largest enrollment and graduating classes in town history were experienced in the years 1965-1971. More Lyman Hall graduates than ever before were going off to college, while many others either enlisted or were drafted into the armed forces, aided by the passage of the Military Selective Service Act of 1967. With the cultural changes imposing their will on the populous, Lyman Hall High School's administration instituted a more rigorous dress code that included that students could not wear blue jeans or striped pants, and girls couldn't wear sneakers. What's more, boys could not have hair of a length considered on, or over the ears and always off the collar.

The year of our Lord, 1968, was indeed two trains racing towards each other on a single track that could only result in upheaval.

FRIENDS OF WALLINGFORD FOOTBALL

In April of 1968, a large group of Wallingford citizens began the formative stages of an organization that would come to be known as the Friends of Wallingford Football. The group, loaded with civic-minded individuals, wanted to create a coordinated effort to build a successful football team at Lyman Hall. This meant efforts to link the Wallingford Junior Football League, the Junior High School League, and Lyman Hall High School football.

The board of directors were local "movers and shakers" who were used to getting things done in their respective professions and making themselves heard and loudly regarding their opinions and concerns. Although the organization's singular goal was to "help promote football at all levels in town," their agenda of action was more than a change agent.

The "Friends" group was instrumental in the removal of Joe DeDomenico as head football coach and made recommendations for the hiring of a new coach in 1968. They advocated for a salary increase for the football coach in order to attract better and more qualified candidates. The "Friends" strongly recommended that the new head coach be a physical education major in college. Not stopping there, they successfully lobbied the Wallingford Board of Education to approve the authorization of four assistant football coaches. All of these proposals were enacted by the board of education.

Although the Friends of Wallingford Football was not directly involved in selecting the new coach in 1968, they would insist that whoever was chosen to be involved with the organization. The first officers and board of the Friends of Wallingford Football included Dan Moran (president), George

Soroko (vice president), Alfred J. Namnoum (treasurer), Marv Garber (secretary), and directors Art Brandl, Keith Bryant, Les Jobbagy, Don Griffin, Dick Johnson, Dudley Warren, Jack O'Brien, and Ray Figlewski.

Chapter 55

Board of Education Finds a Head Coach

With the end of Joseph DeDomenico's three years as head football coach, he became the fourth consecutive coach whose teams won less than ten games during their respective tenures. Despite the lack of on-the-field success of football at Lyman Hall, the school administration and athletic director still wanted no role in the hiring of a new football coach.

The practice of recruiting candidates and the subsequent hiring of a new football coach became the responsibility of "one" member of the Wallingford Board of Education. Just a single member of the board in the spring of 1968 volunteered to manage the recruiting of candidates, the interviews, and the football coach's final selection.

Surprisingly, nine candidates submitted applications for the football post. The applicants included well-meaning coaches of the WJFL, middle school teachers, four other candidates from outside of Wallingford, and one out-of-state candidate.

Of all the candidates for the head football coaching position, not one came close to the football resume of Phil Ottochian. A highly touted assistant coach at Port Chester High School in New York, he was a former All-New York City football player, captaining his football team at powerful Lafayette High School in Brooklyn. This was the high school with the longest football winning streak in the country under coach Harry Ostro. So renowned was Lafayette that when Coach Ostro retired, they hired Sam Rutigliano, who went on to be the Cleveland Browns head coach.

Ottochian, a lineman, graduated high school at 5-9, weighing 185 pounds, matriculating to the University of Nebraska. After a year, he transferred to Trinity University of Texas, where he was honored as one of Texas's top linemen. Indicative of his love for football is this anecdote. His brother was getting married during the fall. Phil refused to attend the ceremony, for as Phil so adroitly put it, "We were playing Texas A&M, and I was starting."

In June of 1968, Phil Ottochian was named Head Football Coach at Lyman Hall High School and hired as a physical education teacher. With a sculptured body and crewcut, the square-jawed Ottochian was right out of central casting. He was terrifying at first glance.

Chapter 56

Ottochian Sets the Tone

Coach Ottochian immediately arranged to meet those boys interested in football in a meeting in the auditorium. There were 81 boys who showed up for the meeting, but Coach Ottochian scared a number of them off after that meeting. "He was matter of fact in everything he said," according to Jim Karl, 1969 co-captain, "He (Ottochian) laid it all out for us. Ottochian was like Patton standing up there on the stage, ten feet above us with his pinched brow. He was intense and talked about losing being a disease".

Barry O'Brien, a three-year starter and Co-Captain with Karl in 1969, "He told us we all needed to get crew-cuts and if he didn't feel the crew-cut was short enough, you didn't practice until it was short enough for him. As for girlfriends, he better not see you even talking to a girl during the season. If he was coming down the hallway and you were with your girlfriend, you left her immediately".

Ottochian was so different from anything Wallingford or Lyman Hall had ever seen. His mere presence in the school was intimidating, and members of the faculty made fun of him, behind his back ... of course. They called him "Biff," a reference to the character in the Archie comic books.

Before the start of school, Athletic Director Fred Schipke was interviewed in the local paper about his thoughts about the coming school year. Schipke was quoted as saying, "The Board of Education hired this Chinese guy as our football coach. I think his name is "Otakatean, but I haven't met him yet."

All these slings and arrows made at Phil Ottochian's expense would have hurt other men, but as Jim Karl, who played on Ottochian's first two teams put it, "Coach was above it all. He only had one thing on his mind, and that was winning football games".

In his first season, Ottochian enacted triple-sessions, a brutal week of football under the August heat, three times a day. Coach Ottochian did not allow water on the field that he expected would result in making his team tougher. Tackling drills were conducted on a heavy leather dummy suspended by a buckle. Players from that first camp in 1968 stated that it looked like a gallows with the dummy hanging there, but they tackled that heavy object until they could stop it from moving back and forth.

Ottochian coached high school football in New York and knew many head coaches from lower Fairfield County. One of the annual powers in that part of the state was Greenwich High School, and Coach Ottochian wasted no time in scheduling them for a scrimmage. The Ottochian Trojans battled the down-staters, moving the ball with great efficiency, quite an improvement from the previous years. Ottochian preached the same line over and over again, "You've got to pay the price, and you've got to make sacrifices." This led to the first helmet logo of the Ottochian years, "P/S," debuting on Thanksgiving Day, which stood for "Pride and Sacrifice."

Chapter 57

The 1968 Season, Ottochian's First

The 42 members of the '68 squad were feeling especially good about themselves heading into the first game of the year against Platt High School with such a successful scrimmage with Greenwich. However, scrimmages are only small indicators along the way, and varsity games are a totally different level of football. At halftime at Ceppa Field in Meriden, Coach Ottochian was disappointed with his team's play and proceeded to punch the metal garbage can in the locker room.

Over the next thirty years, Coach Ottochian would often resort to some manner of physical ferocity on furniture, oranges, or the toughest guy on the team. The Trojans could not pierce the Panther goal line, as the Trojans dropped Ottochian's debut game, 19-0.

On September 29, 1968, Lyman Hall battled with Housatonic League foe, Amity Regional High School in Woodbridge. The game was a combination of good defense or inept offense as both teams entered the fourth quarter tied 0-0. In that final stanza, Co-captain, Mike Moran scored from the five-yard line as the Trojans end the string of 26 games without a victory, dating back to 1965.

The Trojans, with so much to learn about winning, carried their celebration onto the bus and, in the words of John Namnoum, "We trashed the bus." The Lyman Hall team proceeded to use their helmets as hammers and battered the ceiling of the bus with helmet dents. The coaches, one and all, ignored the clanging helmet to metal ceiling all the way back to Wallingford. As it turned out, the parents of the players, happy or not, paid for the damages to the school bus, and Ottochian had his first victory as Lyman Hall head coach.

From then on, the teams of the Housy would show no kindness to the improving, long-standing, "doormats of the Housatonic League." Lyman Hall would have spurts of tough defense in 1968 but would have a difficult time scoring touchdowns. As the Trojans prepared to play Cheshire in the Annual Beanpot game, the team played a scrimmage against faculty members and coaches on the Saturday before the game. Leading rusher, and captain, Mike Moran, breaks his arm in the scrimmage that further limits the Trojan's offense as the Cheshire Rams defeat Lyman Hall, 12-0.

LEARNING TO WIN

The stanchions of team operations and conduct were put in place in 1968 that ended in a one-win season with eight losses, but with the majority of players returning for the 1969 season, there was reason for some optimism. Coach Ottochian was ahead of his time in emphasizing weight training for his players, but there was a problem. There were no dumbbells, bars, or weights at Lyman Hall High School. The only piece of equipment that Ottochian could find was an old medicine ball with leather stitching that probably had never been used in gym classes. Ottochian and his coaches, along with some parents, set to the task of "making weights." Using #10 tin cans, the containers thrown away by the cafeteria staff that held tomato sauce, fruit, and vegetables, each can was filled with cement, and a metal bar of approximately three feet in length was inserted into the cement in the middle of the can. Once the cement hardened, another can with cement was placed on the other end of the pole, positioned there until that one hardened. With patience and fast hardening cement ... "*vuala*" ... Lyman Hall barbells.

With no rooms or areas within the gymnasium proper to conduct weight training, Coach Ottochian staked out a corner of the cafeteria where the members of the team used the handmade barbells. Ottochian instructed the members of the team on the proper techniques of lifting, and with pushups, sit-ups, and squat thrusts mixed in, Lyman Hall had its first wave of weight-training. Everything was so new to one and all, but this was the only way Coach Ottochian knew to build a winning team.

Despite the dramatic demands that Ottochian placed on his team in the first year, the team grew from 42 members in 1968 to 54 in 1969. A seasoned senior class, headlined by co-captains Barry O'Brien (#55) and Jim Karl (#32), both of whom had started every game of their careers, heading into the 1969 season.

Of the benchmarks, the Friends of Wallingford Football had in mind as the Ottochian years got underway was increasing the recognition that LHHS players received from league coaches. In Ottochian's first season at the helm, no Lyman Hall player received sufficient votes by league coaches to be named to the All-Housatonic League team. In fact, only guard, David Friend in 1965, was recognized as a first-team recipient in the 1960's before the '69 season. With the bevy of experienced returning players, the outlook was bright for those who wore the Blue and White and the hope that wins might bunch up and with those victories some manner of acknowledgment from those outside of Wallingford.

Everyone connected with Wallingford football was standing by for some evidence of progress at the high school. Maybe it would come in defeating one of the best teams in the league. There was no doubt that the football Trojans were gaining the Housatonic League's respect, but students and the Wallingford citizenry craved results.

The Trojans opened the 1969 season with back-to-back wins over Platt (28-14) and Amity (6-0), then came Seymour led by All-Staters quarterback Mark Allen and his favorite receiver, Dennis Rozum. This would be the perfect team to notch that first notable or "signature" win under Phil

Ottochian. Quarterback Allen had already thrown 43 career touchdowns heading into the 1969 LHHS game, and Rozum had been on the receiving end of 18 TD ariels from Allen. Seymour turned out to be just too much for the Trojans as the Wildcats won at Fitzgerald Field, 21-6.

Lyman Hall bounced back the following week at Branford, scoring a decisive 35-18 win as tailback, Danny Weed (#31) scored four touchdowns and was named New Haven Register Player of the Week, the first LHHS player to be so recognized since Tommy Theis in 1965.

After a 14-14 tie with Shelton in game five, the Trojans lost three of the following four games by lopsided scores to end the season, but the four victories tied for the most wins for any Lyman Hall football team since the 1931 Orangemen of Langdon Fernald. After the season, David Soroko was named to the first-team All Housatonic League defensive unit at defensive end, the first Ottochian coached player to be so named. Danny Weed amassed 851 yards rushing in 1969 and became the all-time rushing leader in school history.

Under Phil Ottochian, was progress made in 1969? Yes, but the seminal victories of schools with football teams on the rise had not happened ... not yet.

Chapter 58

Finally, A Signature Win

- October 31, 1970

The gradual progression in building a winning high school football team certainly requires the dedication of a head coach who works to overcome the many losses with all of the frustration and sleepless nights that accompany the scoreboard failures. Such a coach must see beyond the residuals, including losing quality athletes to other sports or quits playing football. While the coaches of recent years throw-about terms such as "building a program" or "changing the culture," none of these cliches mean a thing without a coach's unity of purpose in teaching and celebrating the smallest of details in skill development.

The "fun" that some coaches toss out as the goal of the day or game is a hollow word without the satisfaction achieved by being victorious in a single repetition within a drill. To be sure, making this described baby step by baby step progress is about patience on the part of the coach and player. In essence ... be victorious in the individual repetition within the drill, celebrate that victory, replicate it, and move forward to the next small step. It is not about keeping it simple.

It is about making it *possible,* and a good coach creates the environment and circumstances by which tiny victories become possible. In that endeavor, matching a player's intellect and athletic skill to the skills necessary for little victories in repetitions within drills to the form-fitting skills of a unit within the team is pains-taking. It cannot be rushed by the coach's desire to "see how it all looks."

This stated philosophy is not often articulated, even by a good coach, but without the patience to win the repetition, drill by drill, player by player, sustained winning is not possible. Coach Ottochian's practices were never breezy and fun-filled. He directed his coaches, and it took a long time before Phil would develop a trust in individual coaches. Assistant coaches had to earn his trust, and to that end, assistant coaches worked very hard in his varsity practices.

By the third year of Coach Ottochian's tenure as Head Football Coach, opponent head coaches in the Housatonic League were beginning to take notice. Just a few years ago, Lyman Hall was regarded as a soft touch, a time for opposition coaches to look ahead in their schedules; work on some plays or ideas they might need for when they play one of the league's better opponents.

Although the early Ottochian teams were developing a reputation for toughness, there was little evidence of a change in how other schools approached playing the Trojans. What the Ottochian Trojans needed was a seminal win ... an unexpected result ... not a tie game ... not a win against a school in the lower half of the Housatonic League standings ... but a win that clearly demonstrated preparation and determination over a long-standing superior team.

By 1970, Lyman Hall football, under Ottochian, was showing signs of consistent hard-nosed play. The slogans and tough-talk were being replaced by how his teams practiced and approached each game.

The 1970 team of 36 members was a considerable personnel decrease from the 1969 senior-heavy squad, but what it might have lacked in numbers, it made up in tough football players. Toughest of them all was Co-Captain, Billy Cox, a linebacker/fullback who would make his mark on this Housatonic League season. With future Lyman Hall High School Hall of Famer, Danny Weed moving on to perform at the University of Rhode Island, the ball carrying duties fell to Choate School transfer, Alex Murenia.

After a four-win season in 1969 that was a 38-year high watermark for Lyman Hall football, there was a hope that the 1970 squad might reach that victory total. That optimism was greatly diminished after the Trojans opened the season with a 30-0 thumping at the hands of Platt and a 22-0 defeat to Amity. After these two resounding losses, the Blue and White recorded four consecutive wins, a feat never before accomplished in the lore of LHHS football. However, that fourth win will go down as one of the most significant victories in school history.

Although Coach Ottochian's teams were making incremental progress, game by game, what was missing was a transcendental victory, one that could clearly be termed an upset against a seemingly superior team. In the Housatonic League, where one or two teams always made it into the state's top ten rankings, those big-time adversaries were on the schedule each and every season.

The kingpin in the league in 1970 was East Haven High School, more than a formidable opponent with quality players at every position. Their head coach was the legendary Frank Crisafi, who certified that his 1970 Easties were his finest team ever in 23 years as head football coach ... Undefeated and ranked No.4 in the latest New Haven Register State Poll, the Yellowjackets had man-handled five quality high schools in Hamden, Cheshire, Shelton, Amity and Derby. Crisafi's team came into the contest with Lyman Hall having scored 198 points while his first-team defense had allowed only 8 points in the last five games.

At a time when most high school linemen weighed below 200 pounds, East Haven featured a superb defensive line that included Rich Whitney (6-2, 255), Mark Perrelli (6-4, 245), Bob Migliaro (6-1, 240) and Mark DeFabbio (6-2, 245). The fullhouse backfield of Joe Torre, Ken Miessau, and the pile-driving John Tyndall added to the East Haven offense's power, but the Trojans caught a break before kickoff when it was announced that the Eastie quarterback, George Rose, would not play in the game. Interestingly, Coach Crisafi decided to hold out Rose from the Lyman Hall game for fear of losing his services for the last three "important" games of the season.

The first quarter was a sloppily played affair with penalties and fumbles disrupting any game flow. With 2:47 remaining in the first period, Alex Murenia (#24) broke away on a 29-yard touchdown scamper, as Ottochian elected to go for two on the extra point attempt with Rich Figlewski, taking the option pitch from Bob Axon and with a crushing block by Murenia, darted into the endzone and an 8-0 lead. The spirited Lyman Hall defense led by Rich Cavanaugh and Billy Cox stunned the high-powered Easties with ferocious hits.

A 41-yard pass from Bob Axon to John Russell resulted in a touchdown as the Trojans took a 14-0 advantage into the locker room at halftime. The large East Haven crowd at Lyman Hall's Fitzgerald Field sat stunned during halftime as the Lyman Hall contingent didn't know quite how to respond to all that they were witnessing, but something new and very different was happening on the football field before them.

The third quarter was scoreless, but East Haven was moving the ball and racking up first downs. In the fourth quarter Walt Erhler, the East Haven backup quarterback began to hit a few passes, and combined with runs by his backfield mates, the Easties moved right down the field. Joe Torre banged over from the three, and after a failed two-point conversion, Lyman Hall held onto a 14-6 lead. A Lyman Hall pass by Axon was intercepted that set up the last Eastie touchdown of the day. Ehrler hit two passes, one to Tyndall and the other to Perelli, that set up East Haven deep in Trojan territory. With 3:39 remaining in the game, Erhler took the ball over for the score as the two-point pass attempt failed, leaving the Trojans with a 14-12 advantage.

With 1:24 left on the clock, East Haven got the ball back with a chance to keep their undefeated season alive. Forced to pass on third down with time running out, Rich Cavanaugh intercepted Erhler, giving the Trojans a first down on the Eastie eight-yard line. On second down, halfback John Riccitelli carried the ball over for the touchdown, sealing the 20-12 victory for the Trojans.

The 1970 football team would establish a new record for most wins in a season with five. It would be the first Lyman Hall football team with a winning record since the 1931 team of Langdon Fernald went 4-3. The five victories were a plateau for Lyman Hall, and the question was, could LHHS get to six in the seasons ahead.

Despite the apparent progress that the Ottochian Trojans were experiencing, only two Lyman Hall players received post-season recognition. Co-captain Bill Cox was named as an All-Housatonic League linebacker and Alex Murenia as a defensive back.

Chapter 59

Moment for the Esteemed

There is a stark loneliness to a football field below the setting sun on an October Saturday after the game is over. As the breezes blow the crumbled hotdog wrappers and discarded programs, one can be easily overcome by the dramatic contrasts. What a few hours ago were the cheers of the crowd and the bright sunlight that pierced the clouds of fall is now an eerie quiet that makes one wonder if there ever was a game here that day.

A reporter of sorts, of novice status, a stringer for the local newspaper, is the last to leave Fitzgerald Field. Trying to collect his thoughts from the drama that unfolded this day ... for Lyman Hall High School ... where losses on the gridiron had out-numbered the wins more than four-to-one since 1949, there was a solitary figure standing alone, facing the northern brick wall of the school's gymnasium.

Walking slowly in the direction of the locker room that was indeed filled with the smiles of Lyman Hall coaches, players, and well-wishers, the tall gentleman bent slightly forward with his left hand open on the brick wall before him. A lit cigarette dangled from his lips. All at once, he was recognized by the youthful reporter. The man was none other than the immortal Frank Crisafi, the head coach of the East Haven High School football team. He was more than a legend. He was in spirit and persona the most recognizable in high school coaching in Connecticut. Just as his contemporaries in every high school in the mid-20th century, he had coached all the sports. His East Haven basketball teams were of the finest in New England for over twenty years. He had coached the Yellowjacket football team for 23 years.

When this day started, Saturday, October 31, 1970, Frank Crisafi was preparing to take his undefeated football team to Wallingford for a 1:30 pm game against a perennial bottom-of-the-league football team that his teams usually rolled over. His confidence in his team's capacity to beat Lyman Hall's football team was evidenced by his decision not to play his slightly banged-up star quarterback, George Rose, in the game. To be sure, if Crisafi's Easties were playing Derby or Seymour on this day, Rose would have been in the starting lineup, but this was Lyman Hall.

As the 19-year old reporter walked ever slower in his approach to the visibly contemplative Crisafi, his thoughts were to ask him for a post-game quote or just do the Dionne Warwick thing and "Walk on By." As it was some 45 minutes since the game's end, the reporter looked across the parking lot and noticed that the visiting East Haven team bus was not there and surmised that Crisafi sent it on its way, leaving him behind. Instantly, the joy the reporter felt in his heart over the historic victory was replaced with sadness for the man who had celebrated victory in every venue of his coaching life ... but not on this day.

Passing Coach Crisafi by a few feet, the young reporter turned back and asked, "Coach, are you all right"? Crisafi looked at the young man with a tenderness in his eyes that might be mistaken for tears on any other man. The coach just lifted his right hand as if to say, "I'm OK," but he wasn't.

The reporter cleared the corner of the building and headed for the locker room to catch the celebration's tail end and try to get a quote from Lyman Hall coach Phil Ottochian.

Despite the enormity of the victory for third-year Coach Ottochian, the young reporter was overwhelmed with thoughts of Frank Crisafi, whom he had never met, but had seen many times at Lyman Hall basketball games. He remembered Crisafi entering the Lyman Hall gymnasium to scout the Trojans. The coach cut quite a figure, dressed with style and always surrounded by an entourage. Indeed, he comported himself like the legend he was.

Entering the locker room, the revelry was beginning to die down, and Coach Ottochian gave the reporter a rambling quote the reporter did his best to paraphrase. His attention was still with Crisafi, and he exited the locker room, walking back to the side of the building. To his surprise, Crisafi was still standing there with the crown of his head, almost touching the brick wall before him. Once more, the diminutive stringer approached Crisafi and noticed there were cigarette butts at the coach's feet. Wanting to do something, ... anything for the East Haven coach, he quietly asked, "Is there anything I can do for you"? Crisafi never looked up, and shaking his head, the reporter turned and headed to the parking lot to the car he borrowed from his father on this day.

He sat in the driver's seat but did not attempt to start the vehicle and depart. Looking up through the windshield, he continued to watch Crisafi, who suffered in silence. His thoughts were, "What must the coach be thinking now"?

That game and the aftermath with Coach Frank Crisafi are indelible. The reporter became a teacher and a coach, participating in winning some big games while losing others for dear ole' Lyman Hall, but only one game ever reminded him of the depth of loneliness and despair that <u>might</u> have consumed Frank Crisafi on October 31, 1970.

If one coaches long enough, there will be plenty of wins, losses, and disappointments galore, but for any coach to experience what Coach Crisafi probably did that day, one would have to know and be sure how rare a team you coached and how much was at stake that could never ever be approached again. It was not about losing a championship game or any game for whatever reason. This was knowing that as a coach, you and your team were in a hallowed place, and if you coached for another fifty years, you would never have this opportunity again.

Chapter 60

1971, Another Wallingford High School

In what seemed like a mere blink of the eye, the Wallingford decision-makers discarded the original 1955 architectural plans to expand Lyman Hall High School, following its opening in 1957 on Pond Hill Road. With the largest graduating classes ever recorded at Lyman Hall High School, 1968-1971, a second Wallingford high school was constructed with lightning speed, tucked in just above Moran Junior High School on Hope Hill Road. The school named for a long-serving doctor in Wallingford, Mark T. Sheehan, opened its doors in the fall of 1971. A newly designed districting plan assigned students to Sheehan and Lyman Hall based solely on geography (at least at first), in essence, splitting Wallingford in two.

Students who had attended Lyman Hall but lived on the Yalesville or westside of Wallingford would now attend Sheehan. This meant that many student-athletes would now play for the Sheehan sports teams that adopted the mascot, "Titans." Many teachers from Lyman Hall would transfer to the new high school, including mathematics teacher and six-year assistant football coach, Charles Farley who was named Sheehan's first head football coach. John Riccitelli, who was synonymous with Lyman Hall as an all-time great basketball player and head coach of the LHHS baseball team, took his wit and smile to Sheehan as their first athletic director.

Many people believed that the split into two high schools

would create a high tension "rivalry" between the crosstown schools, but it was more hype than reality. The westside school, Sheehan, began varsity football in 1972. Taking advantage of the Beanpot Game lessons, both high schools devised a plan to maximize the money that could be made through a Lyman Hall-Sheehan Thanksgiving Day game. With Lyman Hall still not garnering big crowds for football games and Sheehan just launching its football team, the regular ticket prices were increased for Thanksgiving, with both high schools splitting the game receipts.

The game and its annual trophy were to be named after the second mayor of Wallingford, Joseph Carini, a 1948 graduate of Lyman Hall High School. On Thanksgiving Day, November 25, 1972, the first Carini Bowl would be staged, but until then and beyond, Phil Ottochian sought that sacred place that henceforth, only the Lyman Hall basketball teams and the 1969 baseball team had previously stood.

It was all in keeping with the historical plight of Lyman Hall football since 1926 that just when it appeared that the stars would be aligned and football would finally take its place in the bright lights of Wallingford history, yet another obstacle rises from the ground, the splitting of the town into two high schools.

Chapter 61

Signature Win Two – November 13, 1971

With some quality football players now wearing the jersey of Sheehan, Coach Ottochian and his staff went about the task of piecing together a team capable of reaching a better than .500 record. The 1971 season was a definitive study of inconsistency as the Trojans opened the season with a 41-8 loss to Platt and then shut out Amity 13-0 the following week. A twenty-point loss to Seymour was followed by a 22-22 tie with Branford.

Despite the opening of the new cross-town high school and the gleaning off of some of LHHS's veteran players, the 1971 football team had grown to 49 players in 1971, led by co-captains Richard Cavanaugh and Richard Figlewski.

Still developing the wishbone offense, the Trojans were fickle on offense throughout the season. Heading into the ninth game of the season, the Trojans were sporting a 2-4-1 record and facing the Derby Red Raiders, who had six wins, no losses on their schedule to go along with two ties.

Although the two ties knocked Derby from a chance to win the 1971 Housatonic League crown, the Red Raiders were undefeated and loaded with talent that would sustain them for seasons to come. If Lyman Hall could upend Derby and hold serve against an under-achieving Cheshire High School team in the last "Bean Pot Trophy" game on Thanksgiving, the Trojans would secure another four-win season.

Lyman Hall had dueled Derby in football as well as basketball and baseball since the first year of the Housatonic (Valley) League in 1924 until the removal of football from Lyman Hall High School in 1937, including the classic 1926 battle that resulted in a 0-0 tie, giving Lyman Hall their first and last Housatonic League title until 1974. Since 1950 most games between Derby and Lyman Hall were mismatches, but in the years to come, the annual battle with the Red Raiders would directly impact the quest for a league title.

As the 1971 season unfolded, Derby was undefeated after eight games, ranked 10th in the Connecticut statewide polls with a stout defense and an offense led by quarterback Bill Meyer. To the Trojans' good fortune, just as George Rose, the quarterback for East Haven who was held out of the 1970 Trojan-Eastie game, Meyer did not play for Derby in the 1971 tilt due to a concussion.

With Hall of Fame coach Lou DeFilippo at the helm, the Red Raider rush offense was paced by sophomore running back John Pagliaro, who would go on to record-setting seasons in 1972 and 1973, then break open the record books at Yale University. With Pagliaro, Derby had Tom Palmieri in the backfield, a talented two-way player. Without Meyer, who led Derby with his pinpoint passes, the Raiders would be forced to become somewhat one-dimensional, running the ball at the Trojans as their primary strategy.

The game was a fast-moving affair as both teams relied heavily on the run game. The Trojans scored first, with Rich Figlewski running a power play out of the wishbone formation from nine yards out in the first period. Although picking up first downs, the Derby offense repeatedly committed costly penalties and turned the ball over on fumbles as the first half ended with Lyman Hall on top, 6-0.

After a scoreless third quarter, sophomore Jerry Butler (starting in place of an injured Rich Cavanaugh, playing only guard on offense) recovered a Derby fumble. On the first play of the final quarter, Figlewski tallied his second touchdown, receiving a pitch from Paul Buckanavage, scoring from the

18-yard line. Once again, the Trojans could not convert the extra point but led 12-0 with 11:52 remaining in the contest.

As late in the game as it was, the Red Raiders finally caught fire, putting together a 15-play touchdown drive that included six first downs as Derby banged it over from the one-yard line, still behind with the score at 12-7. A Buckanavage fumble gave the Red Raiders the ball on their own 35-yard line with a chance to win the game. With 1:07 left on the clock and facing a fourth down and long, DeFilippo called one of Derby's many gadget pass plays that the Red Raiders spent time practicing on Thursdays of every game week. Alas, the pass was incomplete, and the Trojans took over, running out the clock. Rich Figlewski earned New Haven Register Player of the Week honors with his two-touchdown performance against Derby, having carried the ball 17 times for 136 yards.

With the 12-7 upset of Derby, the Trojans were set up to record a .500 campaign and another four-win season, if ... if, they could defeat the Cheshire Rams in what turned out to be the final Beanpot game.

AFTERMATH

The dramatic upset of Frank Crisafi's East Haven Yellowjackets in 1970 and Lou DeFilippo's Derby Red Raiders in 1971 proved that Phil Ottochian was of the elite coaches in the Housatonic League. No coach in the league snuck up on these two coaching giants (Crisafi and DeFilippo). Those two were the best and proved it many times in the biggest of games and had the records to prove it. His teams competed weekly, comported themselves well, and Ottochian got the most out of his players that he could.

The All-Housatonic League recognition began in 1960, based on a voting process by the league's Head Coaches. Unlike basketball, where there was usually a clear top five, sometimes six, players in the league, All Housatonic League voting for football was a selection by position on both offense and defense.

Since the beginning of All Housatonic League recognition,

the head coaches agreed to base their decisions squarely on the performance of the players their teams competed against on the field. The head coaches shunned the idea of each high school getting their "fair share" of players on the team. There was no "Pollyanna" proviso to give every team at least one selection from each school. If you were the best at your position, you got selected. The selection process changed over the years, and there were some egregious mistakes as a few outstanding performers were left off the annual all-league team, but by and large, the coaches played it on the square.

As game filming and study became more a part of the coaching process in high school football, coaches had many more opportunities to study themselves and their opponents. Heretofore, not many players of high performance didn't get voted onto the all-league team. The most egregious error ever made was in 1975 when Lyman Hall's Mike Nesti ran for 1,459 yards, a mere 8.06 yards a carry, and did not get selected to the All-Housatonic League team.

Every coach wanted their players to get chosen, especially the players who had endeared themselves to each coach. For the first part of the decade of the 1960's the process was cold and numerical in terms of voting. It was well into the 1970s when league head coaches fell victim to the Coaches All-State team selection process, where coaches lobbied for votes for their players. In the Housatonic League, coaches nominated their own players for selection, but were not permitted to vote for their own players. There were always some disappointments.

By and large, the league coaches voted for the best players in the Housatonic League on both offense and defense. However, through the first few years of Coach Ottochian's career, few deserving LHHS players, if any, were elected. This strongly suggested that the league coaches felt that it was Ottochian's coaching, not his players' abilities, that impacted his team's performance. As a footnote, in Joe DeDomenico's three years as head coach (those years preceding Ottochian's hiring), only one player received All Housatonic League recognition.

Phil Ottochian's career path in coaching was never a

certainty to end at Lyman Hall High School. Ottochian had many friends in the coaching profession, especially on the collegiate level, and a growing reputation within the coaching fraternity in Connecticut. It wasn't long after he started coaching at LHHS that job offers started to come his way. The more college coaches saw film of Lyman Hall games and talked to Housatonic League coaches, the more positive notice Phil Ottochian received. This was all the more notable given that Lyman Hall had yet to even approach a league championship.

Following the 1971 season, three LHHS team members were selected to the All Housatonic League team in defensive back, John Riccitelli, linebacker, Mark Butler, and guard, John "Skip" Hayden.

END OF THE BEANPOT CLASSIC

As with most sports cliches, the word "rivalry" is often overused, misunderstood, and just a convenient verbal crutch for sportswriters, broadcasters, and coaches to use when some added measure of importance to a game seems warranted.

"Rivalry" was a word that had little meaning to a high school with one winning record since 1949. According to all definitions in the King's English, a "rivalry" is a competition between two persons or two teams. Heretofore, any game is a rivalry.

A contest between two teams where there is "a little more" at stake than just who wins and who loses might be labeled as a rivalry. That little more might be in the way of a continuing trophy, named for some object that has a shared meaning or maybe after a person who might have left a mark on a community or school.

Thanksgiving Day football on the high school, college, and professional levels across the country had become a tremendous cash-cow, attracting the largest crowds of the football season with people returning home for that holiday; taking advantage of alumni gatherings; homecoming dances, and ... something special to do while waiting for the Thanksgiving turkey to cook.

At a diner in Cheshire off of Route 10, representatives from both schools met in the spring of 1963 to plan what would be one of Connecticut's many annual Thanksgiving Day football games, starting on November 26, 1964.

As Fred Schipke told the story, "It was an easy thing to plan, but we couldn't think of what to call the game. There were these old beanpots on each table as a decoration at the eatery where we got together. They were brown and white, and people used to bake those Boston baked beans in them. So, we decided to call it the "Beanpot Game." We got one of those beanpots, and each year the winner of the game and the score was hand-painted on the pot."

The 1971 Beanpot Game was an interesting matchup. Lyman Hall (3-4-1) was playing for a break-even, .500 record with a win against the Rams after its upset of Derby. The Trojans operating out of the wishbone possessed one of the better rushing teams in the league in 1971, coming into Thanksgiving Day. Cheshire (1-4-3), a flashy offensive team with multiple formations, was led by their strong-armed junior quarterback, Paul Linehan.

The field was November-typical, muddy and sloppy that affected both team's offensive performance, but surprisingly, Lyman Hall, with its three-back power offense, was largely held in check. After a Trojan fumble deep in their own territory, the Rams moved right in as Linehan scored on a quarterback sneak for a 6-0 lead in the first quarter. With the Trojans ground game stifled (on 35 yards rushing for the game), the Rams began a 36-yard drive, capped by Linehan's two-yard touchdown run around left end and his two-point conversion. The 14-0 Ram victory gave the Beanpot Trophy a permanent residence at Cheshire High School. The teams would continue to compete in the Housatonic League, but never again to face each other on Thanksgiving Day.

Chapter 62

Developing the Elements of a Champion

The 1972 football team had a textbook "up and down" season, racking up three straight wins after an opening season loss to Platt High School. Then four losses in a row to Cheshire, East Haven, North Haven, and Derby before the first Thanksgiving Day affair with crosstown Sheehan High School.

Despite the less than modest record for the 1972 Trojans, the roster of 39 players had a solid junior class, led by Richard DelCervo, Gerry Butler, and Paul Bruton. There was a building toughness within the squad that would set the stage for some of the best football yet seen from a Wallingford team, beginning in 1973.

Tucked in that roster was a tall, thin, blonde hair running back who showed a few flashes of talent. He was a transfer from Notre Dame High School of West Haven, but like a young colt growing into his body, gaining confidence with every sprint, this young man was not quite ready to step into the pages of Lyman Hall High School history. He would become more than a generational player. In a matter of months, his name, number (#38), and deeds would become of the legendary status of Inguaggiato, Horowitz, and Stupakevich. He would change the fortunes of Lyman Hall football forever. His name? Rick Angelone.

Understandably, there was a lot of buildup within the community and the two student bodies for the first Lyman

Hall – Sheehan, Carini Bowl game. It was a curiosity, something that hadn't been seen before. Would it be a great football game with exciting action? Would the game light a fuse for more dramatic games in the years ahead? To these questions and more, the answer was a convoluted ... "who knows."

The game attracted a crowd, estimated at over 2,000. The game itself didn't approach the buildup for this first football game between Lyman Hall and Sheehan High Schools. The play was often slipshod, and the score was close, with the Trojans prevailing 13-7. There wasn't an overly exuberant celebration at the ending, just a handing out of the trophy and a few awards to members of both teams. Lyman Hall co-captain Paul Buckanavage was named Lyman Hall's offensive player of the game, and Jim McLaughlin, the outstanding defensive player for LHHS.

The 1972 season record was another four-win campaign that seemed to be the number that Coach Ottochian's teams were stuck on, but there were elements of something compelling, far more radiant than anything ever seen. There were tough, finely tuned "football players," those who could think the game and command classic hard-hitting play. In the past, that caliber of player at Lyman Hall was rare indeed, but sprinkled throughout the 1972 roster could be the foundational elements of ... "dare we say it" ... a championship team for Lyman Hall.

Without giddiness or happy-apple expectations, there was a fiber of football player that would sew the seeds of winning, not by upsets or blow-out victories over lesser opponents, but by habit and clear intention.

Lyman Hall finished the season with a four win – six loss record, but for the first time, the Ottochian Trojans had four members of the (1972) team, gaining first team All Housatonic League recognition from the league's head coaches. Gus Maningus was chosen as the all-league noseman, John Purcell at guard, junior Gerry Butler a center, and junior Richard DelCervo at defensive end.

WITH ANGELONE ... "WE CAN FLY"

Approaching the 1973 season, Phil Ottochian finally assembled a varsity coaching staff who would be with him for a few seasons and worked very well together. The assistant coaching carousel that is common to most high schools is often difficult for the head coach and his team to navigate in bringing consistency to the daily work in practice and game preparation quality. For assistant coaches, it is not a matter of "what you know" but how you compliment the head coach in delivering his message. In that regard, loyalty is valued above all things and then ... teaching skills. The greatest of educators recognize this truism, "a great teacher can teach anything." An assistant coach must be able to coach/teach far beyond his or her frame of reference. If an assistant coach is lost in their past experiences as a player or coach, that person will be unable to deliver their responsibilities when change and adjustment are required, or adversity happens on the field.

Led by line coach Andy Borelli, Ottochian had a meticulous teacher who had played the game at a high level at Southern Connecticut State University. Borelli was a physical education teacher at Dag Hammarskjold Junior High School who possessed a focused football acumen but with a sensitivity to reach into his linemen's hearts and bring out the very best in every one of them. He did not look at the girth of the linemen as a predominant measuring stick of potential. Rather, he measured their hearts by their commitment to the skills he taught every day in practice. Coach Borelli was loved and beloved by everyone on the Lyman Hall teams he coached since 1967.

In Sean Meehan, a social studies teacher, Ottochian had a rah-rah coach who always had his wry Irish wit rolling, inserting a staccato laugh in his words of encouragement and critique. He was a pleasure to be around, and no matter what the name of the player or coach he was addressing, he would often add an "ie" or "y" to their name and extend the final syllable. Coach Jim Lynch was "Jimmmmmmie," and Phil Ottochian was, "Philieeeeeeeeeeeeeee."

Jim Lynch was the 1961 captain of the Trojans, now a history teacher at LHHS who began coaching the freshman team and then easily transitioned to coaching the secondary on defense. The best-dressed coach in the Housatonic League, he could make a winter parka look like a dinner jacket. Rarely showing much emotion, he brought a wonderful teaching style with a smile of encouragement and a bark when his defensive backs needed it.

Nick Economopoulos was the head freshman coach and displayed a knack for organization. John Ryan had been the secondary coach in the past, and 1973 would be his last season coaching football at LHHS.

Coach Ottochian enjoyed the comradery he had with his coaches, especially Borelli, Meehan, and Lynch. They were all close in age and enjoyed their hours together. The players embraced the togetherness that their varsity coaches demonstrated, and it made the team environment that much more of a "togetherness" rather than a shared responsibility.

The 1973 Trojans possessed a depth of quality players capable of vying for a Housatonic League championship. The team had a seasoned senior class and arguably the best junior class any Lyman Hall football team ever had.

AND … The 1973 Trojans had one more ingredient, never seen on an LHHS football team ever before. 1973 was the coming-out season for Rick Angelone (#38).

The Lyman Hall offense began to adopt the wishbone as its offensive philosophy in 1970. A significant change for Ottochian, it places a great deal of responsibility on the quarterback to read the defense on most plays, making the decision to handoff, pitch out or keep the ball after the ball is snapped. The wishbone offense had incredible potential, but like all offenses in the game of football, to be explosive, you needed players who could run and block.

After three seasons in the "bone," Ottochian's offense showed flashes of brilliance but never a sustained level of success that might make Lyman Hall a contender for the league title and a dominant force week after week.

As the pre-season scrimmages unfolded against Bristol Central, Danbury, and Stamford Catholic, three-annual tough guys in Connecticut schoolboy football, it became clear that the Trojan wishbone attack finally had the big weapon in the backfield, Rick Angelone.

The 1973 Trojans opened their season at home against Platt High School. With junior Ron Suplinskas providing the leadership at quarterback, the Trojan offense was a machine of power, speed, and quickness. Angelone was spectacular right out of the gate, running for 90 yards in the first half and, with limited carries in the second half, ended his day with 108 yards.

Lyman Hall amassed 271 yards rushing in the game, and as a New Haven Register sports writer proclaimed in the tiny LHHS pressbox, "With Angelone, they (Lyman Hall) CAN FLY." With the final 41-6 victory over Platt, there was an instantaneous excitement in Lyman Hall High School. However, it didn't last long as Amity upended the Trojans, 14-9 in game two, as the Spartans keyed on Angelone. Despite a second 100-yard rushing game for sophomore halfback Papo Diaz and a 9-0 halftime lead, Lyman Hall could not hold down Amity's passing game in the second half.

With a renewed energy, LHHS outlasted Seymour in the third game of the season as Angelone rambled for 189 yards on 16 carries for a 28-12 win. The Trojan wishbone was flying high against Branford High School the following week as Angelone ran for 200 yards on 18 carries.

With a 3-1 record, the Lyman Hall student body began to show up in earnest for the football Trojans on Saturday afternoons. The excitement that Angelone brought to Lyman Hall football was only reminiscent of the edge-of-your-seat court wizardry of (Mel) Horowitz and (Fran) Stupakevich. Never before had a football game in Wallingford beheld a player who caused the crowd in the stands to rise, even before touching the ball.

Without any coaches' prompting, the team's buzz was that

this team, the 1973 Trojans, could just win the Housatonic League Championship. Heading into the Shelton game, the offensive line was brimming with confidence with Steve Giordano at center, Tony Marotta and Steward Crawford at the guards, and Paul Bruton and Carmen Arisco at the tackles. Arisco was a "Coach Borelli special" who was 5-8 and weighed 165 pounds.

As the Trojans prepared to face long-time Housatonic League nemeses, Shelton, one of the largest crowds since football returned in 1949, was anticipated.

SUPLINSKAS HURT, WON'T PLAY VS. SHELTON

Junior quarterback Ron Suplinskas (#7) was the magnificent leader, and a tough "hombre" as Coach Ottochian would say many times. The nature of the wishbone offense with the quarterback being the decision-maker on virtually every play. To defend the wishbone, opponent defenses would viciously hit the quarterback on every play. The strategy for opposition defenses would be to drill the quarterback before he could make a decision to pitch or keep the ball. Additionally, defensive tactics included hitting the quarterback every play and wear him down or put him out of the game. Henceforth, even after four games, Suplinskas, a sturdy 6-1, 180 pounds, had taken more than his share of hard hits. After the Branford game, Captain Ron was banged up and would not play against Shelton. In his place, sophomore Dave Buckanavage would start at quarterback.

With Rick (Angelone) doing what the Lyman Hall students came to see, and with Ottochian calling on Buckanavage to throw the ball (just five times), the Trojans beat the visiting Gaels, 21-14.

Incidentally, Lyman Hall had just two passing plays in their limited playbook, "veer blue," a pass to the split end, and "veer red," a pass to the tight end. Both of these plays began with a run-fake as opponent defensive players would quickly move to their individual responsibilities to defend each piece of the option (dive, pitch, QB keep). The more prolific the Lyman Hall option attack became, the more vulnerable opponent defenses became to those basic pass plays of Ottochian. In the Shelton victory, a first-time starter, Buckanavage, completed two "Veer Red" passes to tight end Richard DelCervo, resulting in a 39-yard touchdown and the other a 47-yard scoring toss. It all looked so effortless, but passing the football was never easy for the Trojans. What made it all possible(?) ... Rick Angelone had carried the ball 18 times for 132 yards, including a 34-yard touchdown and now led the Housatonic League in rushing with 677 yards at the mid-way point of the season.

For the growing number of "Lyman Hall football believers," and there hadn't been many throughout the years, the Shelton victory seemed to signal the notion that a championship <u>was possible</u>. For the first time in school football lore, at least since 1949, this mid-season victory against a formidable foe was not a "once in a blue moon" event or a shocking upset. Instead, it was a methodical game, where a backup quarterback throws two touchdown passes, and your larger-than-life halfback turns in another herculean performance that had become "*a predictable.*"

TRAINS PASSING IN OPPOSITE DIRECTIONS

Winning championships in football at LHHS was so far beyond the realm of comprehension that people in the bleachers and standing in the endzones who might have let such a reference pass from their lips evoked giggles from those nearby. The LHHS basketball teams that had fallen on hard times in recent years were still viewed as a title contender if "they got some breaks," such as getting a few taller players. No one ever laughed about the basketball team's potential to win a Housatonic League crown or make a deep run in the state tournament, but football was another matter. There was no state tournament in Connecticut high school football or state championship to pursue, not yet anyway.

As the basketball teams of the high school dipped into mediocrity after the 1967-68 season, Phil Ottochian was slowly building football into an entity that might someday, some season, reach a sort of nirvana, ... a championship year. As the Trojans of Ottochian first got to a .500 record, then defeated a couple of teams ranked in the top ten in Connecticut, and a few players of the Blue & White received post-season recognition, there was "hope," yet not "belief" on the part of the faculty, staff, the community at large that the summit of team achievement might ever be reached.

Soccer was introduced just at a time (1967) when the best athletes in the school should have been encouraged to play football, or at least there should have been a fair and balanced physical education recruiting effort with that which was done for soccer. Once again, football was left for dead. The commitment to do what was best for all students (athletically) was marginalized by outright disdain and benign neglect. Phil Ottochian, hired as head coach in 1968, was a man who knew nothing of the history of the school as it related to football, nor the lack of deference shown to those who only wanted to do their best for their players.

As Ottochian finally had a quality coaching staff and the stanchions of quality high school football teams in place, such as weight training, film study, coaching clinics, and youth programs to teach the sport, a new obstacle emerged ... a second high school.

As Ottochian's former players have repeatedly asserted, "Coach O" was above it all. His level of commitment always exceeded his adversity and adversaries. Like all men (and women), Phil Ottochian would face that tipping point in the future and decide to pursue another coaching position or stay at Lyman Hall. However, in 1973 Coach Ottochian indulged himself in a steady diet of blind faith when the world of Lyman Hall around him offered only half-baked smiles.

The sport of basketball that had contributed to keeping football down for decades was now a lot less potent with no championships since 1968, and Ottochian's football teams were about to step into the void. Basketball and football at Lyman Hall High School were two trains passing each other, going in opposite directions.

THE 1973 CHESHIRE GAME – END OF HOPE

Sporting a 4-1 record, Lyman Hall was tied for second place in the Housatonic League, the highest league ranking since football returned in 1949. Even though the Trojans would still be without starting quarterback Ron Suplinskas, Ottochian was encouraged by the play of backup Dave Buckanavage in the Shelton game. Papo Diaz, who injured his ankle in the Amity game four weeks ago, was ready to return to the backfield with fullback Gerry Butler and the incomparable Rick Angelone.

Cheshire's defense had only allowed 51 points heading into the contest and was primed to stop the vaunted Trojan run attack. All was business as usual early in the first quarter as Lyman Hall drove for a touchdown, with Angelone picking up 23 yards on three carries during the 55-yard drive with Butler carrying it in from the one.

AND THEN ... In the second quarter, leading 7-0, Rick Angelone carried the ball off-tackle. As the tall back hit the line, a Cheshire defender got into Angelone's mid-section and drove Rick's right shoulder up, badly damaging the shoulder. There was a breathless pause all about the field as the LHHS team and coaches waited for Angelone to regain his feet and return to the huddle. With the suddenness of the tragic knee injury to Fran Stupakevich in 1967 that all but ended his season on the basketball court, Rick's football season and the Trojan's hopes for a league crown were over. Yes, others who wore the Blue & White would play Angelone's position for the rest of the game and the remaining four games, but no one could fill the extraordinary Angelone's shoes. The emotional loss of Angelone and a steady running attack by Cheshire aided by Buckanavage's four interceptions and a lost fumble led to a 27-7 victory for the Rams.

The Trojans did not bounce back quickly from the Cheshire game, losing the East Haven, 27-7, tying North Haven, 14-14, and suffering a 27-0 beating against the Red Raiders of Derby.

Just as the first Lyman Hall-Sheehan encounter, the 1973 game was anything but exciting football as neither team could mount much offense. The Trojans lost five fumbles in the Thanksgiving Day affair, and Sheehan was intercepted four times. The leading rusher for Lyman Hall was future standout halfback Dave Biega, who ran for 65 yards on nine carries as Trojan quarterback Ron Suplinskas was masterful in engineering the Blue & White offense to 234 rushing yards.

The 1973 Trojans completed the season with a winning record of 5-4-1 as eight juniors, and four sophomores were starters. Most importantly, there were prayers a-plenty that Rick Angelone would return, fully healed for 1974.

Gerry Butler and Richard DelCervo were voted onto the All Housatonic League first team for the second year in a row, and both were named to the roster of the 1974 Nutmeg Bowl team.

As captain Rich DelCervo stated years later, "If Rick doesn't get hurt in the Cheshire game, we win the Housatonic League title in 1973".

Chapter 63

Shall We Dare to Dream

There were moments since 1949 that a few victories and a tie on the seasonal ledger of the football team would provide a winter full of fond memories. For so many football seasons past, one of the measuring sticks of a successful gridiron campaign was not to let a basketball player get hurt if you even had a basketball player on the football team. Yes, there was always pre-season optimism, and indeed every game was approached as an opportunity to win, but the facts spoke to a different reality.

From 1949 to 1968,... 20 consecutive seasons were played, resulting in 20 losing records in a row under four different head coaches. In 1969 Lyman Hall experienced its first football .500 record (4-4-1) since 1934. The 1970 season brought the football team its first five-win campaign since 1929, and the first year in which wins exceeded losses (5-4) since 1930. Unfortunately, the 1971 (3-5-1) and 1972 (4-6) seasons returned to losing record status.

There were obvious strides of improvement under Coach Ottochian, culminating with his second five victory season in 1973 (since 1968), but as the fall of 1974 approached, the question that hovered above those who engaged in the cavalier prognostication of Lyman Hall football was if there was real reason for optimism. Might a unique fall campaign be possible, or should we all just anticipate a near .500 record, enjoy the games, and hope for another surprising win. After all, at best, Lyman Hall football teams were always historically near the bottom of the league standings, with an occasional "middle of the pack" season.

As the 1974 season approached, Coach Ottochian felt that this team was "going to be good," but this was Lyman Hall football, and "good" historically was code for "we will be in every game."

The facts were that the '74 Trojan football team was returning more starters who could play more different positions than any team during the Ottochian years. Carmen Arisco, Pat DiNatale, Tony Marotta, and others returned with varsity time on the offensive line. Linebackers John Wallace, Bob Martin, and Mike Puig were all back, a year older and stronger. However, what was most attention-grabbing was the number of "skill" position players who could and would play on both offense and defense from time to time.

Tri-captain Ron Suplinskas (#7), who brilliantly directed the wishbone attack at quarterback in 1973, was back in the fold. Mike Nesti (#21), who had started as a defensive back since his freshman year, was named the fullback, and the powerful running Dave Biega (#33) would be one of the halfbacks. The news that made the grass grow greener on Fitzgerald Field was the return of Rick Angelone (#38) back from that horrible shoulder injury. Adding to the backfield's depth was Papo Diaz (#22), who ran for two 100-yard games to open the 1973 season, but was slowed by an ankle injury that led the way to Biega's being inserted into the starting lineup.

Other outstanding players would return in 1974 to give Lyman Hall its most experienced team in the early Ottochian years. Jim Silvestri, Kevin Gauntlet, Brenden Feeney, Stuart Kosnoff, and Neal Heffernan would play significant roles in the season about to unfold.

READY TO WIN

Since his arrival at LHHS, Phil Ottochian placed a high value on scrimmages, scheduling the highest regarded high school football teams to go against his charges in pre-season. Each team that Coach Ottochian scheduled for scrimmages seemed to have a head coach who was highly competitive, exceedingly emotional, demanded confrontation, and a few of them were just plain "nuts." The scrimmages held in the final weeks of August and the first week of September meant scorching temperatures in the high 90's with the humidity of a rainforest. The pretext was basic for Ottochian. Make his Lyman Hall team's as tough as possible, getting them in the highest mental and physical condition possible that would see them through the back-breaking Housatonic League schedule. Heretofore, the 1974 "Housy" (Housatonic League) had at least four teams capable of capturing the league title.

Each scrimmage in 1974 was more backyard brawl than football teaching and learning opportunities. Of the scrimmages, two memorable scenes took place. Bristol Central High School brought a big, physical team to LHHS in 1974, led by future All-Staters, linebacker Rocco Testa and tackle Tim Bachman, along with the multi-talented quarterback, Brian Stranieri. With both head coaches perched close to the action ... if a Bristol Central (B.C.) player was beaten on a block by a Lyman Hall player, the scrimmage was stopped by the B.C. coach. He then ordered his own player and the Lyman Hall player to do battle between both teams, one on one. This slowed the scrimmage to a crawl, but it made every play a life and death matchup. Periodically, punches were thrown, and inevitably, the scrimmage was halted more than a few times before its scheduled end.

The Stamford Catholic scrimmage was held in Stamford, requiring a steamy hour drive in a school bus. As safety, Jim Silvestri remembers it, "Coach scheduled us for a scrimmage with Stamford Catholic at their place, and this was a state football power, and they could hit. It was a war from the first play".

Noseman and guard Tony Marotta recalls, "We ran basically the same play maybe ten times in a row with Mike Nesti, (fullback) carrying the ball. Coach was all over us. Coach (Ottochian) not only told the Stamford Catholic defense who would be carrying the ball, he pointed to the exact place where we were going to run the play".

Although Lyman Hall moved the ball on offense with its option offense, Coaches Ottochian and Borelli were steadfast in demanding that the team ran the ball directly at the green-clad Stamford Catholic defense. Ottochian's obvious objective, although not verbally stated, made the Lyman Hall squad as battle-hardened as they could be heading into the traditional season opener against Platt High School.

Chapter 64

The Fall That Changed It All, 1974

With all of the bravado coming from Coach Ottochian regarding the start of the 1974 football season, it seemed as though we had all been down this road before. For most Wallingford citizens, high expectations for Lyman Hall High School athletic teams were best directed at basketball. Over the many decades, the presence of just one or two handlers of the round ball on the hardwood was enough to raise the tide of enthusiasm for yet another Housatonic League crown. As for LHHS football, there was no community frame of reference that would lead anyone to believe that a gridiron team of the Blue and White had any realistic chance of winning a league title, so it was best to just have a "Coke and a Smile" and wait for basketball season to start.

Football at Lyman Hall had been the hapless victim of so many adverse events and people since 1926 that there seemed to be a perpetual cloak of darkness, ensconcing the sport at the high school. At the beginning of some seasons, a tease of sorts was perpetrated on the Trojans' hopeful patrons with a few double-digit early-season victories. The traditional black helmets 1916-1965 (no negative inference suggested) were replaced with white helmets, 1966-1968, and then, low and behold, the Trojans had navy blue (the accurate school color) helmets with a limited variety of stripes and decals, but no logo or uniform design ever generated a sustaining presence until 1974.

Athletic Director, Fred Schipke as a tribute to his former coach and principal, Langdon Fernald, introduced orange as an accent color, first on the thread of the numerals in the tackle-twill uniforms of the early 1960s. Then an orange stripe on the football pants made its appearance in 1973. Somewhere in the annual helmet logo du jour of the early 1970s, a bold orange "T" (Trojans) made its debut onto the football helmets and became THE prominent logo for many years to come. However, it never would have had any staying power without the happenings of 1974.

As the football season began, the student body, faculty, administration, and the long-suffering Lyman Hall alumni, at least those that had the slightest scintilla of interest in the football team, needed evidence that there was some reason to believe that the football squad had half a chance to be "pretty good," whatever "pretty good" might mean.

As the Lyman Hall team of 49 players lined up for pre-game stretching for its opening game, led by captains Ron Suplinskas (#7), Rick Angelone (#38), and Pat DeNatale (#77), there were no rah-rah chants and demonstrations of false-machismo. This was the nature of the 1974 team. It was all an intelligent approach to all aspects of the game before them. As the game and the season unpacked itself, this team took the field with only business to be done in their faces and in their actions.

There were no first-game jitters for the Trojans against a quality Platt team. From the opening kickoff, the Lyman Hall offense ran their plays with elegant precision. Both halfbacks, Angelone and Biega, were equally superb at running and blocking for each other. With the defense limiting the Panthers to few first downs, led by the lightning-quick noseman, Tony Marotta, the Trojans ran away with a 28-0 victory.

In 1974 high school teams could add an extra game to their schedule due to the calendar's extra week. Lyman Hall decided to invite ole' basketball foe, Hillhouse, for the 11th opponent. The "Hilltoppers" were no match for the Trojans as

Lyman Hall overwhelmed the New Haven team, 35-6. With confidence brimming for the Blue and White, the Trojans completely shut down and shut out the Amity Spartans, 35-0 in game three.

THE TAPESTRY TROJANS

For those who witnessed the first three games of the 1974 season, something was very distinctive, totally atypical. It was not just that the LHHS football team was winning by decisive scores. No, this was diametrically different. It wasn't a matter of seeing a high school athletic contest, ... it was a feeling, unlike nothing ever seen before in Wallingford.

With a long breath and a scant glance to the heavens, one could feel a churning internalization viewing the 1974 Lyman Hall football team. It was a tapestry in creation. Emerging stories that would last forever were being woven into its fabric. Sensation without sound as Mike Nesti would glide through the quarterback to fullback mesh with Ron Suplinskas, his eyes affixed to the raging opponents before him. Halfback Dave Biega would seem to float to the wishbone formation's edge, drawing a confounded defender to him. Then with the stroke of a master chef, julienning his fare, Biega would chop down the approaching cornerback, freeing Rick Angelone to carry the pigskin upfield. With opposition jerseys converging, Angelone would assert a sudden change of direction, a falcon into the wind, causing defenders to chase on.

The men of the '74 football Trojans were a 48-minute play of elegance, a beauty to behold. Variations in weather and fields of play only added additional pigment to the intricate weaving of this Wallingford tapestry.

After a few outings, the 1974 Trojans were a must-see happening in Wallingford, now drawing enormous crowds at Fitzgerald field, equal to or exceeding those of the first two Thanksgiving Day games with the new high school team across town.

It was with a sense of delicacy that one followed the Trojans in 1974. By God, ... what if Angelone got hurt again? What if

Suplinskas, Nesti, or Biega fell victim to injury? There would be challenges to be sure, enemies seen and unseen, but this was a tapestry to be clenched no matter what cometh.

HEART OF THE HOUSY

With a 3-0 record, the best of the Housatonic League schedule lay ahead for the 1974 Trojans. First up ... game four, the Seymour Wildcats, the sophisticated offense of Head Coach Dan Heffernan. Although the Blue and White were able to run its offense, moving the ball almost at will throughout the contest, the Trojan defense could not stop Seymour's passing game. Safety, Jim Silvestri remembers, "We could not stop (Matt) Wozniak." The 6-3 All-State receiver made more than a few acrobatic receptions on this day, keeping the Wildcats within victory's reach right to the end of the game, but the Trojans prevailed, 26-25.

Branford High School was next in line, but the Hornets were no match for Lyman Hall as the Trojans recorded one of the highest point totals in school history, blasting the Hornets, 47-14. With five wins against no defeats, the Hartford Courant and the New Haven Register finally started to pay attention to the traditional Housatonic League "also-rans."

Wonder of wonders, the Lyman Hall High School football team started the 1974 season with five wins. This had never happened before in school history. The victory total already equaled the most in any season past, and there was a half of season yet to play. It was all so different, so terribly exciting, and although Connecticut had no state championship games in football, there was a buzz around everything football at Lyman Hall.

Rick Angelone recalled the fiber and substance of the team, "We were workman-like and confident. The team was so close ... we often sang together and expected to win every game. There was so much camaraderie in the school, at practice, and during games. We had some guys from out-of-town, like Tony Marotta from North Haven, and they fit right in. We knew early on we had good players. We just have to stick together".

Defensive back, receiver, and halfback, Papo Diaz recalls the attitude of the team, "Every day in practice, we tried to make ourselves better. We always went hard in practice, and we just kept getting better and better".

All seemed right in the world on October 19, 1974, as the Trojans traveled to the valley to face the Shelton Gaels that were among the high schools favored to win the '74 league title.

Shelton was playing at their best entering this contest. On the first play of the game, as a portent of things to come, the Shelton offensive tackle fires out to block Stu Kosnoff, who was playing defensive tackle for the Trojans. On the head-to-head confrontation to begin the game, Kosnoff jacks up the 230 pound Shelton tackle, lifting him right off the ground. Even to the casual observer, it was clear this game would not be your typical "popcorn league" high school football game.

The Gael fans surrounding the field were loud and belligerent throughout the game, but as the Trojans were unable to score in the first half, Shelton opened up a 14-0 lead. It appeared that the magic carpet ride of 1974 might be disappearing into the mist as the Lyman Hall team left the field. Dave Biega recalls the scene just at halftime, "Shelton fans were throwing beer bottles at us as we walked off the field and calling us over-rated."

With the Lyman Hall team down in spirit and on the scoreboard, Mike Nesti remembers what happened at halftime to flip the switch on the Blue and White, "(Coach) Borelli goes crazy at halftime. He was all over us. It was like our hearts started beating for the first time. We would have run through a wall at that point".

Coach Borelli tells the team that they will run back the second-half kickoff for a touchdown and turn the game around. This is precisely what happens as Dave Biega runs back the second-half kickoff for a touchdown and begins the comeback that sees the Trojans score four second-half touchdowns. In this physical Housatonic League confrontation with so much at stake, Rick Angelone plays most of the game at defensive end as quarterback, Ron Suplinskas plays strong safety (monster back). On one key play, Suplinskas intercepts a Shelton ariel and runs it back close to the goal line, whereupon Angelone runs it in for the score on the next play from scrimmage. The Trojans stay unbeaten, winning in Shelton, 28-14. Dave Biega sums up the victory this way, "Coach Borelli was the reason we came back and won."

A HOUSATONIC TITLE ... IN FOOTBALL?

The Trojan football juggernaut rolled on after the Shelton game with another hard-fought league game against Cheshire, led by their star running back, Jon Rogers, who would go on to many record-setting performances. The Trojans prevailed 14-12 against Rogers and company as Lyman Hall received its first group of votes in the state high school polls. The talk of the town began to speak in the most positive terms about the real shot LHHS had to win their first Housatonic League Championship in football since 1926. There were banners in the stands proclaiming, "WE CAN DO IT," and these were signs stating the belief that LHHS might be standing in the winner's circle of the league at season's end.

East Haven was next up for Lyman Hall, and once again, halfback Dave Biega took center stage. In a performance that would earn Biega New Haven Register Player of the Week honors, Dave runs for three touchdowns, one of 64 yards, another of 74 yards, and a breath-taking 80-yard kickoff return for a TD.

Mike Nesti credited Dave Biega (#33) this way, "Dave never received a fraction of the credit he should have gotten. Dave was as fast and athletic as anyone. If a defensive player was closing in, Dave just leaped over him". Rick Angelone stated, "Biega was a great blocker. We are running triple option, and Ronnie (QB, Ron Supplinskas) pitches to me, and the corner comes up (to tackle me), and Dave chops him off his feet".

North Haven High School, always a harsh foe for Lyman Hall to face in any sport, played a terrible role in the 1974 football season. With Lyman Hall way ahead in the game, Angelone and Biega are still in the game in the fourth quarter. In rapid succession, both Angelone and Biega suffered ankle injuries in the final period of play that would force both to miss the Housatonic League showdown against the Derby Red Raiders for the league championship.

Since Lyman Hall returned to football in 1949, Derby was usually the final opponent for Lyman Hall before Thanksgiving Day. In this year of the Trojans, Derby and Lyman Hall both held identical, 9-0, undefeated records going into this game that most felt would determine the 1974 Housatonic League title.

Derby was at full strength, playing at home on Ryan Field. Lyman Hall is in the biggest football game since the 1926 Derby game that also determined the league championship. Despite the best efforts of trainers and medical experts, Rick Angelone and Dave Biega could not play in the game. Once again it was that historic recurring nightmare in which adverse circumstances and people forced bad things to happen to Lyman Hall football. As the 1974 Trojans rolled along through an undefeated season thus far, it seemed safe to dream the big dream, but now in a twinkling, all the wrongs perpetrated on LHHS football in the past reared their ugly presence yet again.

Coach Ottochian decided to reposition all-league quarterback Ron Suplinskas to fullback with Mike Nesti and Papo Diaz at the halfbacks. Dave Buckanavage, who filled in for Suplinskas in 1973, was again inserted at quarterback to face the Red Raiders.

It would have been a classic football game at full strength, but the Trojans faced more than an insurmountable foe without the two running backs. Unfortunately, the Trojans did not play their best of games on defense as Derby moved the ball effectively. It was never a close game as the Red Raiders prevailed with a 29-13 win, securing at least a share of the league crown if they could defeat Shelton on Thanksgiving.

After the Derby defeat, there still was a ray of hope to win the league title if Shelton could upend the Red Raiders and

Lyman Hall could do away with Sheehan. In the preparations for the Sheehan game, Coach Ottochian shocked his team by deciding to start All Housatonic League quarterback Ron Suplinskas at fullback, sitting down regular starter Mike Nesti. Biega and Angelone were healed and back in their halfback slots as Buckanavage would start at quarterback. Whatever the reason for the move of Suplinskas to fullback, it was never revealed to members of the 1974 team.

As most anticipated, the '74 Trojans ran rough-shod over the Sheehan Titans, 35-0, as Angelone scored 26 of the 35 Trojan points in the game in the shutout victory. The highlight of this Thanksgiving Day was the news that the Shelton Gaels had indeed upset the Derby Red Raiders, making Lyman Hall and Derby Co-Champions of the Housatonic League.

Chapter 65

The Meaning of 1974

The captivating season of the 1974 football team brought forward a now believable narrative that there was a fresh dynamism relative to Lyman Hall High School's football efforts. Before this year, few, if any locals, or those who followed school-boy football, might have thought it possible. The uncovered dynamic that took years to discover brought forward the preposition that internal change, made with marginal supports methodically and not without discomfort, could result in an unimagined outcome.

In the subdued revelry that followed the league crown, no one familiar with Lyman Hall High School's history would ever suggest that success was sustainable. The locker room theorists who spew terms such as the cheeky jargon "program-building" and "changing the culture" have never faced the bondage of school and community history such as those that held fast Lyman Hall High School football and its head coaches.

The 1974 football team classically certified that a championship football season was possible in the face of the reigns of history and a challenging schedule of opponents. The prior years under Phil Ottochian might have ended in a similar fashion of those of his predecessors had it not been for Ottochian's mien to ignore all that was a distraction to winning a single football game. He saw right and wrong with a black and white lens and shrugged off the disloyalty and the absence of supports that often surrounded him.

Wallingford's citizenry came to see the 1974 football team. Most weren't football fans, much less Lyman Hall devotees. They didn't attend because of habitual fall functionality or because they, their children, or their children's children had walked the halls of LHHS. The '74 football team was an experience. They had true stars that burned in beams of passion and subsequent joy. Children across town, ... yes, even those on the westside of Wallingford, played touch football in parks and their backyards. Some insisted that they play Angelone, Biega, or Nesti. They knew their jersey numbers, and some etched the numerals on classroom desks and on book covers. For the first time, football was a **Wallingford Fieri**, a happening that had previously been reserved for only basketball.

RECOGNITION AND REFLECTION

The 1974 Lyman Hall High School football team completed the season with a 10-1 record as the Housatonic League Champions, finished 4th in the Final State Polls, the first time a Lyman Hall football team had ever been ranked.

Captain and quarterback Ron Suplinskas became the first Lyman Hall High School player to be selected as a National Football Foundation Scholar-Athlete.

Rick Angelone ran for 1398 yards on 163 carries in 1974, averaging a staggering 8.5766 yards per carry. Additionally, Angelone led the state in scoring, totaling 152 points, and was a first team All Housatonic League choice and a first team All-State running back. Tony Marotta completed his three years on the LHHS defense, recording 225 tackles, including 26 tackles behind the line of scrimmage (CBL), and was chosen  as a first team All Housatonic noseman on defense in 1974.

Ron Suplinskas was a first-team, All Housatonic League quarterback.

Although not selected for all league recognition, halfback Dave Biega finished the 1974 season with 887 yards rushing on 119 carries, a remarkable 7.4537 yards per carry average.

The Housatonic League in 1974 was brimming with outstanding teams and individual player performances, a more remarkable testimony of how incredible the Lyman Hall team had performed.

Years later, Michael Puig recalls the 74 team, "There was such great leadership and experience, no bickering or big egos, just people wanting everybody on the team to play their best and win the games".

The 1974 football Trojans set the standard for all teams of the future. They placed the bar very high, and every subsequent season would be measured against the 1974 team and individual record of achievement. The residual of 1974, maybe the most meaningful of all, was that the 1974 football Trojans transformed what seemed impossible to the realm of possible.

Chapter 66

After the 1974 Title

As in most seasons under Head Coach Phil Ottochian, the football team passed into and sometimes out of new stages of development. After winning the 1974 Housatonic League championship, the first since 1926, a whole new uncharted territory stood before the 1975 team. The question was simply ... "What do we do now"?

The '74 seniors were an exceptional class in so many ways. They were highly intelligent, tough in the game's true spirit, and grew together as a wonderful group of young men since their freshman year.

The 1975 team was a composite of a fine group of seniors, who were contributing juniors in 1974 and many high-quality '74 freshmen team members. The most dominating storyline to come from the 1975 season was the performance of Mike Nesti (#21). In 1974 he was a 5-7, 145-pound fullback who was often overlooked in the afterglow of Rick Angelone and David Biega. Once freed to stand on his own stage, Nesti was one of the most sensational running backs in LHHS history. Angelone established records that no one thought could ever be broken, especially his achievement of carrying the ball for 2,106 yards for an eye-popping average of 7.9471 yards per carry. In perspective, Rick almost ran for a first down every time he touched the ball. It was an astronomical figure. As the legendary Maloney High School football coach, Rob Syzmaszek, was quoted as saying, "If you give a good back enough carries, he'll run for 1,000 yards, but it's the yards per carry that separates the great back from the rest". When Rick made his last high school carry, no sane thinking person would ever think that his yards-per-carry record could ever be even approached.

With Nesti now at one of the halfback slots with an almost new offensive line, he became the go-to back in the Trojan offense. Although the 1975 football squad battled through a six-win, five-loss season with many close games, Nesti was brilliant. In this season alone, he carried the pigskin 181 times, gaining 1,459 yards, breaking Anglone's single-season record set one year earlier of 1,398 and approaching, while not breaking the yards-per-carry record. Mike Nesti averaged 8.0607 yards every time he touched the ball.

The fleet Nesti possessed the quickest of steps that allowed him to evade would-be tacklers with amazing grace. While Angelone ran to glory with the elegance of the Great Egret, Nesti carried the ball with the grace and style of the great Nureyev. Nesti possessed the ability to sprint to a near sideline as defenders closed in and, with a football version of an **en l'air**, would plant his upfield foot mere inches from the boundary, shift his weight from outside to inside and whirl seamlessly to open ground, leaving all who would chase in his wake.

There was no league championship to be won heading into the final game of the season, but the Trojans had Nesti to keep them in every game and inside linebacker Michael "Maddog" Puig to anchor their defense. Puig would record 159 tackles in 1975, making him the most prolific tackler in a single season in school history to that point and becoming the only member of the LHHS team to be selected to the All-Housatonic League first-team defense. Tragically, despite the all-time record-setting rushing performance of Mike Nesti, he was passed over for All-Housatonic League recognition.

After 1974, winning football games became a more common occurrence at Lyman Hall as the 1976 team equaled the win total of 1975. In the third game of the year, the Trojans established a school record for most points scored in a single game with a 54-21 win over Seymour. With a final 6-4 slate, the Trojans earned their fourth consecutive winning season, at the time a school record. Michael DelCervo was selected as the all-league center, as junior Alan Suplinskas earned first team All Housatonic League recognition at defensive end.

1977 LEAGUE CHAMPIONSHIP

The 1974 Freshman team was loaded with superb talent, and as seniors in 1977, they gave Lyman Hall High School its third Housatonic League crown with a 9-1 record. In a season of exciting finishes, Lyman Hall won five games by a touchdown or less with outstanding performances from several team members.

Starting quarterback Carl Schmitt (#7) began the season without participating in any pre-season scrimmages due to injury. None of that missed time seemed to slow down the 5-7 swift signal-caller as he was recognized as a New Haven Register Player of the Week, a National Football Foundation Scholar-Athlete, and the 1977 All Housatonic League first-team quarterback.

Schmitt returns to the opening day lineup just in time to lead the Trojans to eight victories in a row. Alas, it was Derby once again who denied Lyman Hall a perfect season as the Red Raiders downed the Trojans, 26-22. Connecticut was still a year away from beginning state championship games in each of the four classes (S, M, L, LL), but the '77 Trojans certainly gave the student body some thrilling moments.

The 1977 league titlists were led on the ground by Alan Angelone, who rushed for 978 yards, and Schmitt's 658 yards. The All Housatonic League first team included Alan Suplinskas at defensive end, Bruce Hecklinger at noseman, and the aforementioned Schmitt. Suplinskas went on to be named as a first-team, All-State selection at defensive end, only the fifth first team All-State player in school history.

With the second Housatonic League championship in four years and the fifth consecutive winning season, Lyman Hall was now in a new place in the minds of league and state high school coaches. In league coaches' opinions, the Trojans were no longer a soft spot on their respective schedules but rather a formidable, physical annual opponent that had learned how to win.

The '77 title would, hopefully, galvanize LHHS football as a Housatonic League upper-tier school, but if history taught us anything, there would still be difficult times ahead for Lyman Hall football.

Author's Note ...

Having accepted and fulfilled many responsibilities in the service of Lyman Hall High School over many decades, few were as rewarding as serving as an assistant football coach from 1978-1999. In the reporting of this historical piece, I shall, from this point on ... at times, move from the third-person observer to a first-person participant. My writing may now shift to a delicate balance of absolute fact to a personal and impassioned conveyor of the events so chronicled. I beg your indulgence in the hope that this parry of tenses will add further resonance to the tale told herein.

~Stephen W. Hoag, Ph.D.~

STAYING IN THE WINNING SEASON GROOVE

The 1978 and 1979 editions of Lyman Hall High School football each notched six-win seasons, running the consecutive winning-season streak to seven. Who would have dared to imagine this level of winning in the 1950s or 1960s, but this metaphorical plateau that supported the feet of the Trojans was about to slide into subsidence in 1980.

With a revamped coaching staff under Ottochian, the Trojans were hard-pressed to cross the goal line, being held to a touchdown or less in eight of the eleven games played, ending the year with a 3-5-3 record. Even with the influx of a talented sophomore class, the 1981 Trojans could not find ways to score, being shut out in five straight contests and scoring only one touchdown in two other games. For the first time since the westside high school (Sheehan) began varsity football, Lyman Hall was a decided underdog entering the Thanksgiving Day game. Led by captain Frank Ruotolo and sophomore linebacker Justin Toomey, the Trojans hold Sheehan to just a kickoff return for a touchdown, as the Trojans prevail, 12-7.

Very little within an athletic team happens all at once. The decisions of players in season, out-of-season, on the field, and off the field determine the destiny of many a team. There is no shortcut to winning, nor is there one for losing. Varsity football has never been about a pre-determined intention to "enjoy yourself" or "just have fun," as the cost of mental and physical challenges is far too high for the manifestation of a fortuitous attitude.

Henceforth, the ill-advised decisions of play and comportment have consequences on teams far into the future. Athletic coaches often use the word "tradition" as something one hands down to others, like a pair of ski-gloves, but in truth, it is a pattern of thought and behavior that supports planks of stability, leading to sustained success.

Chapter 67

Depreciation and Defiance

The 1982 football Trojans experienced the depreciation of created scaffolding that had gradually been put in place since 1968. More than rules, but less than dictatorial mandates, these were ways that one prepares to face challenges, meet the daily tasks of learning and skill acquisition. One might call it "doing what's right." In fact, the pure significance of all that is implied in that word "tradition" is making daily incidental decisions, founded by the basic integrity of putting others and shared goals above yourself.

The 1982 football Trojans of thirty members won their first three games, led by captain, fullback, and cornerback John Gawlak. The defense was a sturdy group fortified by several underclassmen. During the campaign, the '82 defense forced the opposition to cough of the ball nine times inside their ten-yard line. A tragic occurrence, maybe better left forgotten, but having long-term, negative consequences for Lyman Hall football was the North Haven High School game at Fitzgerald Field on Saturday, October 23, 1982.

Always more than the athletic competition, whether it was basketball, baseball, or football when playing North Haven High School, this day the temperature reached the boiling point fast and never cooled down. Almost from the first few minutes of the contest, the referees warned the coaches to "calm their teams down." Members of both teams were warned to cease all antagonistic byplay that was laced with profanity and threatening intentions, or penalties would be assessed; however, no penalties for unsportsmanlike conduct were ever flagged.

Running plays into the line resulted in the normal pile-up of players, but in this game, players were in no rush to regain their feet, and more than a few punches were thrown by both teams in the scrums, without penalties being assessed. Late in the game, with North Haven hanging onto a 14-12 lead, one of the Lyman Hall players intercepts a North Haven pass, proceeding to spike the ball in front of the North Haven bench in an overt demonstration of taunting. Within seconds the words turned into punches as both teams entangled in an all-out brawl. While some players heeded their coaches' screaming to get off the field, the violence escalated with players swinging their helmets to do harm.

The brawl got out of hand so rapidly that spectators of both teams standing in the endzones and on the sidelines poured onto the field and entered the fray. As coaches literally pulled their players off the field, Lyman Hall assistant coach, Jim Lynch, ordered the Trojans to immediately get in the locker room as Coach Ottochian looked for police assistance to restore order.

When Coach Lynch finally got the team in the locker room, the always classy Lynch unleashed a tirade of anger and disappointment, flinging his megaphone across the locker room, shattering the cone-shaped device. There was little that could be said to right the wrongs, but Lynch, with stern eloquence, turned down the temperatures.

The immediate reaction to the chaotic event by school personnel and coaches was that many players from both high schools would be subjected to suspension from school. "Fighting" is a school policy offense, commonly resulting in an "in-school" or "out-of-school" suspension.

With all of the events that led up to and transpired in the game-ending brawl, the recorded game film would clearly show all of the players on both teams who participated in the slug-fest that resulted in the game being terminated before the end of regulation time. This would logically necessitate mass suspensions of many members of both teams, as the game film would show.

With a new school week beginning, players, parents, and coaches held their breath, waiting for the administration's decision on disciplinary measures to be exacted upon the participants in the North Haven football game fight. Monday and Tuesday passed without a word from the administration regarding the consequences to be exacted. Questions abounded ... "Would the rest of the season be canceled? Would Lyman Hall suspend the team from playing for a week or more, forfeiting subsequent games? Would North Haven High School take comparable disciplinary action against the combatants from their school"?

By mid-week, and no disciplinary decisions forthcoming from school or district administrators, the Trojans tried to return to the practice field, but only a fraction of the team attended. No disposition regarding the next game's status against Seymour was known, but the Trojans did what they could to practice.

On a normal week, Wednesday was a day to complete all team adjustments for the next game. In this topsy-turvy two weeks, yet one more team catastrophe exploded within the football team. Several starters on the football team were caught and subsequently turned in for participating in a drinking party in a place known as the "canyons" not far from the school. One would think that this was the final straw as all the players caught drinking, most of whom had also been in the North Haven game brawl, would be suspended from school or at least removed from the team.

In a moment of disbelief and total confusion, word came down that "no one was to be disciplined for anything." No one will ever know on what basis or lack thereof that decision was made, but it surely was not for the good and welfare of Lyman Hall High School and the football team.

With that lack of exacted judgment, a precedent had been established, or at the very least, a kind of message had been sent to future students engaged in athletics that accountability for conduct on and off the field was open to interpretation, and no rule was firm enough where it could not be violated with impunity.

The Trojan football team had one full team practice that week. Distractions are never a good thing for an athletic team, and the 1982 team had enormous distractions, leading up to the away game in Seymour. There was no way that the football team was even remotely prepared for this contest against a very good Seymour Wildcat team. Remarkably, the Trojans won on the field that day, defeating Seymour 29-15, which further reinforced **the wrong message** ..." that no matter how many rules you break, you can get away with it."

The actions of team members were beyond the pale, yet no positive life lesson was forthcoming. Unfortunately, the legacy of the '82 Trojans was not the winning record, rather the decay of principles and practices that Coach Ottochian had so committed himself to building. The rebuilding, if possible, would be dubious at best, but Ottochian and his coaches would face the deleterious aftereffects of the 1982 season, in both 1983 and 1984.

In the gestalt, the 1982 team completed the season with a 6-4 record. John Gawlak becomes the seventh player to go over 1,000 yards rushing in a career and the first fullback to accomplish that feat. Richard Condon is selected as a first-team All Housatonic League guard, as Tony Cerrotti and Justin Toomey are chosen first-team at noseman and linebacker, respectively. Cerrotti, a senior, and Toomey, a junior, are honored as first-team selections on the Connecticut High School Coaches Association All-State team.

1983 WINNING AT A COST

The senior class of the 1983 LHHS football team expressed their belief that they could win a Housatonic League title, and as coach, Jim Lynch often exported "play in December," which meant playing for a state championship. The seniors of this version of the Trojans were a very "different" type of player. Their talent was unmistakable, and they had size and speed, but in those intangible areas of team identity, they were, as Coach Ottochian often stated, "the most difficult team he ever had to coach."

Undisciplined, this was an intimidating group whose conduct off-the-field as well as in varsity games was often savage. The methods of coaching and game preparation, long-established by Coach Ottochian, were challenged daily. The sacrosanct rules of general conduct off-the-field, before and after practice, were largely disregarded by the upperclassmen of the 1983 team.

This made the daily grind of practices most distasteful for the coaches, resulting in an almost new coaching staff in 1984 and Ottochian seriously considering leaving Lyman Hall High School for other coaching opportunities. Of the roster of 36 players to start the season, eight were sophomores, with only Ralph Riley and Greg Myerson splitting starting duties during the season.

The menacing yet talented nature of the senior-laden '83 Trojans could not keep the Blue and White from a defeat in the first game of the year against out-of-league opponent, Platt High School, 19-7. Having abandoned the wishbone for the I-formation, LHHS was led on offense by quarterback Joe Tuscano, fullback Bill Pello, and tailback, Billy Bridgett, beating Seymour 28-21 in game two. Weeks later, holding a 3-1 record in league action, the Housatonic crown was still in the offering, but a 14-13 loss to Amity on a gadget passing play, severely dimmed the championship hopes of the Trojans.

Following the loss to the Spartans of Amity, the '83 Trojans limit their final four opponents to eight points while Bridgett runs for 565 yards, and quarterback Tuscano throws for 267 yards, leading Lyman Hall to the 1983 Housatonic championship. Guard Richard Condon earns a first-team selection on the Jackson Newspapers and the Connecticut High School Coaches Association All-State teams. Bill Bridgett is recognized as a first-team All Housatonic selection, running for 1233 yards in 1983. Justin Toomey completes his record-setting Lyman Hall career with 434 total tackles, including three seasons of over 100 tackles each. He is a first-team

All-State inside linebacker on the Jackson Newspapers and Connecticut High School Coaches Association All-State teams.

HITTING THE BOTTOM

The 1984 LHHS football team of 36 members with only eight seniors had few returning starters from the '83 championship season. From the beginning of fall camp, it was clear that replicable player leadership from seasons long past had vanished for reasons aforementioned. The new coaching staff, most of whom had played for Lyman Hall in the recent past, would *mention en passant* that maybe the winning attitude might never be recaptured.

The acts of negativity that were so prevalent in 1983 still hung like an albatross around the team. After an opening game, a 21-14 victory over Platt High School of Meriden, the Blue and White suffered through eight consecutive losses with few games that could be considered close. With each loss came a more demonstrative defeatism, especially in some senior members of the team. Maybe the lowest point of the season was the 35-20 loss to Seymour in the next to last game of the season.

One player was heard saying the term "won nine" on the bus ride home," an inane attempt to poke fun at the team, suggesting that they would lose to Sheehan and be 1-9 for the season. The fact that it evoked laughter from other team members indicated the depth of defeatism that had grasped the thinking of one too many members of the team.

As junior and future captain Ralph Riley put it, "I remember the bus ride vividly back from Seymour, exhausted and depressed at another loss being hung on our team and overhearing one of the players saying about playing Sheehan on Thanksgiving that he would describe this season at the end of the year as "Won 9" (1-9), effectively assuming that a loss on Turkey Day was a foregone conclusion. Such was the mindset of our team".

Chapter 68

One Game to Begin a New, 1984 Sheehan

Coach Ottochian was well-aware of the internal problems the 1984 team faced. One week before the annual matchup with Sheehan, knowing that his team needed something, as he said, "to hang their hats on," he was awakened in the middle of the night with an idea. It was a quirky idea, probably manifest from his many years in the game, a cross between the Miami Drive Series and the Box-Formation.

Coach Ottochian called it the "VEE". In layman's terms, the flanker (usually split out wide) was required to place his head between the guard and tackle to the tight end side. The tailback was then stacked behind the flanker (or Vee-back), with the fullback in his accustomed position behind the quarterback. In the "Vee," there was, in effect, an unbalanced line that provided a new power element to the offense. Most of the offensive plays that Lyman Hall utilized throughout the I-formation season could be run from the "Ottochian Vee."

The Vee was a perfect fit for the Trojan personnel and gave them a fresh feeling that maybe they could give the Sheehan football team a game.

The westside high school, under its Head Coach (long time Lyman Hall assistant), Andy Borelli were on the precipice of its first-ever .500 season. At 4-5, they had played some quality football under Borelli. The key matchup in this final game of the 1984 season was the talented Sheehan offense versus what had been a hapless Lyman Hall defense.

WORTHY OF RECALLING – 1984 SHEEHAN GAME

Sheehan fumbled on its first possession, and the Trojans took advantage of the miscue as junior Vincent Poggio ran for a 39-yard touchdown. The crosstown team tied the score at 7-7 when their own back fumbled into the endzone, and the Titans recovered for a touchdown. When Sheehan was forced to punt, junior Greg Myerson blocked the Sheehan kick. Moments later, Poggio took the pitch on the option play from quarterback Joe Tuscano for the go-ahead touchdown.

With the score 14-7, Sheehan's Mark Bencivengo gathered in the ensuing kickoff and ran it back for a 97-yard touchdown. In the second quarter, Tuscano threw a 15-yard touchdown to split end, junior Todd Barket as the Trojans advanced their lead to 21-13. Defensive end Myerson intercepted a Sheehan aerial that set up an apparent Tuscano run for a score before halftime, but a holding penalty negated the touchdown.

The white-clad westsiders began the third quarter with a long eight-play drive, but junior Matt Schmitt intercepted a Sheehan pass that ended the threat. With the Ottochian Vee-formation befuddling the opposition, the Trojans put together a 79-yard drive with Poggio carrying 62 yards. Another interception by Schmitt and in the fourth quarter and then a diving Myerson interception put an end to the Sheehan hopes of victory.

The 41-19 victory over the favored Sheehan team set in motion the "Together" theme for the phenomenon of the 1985 season as the '84 Trojans ended the season with a 2-8 record. On this day, November 23, 1984, it was a day for the juniors to shine as Vincent Poggio ran for 216 yards on 27 carries, capping the season with a total of 1,006 yards. Juniors Dave Klaverkamp, Ralph Riley, Greg Myerson, Todd Barket, and Matt Schmitt performed brilliantly on offense and defense.

The Vee-formation that new fangled thing of Coach Ottochian would be brought forward in the coming year with a renewed feeling of "togetherness" for all that would transpire in 1985.

Although no LHHS football player was chosen for All Housatonic League honors, Tri-Captain, Bill Pello became the fourth football Trojan to be selected to the National Football Foundation as a Scholar-Athlete.

Chapter 69

The 1985 Season ... Impossible, Inconceivable, And A Miracle

With all of the words in the pages thus far offered in this historical narrative of the actual deleterious events, decisions, and circumstances aimed at the heart of football at Lyman Hall High School over 68 years, the ludicrous proposition that a "State Championship" might ever be won in the sport of football, at Lyman Hall High School of Wallingford, Connecticut is of the most irrational and preposterous of declarations.

Fresh off of a two-win, nine-loss season in 1984, the 1985 football team would be beset with the smallest varsity football roster (24 players) in Lyman Hall High School history. The '85 team would have to overcome a hurricane, torrential rains and snowstorms, game postponements, and the strongest Housatonic League ever, filled with teams that could not only challenge for the league title but three division (determined by enrollment) state championships.

This edition of the football Trojans required that at least nine players start on offense, defense, and all kicking game phases. Any injury could be catastrophic, and although most of the starters suffered from various injuries, only one member of the team would miss a game.

Every high school football team is confronted with

challenges during the course of a season, but the 1985 Lyman Hall football Trojans had to overcome the effects of history, weather, the fragility of its own roster, and a torturous schedule. For most of the season there would be insufficient numbers of team members to field a practice or scout team, so a rather ingenious method of practicing would have to be implemented. With all of that, and a lot more, when the '85 Trojans finally reached the summit, they were compelled to face the greatest test any Lyman Hall High School team, in any sport, had ever had to overcome.

If this introduction to the 1985 football season of Lyman Hall High School seems a tad too dramatic, let me offer this, in the etymology of the term, "miracle," foraged from the Greek word, **thaumasion** and the Latin term, **miraculum**, is an event that can only be defined as extraordinary and is inexplicable by normal paradigms.

ALMOST AT AN END, BEFORE BEGINNING

After the distressing 1983 and 1984 seasons, Coach Ottochian's spirits were lifted by being offered opportunities to coach elsewhere on the high school and collegiate levels. Phil Ottochian had gained the reputation across Connecticut as a high-performing football coach, winning at a school that had not won in more than a half a century. He was an effective teacher with great attention to detail. Unlike many other high school football coaches, he always maintained his integrity, never falling victim to the use of profanity or leveling degrading criticism at his players. He was weighing his options, and the extremely low turnout for weight training and spring football practice almost left Ottochian with no choice, but to seek greener pastures.

In the spring of 1985, Lyman Hall convened the football aspirants for the annual spring practice as permitted by the C.I.A.C., the school's governing body in Connecticut. Due to conflicts with other spring sports, the attendance for the ten days of spring practice at LHHS was more than slim. There were 16 players at the first spring practice, and it didn't get much better as the two weeks progressed.

Despite the low numbers, the future seniors for the 1985 team, mostly linemen, worked well together, and even though a full 11 on 11 scrimmage was not possible, the size and synergy of the offensive line were most impressive. Among the problems facing the formulation of the 1985 team, the No.1 goal of the spring season was to find a quarterback. Glenn Root was the favorite to claim the position with good size and a decent throwing arm.

Never to be ignored, Todd Barket, a starter at defensive back and wide receiver in 1984 who had a fantastic intellect and understanding of the offense, was in competition for the job. Todd was the freshman quarterback in 1982 but never had much of a chance to play the varsity level position because of the presence of since graduated Joe Tuscano. With Vincent Poggio (1,000-yard rusher in 1984), the only returner with varsity playing time in the offensive backfield under his belt, Coach Ottochian had to find a fullback and backup players.

At the beginning of his 18th season as Head Football Coach at Lyman Hall, the extremely low number of players and the recent turnover in assistant coaches further negatively fueled his decision-making on whether to remain at Lyman Hall or take advantage of the football coaching opportunities elsewhere.

A NEW COACHING STAFF

As with all high school football teams, there is a steady turnover in assistant coaches. The shine comes off the apple rather quickly for assistant coaches as you toil in drilling the same techniques day after day. For most assistant coaches, there are few decisions to make. Just as with all teaching, not every player learns at the same pace, and with the same learning style as the player standing next to him. In Connecticut, most assistant coaches are not trained teachers, so the pedagogy or methods of successful instruction have to be carefully monitored by the head coach, a sizable challenge. To wit, while most assistant coaches claim a love for the game, the grind of "teaching the techniques of football" are something less than fun.

This is primarily due to the necessity of needing an individual coach to teach the specific techniques for each of the many positions on offense, defense, and the kicking game. Varsity basketball at Lyman Hall High School flourished with only one varsity coach for almost half a century. Football with its positional demands required several coaches, each with different responsibilities.

In terms of time management, so critical in teaching and learning, a head coach must plan for the maximum use of practice time so that all members of the team are improving at their respective positions. This means that there is a teaching plan for the instruction of fundamentals, group work (i.e., offensive line, backfield, defensive backs, etc.), and a team drill period when everything comes together. As a beginning point, the head coach must teach each assistant coach precisely the techniques that need to be acquired by the players at each position. Just as importantly, the assistant coach must assume the professional teaching demeanor and not become a caricature of some image of one of his coaches he had as a player. To be sure, just because you played the game doesn't mean you can coach it.

COACHING STABILITY

When there is stability on a high school football coaching staff, it usually indicates the team is winning with some regularity, and the coaches get along rather well together. Not too many assistant coaches hang around a losing team for very long.

At Lyman Hall High School, it took Head Coach Phil Ottochian some years to assemble a coaching staff who were first and foremost loyal, got along well together, and worked very hard to meet Coach Ottochian's demands. The varsity coaching staff of Andy Borelli, Jim Lynch, and Sean Meehan were together for seven years, and the success of those teams reflects their collective efforts. One by one, each left for greener pastures. By the end of 1983, all were gone from the staff along with others who made coaching contributions to the freshman teams.

All at once, Coach Ottochian was fresh out of seasoned coaches with no defensive coordinator. I had been on the coaching staff for seven years, coaching defensive backs and scouting our opponents each Friday and Saturday, rarely seeing one of our own games. Initially, Coach Ottochian was reluctant to turn over the defense unit to me, even though I had been with him longer than anyone. Then all of a sudden, Coach Ottochian was fresh out of coaches. In 1984 a new coaching staff had been assembled. They were young, enjoyed each other's company, and each had a nuanced understanding of the game, along with being excellent teachers.

The staff included Bobby Corazzini (line coach), Scott Ottochian (defensive end and receivers coach), John Gawlak (freshmen coach), John Wallace (freshman coach), and me (defensive coordinator). I had been one of Phil Ottochian's earliest friends in Wallingford, and I spent many hours with Phil during my first seven years on staff learning the nuances of the game.

For detail and my thousands of questions was Tony Marotta, who was on the staff from 1977-1980. Tony had incredible patience with me and encouraged my creativity in the game. Since I had no reference frame as a former player, Tony Marotta found me a sponge for information, and he was my go-to guy whom I would often bounce ideas and concepts without fear of criticism.

Once given the responsibility, I threw myself into the position. I had learned a lot over the years, but the most significant lessons learned was to build a defense (or offense) on the skills of the players you had on the team, not the flashy "coachingeese" espoused at coaching clinics.

As the 1985 Spring practices began, the formulation of a new defense was taking shape, but until it was done and ready to be unveiled by me to Coach Ottochian, we had to work with the defensive plan of the previous season, a 4-3 defense, that was appropriately named, "Weak."

SPRING PRACTICE – HALF LINE FOOTBALL

Unlike most sports, high school football coaches must adapt to their circumstances. While it is true that some secondary schools have field houses and artificial fields on which to practice and play, Lyman Hall High School had no such facilities in 1985. With the advent of women's sports, the varsity football practice field was tucked between a fenced-in softball field and another non-fenced softball field. The freshmen football practice field was a tiny land plot over the fenced west end of the varsity game football field. The varsity practice area had one metal crossbar. When it rained or snowed, the practice field became an instant bed of mud. It was always a head-shaking dichotomy that a crew of workmen would prepare the two adjacent softball fields and gingerly avoid even putting lines on the football practice field. Such was the continuing saga of Lyman Hall football, but Coach Ottochian rarely complained, choosing to find an area of grass somewhere in the area, avoiding the worn-out dirt surface or the sea of mud.

Most of the spring sessions were spent on the offensive side of the ball. From the first day of spring practice, one could see how talented the offensive line was and how they worked so well together. What was most compelling was how amazingly intelligent the entire team was, and the offensive line was nothing short of brilliant. As they were taught the techniques and adjustments necessary against various defensive alignments (fronts), they internalized the information and rarely needed a mental refresher course. The starters on the offensive line materialized rather quickly in 1985 with Greg Myerson at the center, David Klaverkamp, and Kevin Distante at the guards with Bill Goldstein and Ralph Riley at the tackles.

The newly constituted coaching staff were blunt in their spring assessment of our defensive team. As we installed the 4-3, "Weak" defense, a gap-control concept, the candid talk directed at me made it clear that we had no linebackers, which was alarming with a three-linebacker defense. However, what was apparent to me was how mentally sharp this group of roughly 20 guys were. They picked up everything so quickly, and it was clear that no matter what the final product of the defense turned out to be, they would understand it. Clearly, this was the wrong defense for us at this time.

Although we added some seniors that we greatly needed in Bill Sheridan, Ray Cormier, and Bob Lampo, we were severely undermanned with the shortest roster in the history of Lyman Hall High School football as we held our final Spring practice session with 19 players, so we were unable to conduct a meaningful final scrimmage, opting for a half-line scrimmage.

During the summer months, most of the team attended a football camp in New York where they were matched up against some good teams. This was the first time that the 1985 Trojans would employ the concept of everyone plays both ways. While the New York teams had ample players to play two-platoon football, one group to play offense and another defense, the Lyman Hall players lined up for offense and then turned around and played defense with essentially the same players. The camp was a productive experience at least on offense, but the defense plan would have to be dramatically altered.

THE SUMMER OF RESERVATION & RIGOR

After the return of the members of the team who traveled to New York for football camp with Coach Ottochian, weight training and conditioning became everyone's focus. (That is except me.) After their positive experience in New York, moving the ball on offense against talented teams whose players went one-way (offense or defense), the team members knew they could be a good team in 1985. There were still decisions to be made about positions, and there were missing pieces. The members of the '85 team were most diligent in their weight lifting and conditioning, realizing that any member of the team could, and probably would be, required to play both offense, defense, and in the kicking game.

Coach Scott Ottochian pushed every man in the weight room. If someone didn't have rides to and from the school, Scottie never hesitated to give them a lift. He was intense, ensuring a serious attitude from every member of the team. For members of the '85 coaching staff, a player's byplay or occasional portent to socialize was not tolerated.

Chapter 70

Do What You Do Best

As I have stated in previously written works or in speeches I had made since my undergraduate days around the country, I often articulated an edict that finding one's strength is only worthwhile if you learn how to use the gift to serve the greater good. Once Phil Ottochian officially asked me to "run the defense," it was as if Newton's concepts of gravity were no longer applicable to my feet. First and last, I was a teacher, and the beauty of teaching for me was the application of creativity that could be brought to bear to teaching and learning.

Since my earliest days, watching the big men with black helmets at Doolittle Park, all I wanted was to wear a Lyman Hall shirt with a number. Unfortunately, that privilege was denied me when I was a student at LHHS. Now, in this place and time, I had been given the privilege I so ardently prayed for those many years ago. No, I would never run with a football like Rick Angelone or Mike Nesti. I would never sink a 30-foot basket like Fran Stupakevich or blast homeruns like Charlie Inguaggiato ... but maybe now, with the gifts that I had been so blessed, I might serve my school and the young men who are privileged to wear the blue and white.

As my daily chronicle (writing each day since I was 12) so attests, I watched the brittle super-8 films of our opponents with every moment that I wasn't with my twin daughters. It was obsessive, and my tool of choice was a super-8 movie projector and a roll of scotch tape. Those frail strips of super-8 movie film broke with regularity, and I constantly taped them back together. Next to me were stacks of lined pads where I inscribed every formation, first opponent steps, and blocking schemes. I didn't know a lot of common coaching terminology, except that which Phil (Ottochian) and Tony Marotta taught me. In my relative pretensive manner (a fault since childhood), I thought most of it archaic anyway. I began to use more clearly descriptive jargon that I might use to categorize propensity, decision-making more efficient to design a common language more capable of teaching from a place of understanding.

As the concepts for "the best possible defensive plan" crystalized with every hour I toiled at the projector, I knew that no matter what I came up with, I would have to be able to sell it to Coach Ottochian. As I learned from the seven previous seasons with Phil, he would ask specific questions of me. They were predictable, but if I could not answer those questions, it was back to the projector, my scouting charts, and the data they generated. In the past, his most common question relative to the scouting I performed and the scouting reports I wrote was, "... How do you know this"? You never guessed when answering Phil. Although I was rarely involved with any decision-making before becoming defensive coordinator, I learned to look at football decisions from every angle and then finding more angles to evaluate. You had to earn Phil's trust, and it never came easily. The collection of data, analysis, leading to planning had always been something I relished in life, but serving in a decision-making role for my dear ole' Lyman Hall High School was on the edge of a dream for me.

As with most ideas that take form, there is usually a "jet-stream" moment when there is a breakthrough, and you know you got something special. I kept asking myself the questions Phil would pose to me, such as "what if the offense gives you two tight ends"?

Finally, on August 11[th,] it was all done. At least all the pieces and concepts were on paper. I went over to Phil's home on Courtland Drive and found him working in his yard. He knew I was coming over, and we adjourned to his kitchen table, where I showed him my ideas. Phil was skeptical from the beginning, and although I was prepared for his battery of questions, he would not endorse the blitzing game formula ... at least not yet. He told me I could spend a *little* time on it in practice, but we would stay with the "Weak 4-3 defense". Thank God for small victories.

GUY RUSSO

An obscure event occurred near the end of spring practice that I dismissed as momentary enthusiasm. Guy Russo, a senior who had played on the scout team in 1984 as a lineman, approached me after practice and boldly stated that he was the starting middle linebacker, a position he had never played. The brief conversation was overheard by Coach John Wallace, who walked with me a short distance and stated, "Hoager" (his nickname for me), I told you ... you have NO linebackers on this team".

Guy's declaration that day began an incredible side-story of the 1985 season, a magnificent singleness of preparation. With guile, dogged determination, and an unparalleled level of commitment, Guy subjected himself to a grueling daily schedule of weight training, distance running with weights on his back, and intense study. He transformed himself into a magnificent and dominating linebacker who fully understood the rather revolutionary new Lyman Hall defense in a matter of months.

Guy came to my home at least twice a week, drinking gallons of ice tea as I taught him every aspect of the new blitzing defense. He was relentless in his questions, asking about the responsibilities of every member of the defense. From one meeting with him to the next, he retained everything I brought before him. Guy knew the defense in and out before any of the coaches even heard an opening introduction about the concepts.

The season neared as we participated in the regular grind of double days, circuit training, and scrimmages in heat and humidity, I was still compelled to install the "Weak 4-3" defense that Coach Ottochian wanted, but Guy Russo was constantly in my ear to, ... "stop wasting time with the "weak" and put the new defense in." We spent far too little time on defense in pre-season practices, but I installed the new defense, stage by stage. I never went fast enough for Guy, whether in the classroom or on the practice field. Guy was indicative of the 22-member team who completed double-days in 1985. They were brilliant, challenging, and confident.

BRAINS ARE US

As we entered the long double days of pre-season practice with intense heat and humidity, we had to alter our planning to accommodate so few players. As we started the first day of pre-season practice, we had 22 persons in uniform. This meant that each team member received plenty of individual repetitions on the various positional techniques. The strength of the team was our offensive line, led by their coach, Bob Corazzini. Bobby was a defensive back in his high school and college playing days, but like the other coaches, he had great teaching skills.

Coach Corazzini would often remark, "All (the offensive linemen) were savvy and football smart." He was particularly impressed by David Klaverkamp, stating, "David usually led the discussions and would ask if they (the linemen) could make certain adjustments or block plays in a different way. If they proved that they could do what they wanted to change by the end of a Tuesday (installation day), we would go with it".

Corazzini was most adept at preparing for the hazards of weather, especially on the dirt, mud, and stoney fields on which we were forced to practice and play many games. He prepared his large and athletic linemen to execute their many finesse blocks (pulls and traps) no matter what the circumstances, especially rain and snow. As Corazzini described his linemen's work, "To make sure we did not have to limit ourselves in bad weather games, we would spend individual drill time on something we called the "mud pit." Outside the concession stand/equipment storage room, there was a water faucet. I would take the hose and wet down the grass (if we had any), and we practiced our steps and blocks in something less than ideal conditions. Mud became second nature to these thoroughbreds (the offensive linemen)".

Chapter 71

Installing the New Defense

The defense that I had put so much time in developing since last December (1985) had a whole new nomenclature. It was not a read and react defense that was commonplace in high school football. In concept, it was a fast-attacking approach that made offensive linemen vulnerable to blocking *the wrong man*, no matter how well-drilled they happened to be. The key was knowing how an opponent blocks their offensive plays, especially their passing plays. That required study, but it was one of the few things in life I did well.

Coach Ottochian usually gave me 30-45 minutes a day for defense that included individual technique work, group drills, and a team period reserved for opponent preparation. We did a lot of our adjustment work on the blackboard in the locker room, but Coach Ottochian would always throw a lot of "maybe's and what-if's" at me, so it became part of our coaching methodology to prepare for the most bizarre possibilities.

Led by so many highly intelligent and perceptive young men, I was able to teach the new defensive schemes quite rapidly while still paying archaic homage to the "Weak 4-3 defense".

I had some options for pass coverage in this defensive plan, but for the most part, this was a man coverage defense, and it counted on our blitzing linebackers and defensive linemen to get to the ball carriers behind the line of scrimmage.

Although redundant, we couldn't afford to get anyone hurt on the defensive unit. It seems foolhardy to say it, but if we lost almost any member of the defense, we had far too few replacement players.

It all started with middle linebacker Guy Russo (#56), who had learned every person's responsibilities on the defense. He knew who had coverage on what potential receiver and worked as hard or harder than anyone else studying our extensive scouting reports ... and Guy played only defense but was a backup offensive guard. At the strong or (SAM) linebacker was Randy Pelletier (#40), a junior, who at season's start was also our starting tight end. Randy was aligned to our opponent's tight end side (3-man side in most formations). The open side linebacker or (WILL) was the lightning-quick, Eddie Charbonneau (#24), who was our backup tailback. I do not recall any of these three linebackers ever coming out of a game, and they played every snap of the season.

In the secondary, our quarterback, Todd Barket (#5), was the free safety. The strong safety (aligned to the tight end or strong side of the offensive formation) was senior Tri-captain Matt Schmitt (#35), who was our starting fullback. At the cornerbacks were starting tailback, Vincent Poggio (#33), who I usually assigned to cover the opponent's best receiver, and the cunning Scott Audet (#4), whom our opponents often targeted, but Scottie (Velcro was his nickname) made a few of the season's most significant interceptions. The only substitute for any of these defensive backs was the extremely versatile Al Ferreira (#7). Al was our punt returner and started at split end for much of the season. Chances are if we needed to substitute for one of our three inside linebackers ... it would have been Al Ferreira.

The defensive linemen were uncompromisingly outstanding. Each of them started on the offensive line. Bill Goldstein (#55) was at one defensive tackle, the only junior at 5-11, 255; David Klaverkamp, defensive tackle, was 6-2, 210; Greg

Myerson, the defensive end, was 6-3, 230; and Ralph Riley, the defensive end was 6-3, 245.

Of the eleven starters on defense, only Ed Charbonneau and Guy Russo played only defense. As we began an 11-game season (there would be a 12th game), the proverbial house of cards that existed if we lost a player to injury was a constant cause for concern, but Coach Ottochian insisted, "play 'em all for as long as they last." As it turned out, with a few injuries to deal with, these men of 1985 went the distance.

Chapter 72

Starting Unusual for an Unusual Season

Generally speaking, pre-season scrimmages for high school football teams are designed to finalize the starters at each position and compete against other teams in a controlled environment. For the 1985 Trojans, there was an additional priority, "Don't get anyone injured." If just one member of our team with starting responsibilities got injured, it would impact other parts of the team.

Although the coaches carefully evaluated every one of the 24 members of the team to find starters and back-ups players at each position, it was clear that the starters on offense would likely be the starters on defense. Additionally, starters at the skill positions other than Vincent Poggio at tailback were not finalized as we approached the preparation week for the first game of the season.

During the scrimmages, both Glenn Root and Todd Barket split time at quarterback, but Ottochian was having difficulty deciding who his quarterback would be to open the season. After the last scrimmage, Coach Ottochian talked with the team's senior members and asked for their input as to who the starting quarterback should be. They endorsed their classmate, Todd Barket, who had been playing wide receiver.

The scrimmages revealed a couple of team facts worthy of note. The LHHS offense had little trouble moving the ball in the scrimmages as the offensive line of Klaverkamp, Riley,

Myerson, Goldstein, and Distante were able to block any defense, no matter the players who opposed them. Although Ottochian insisted that we continue to utilize the "weak 4-3" defense, it proved to be exactly as its namesake suggested .... "weak."

Interestingly, on the day of the opening game, September 13, 1985, the Record-Journal (morning newspaper) ran a pre-game story that reflected how uncertain the Lyman Hall starting lineup was in the mind of Coach Ottochian. In the article Todd Barket was listed as a probable starter at wide receiver, along with Matt Schmitt and Scott Audet. It also indicated a starting fullback, who had quit the team before the season began. When the Trojans lined up for their first offensive snap of the new season against Maloney High School, Barket was the quarterback, Schmitt was the fullback.

There was a keen sense of uncertainty as we prepared for our first game. For the first time, Wallingford and Meriden high schools would participate in an unusual Friday evening double-header at Ceppa Field in Meriden, the only area field with lights. The first game was to be Lyman Hall versus Maloney High School, and Sheehan High School would be opposed by Platt High School in the nightcap, usually the opening game of the season for Lyman Hall.

As this was my first foray as defensive coordinator and given Coach Ottochian's commitment to the standard 4-3 defense, I wasn't sure how much decision-making would be required against Maloney.

Chapter 73

Maloney High School

– First Game
September 13, 1985

The opening moment of discovery for the 1985 Lyman Hall football team began this day, at Ceppa Field in Meriden against the Maloney Spartans of Head Coach Rob Syzmaszek. Rob was an outstanding coach (and a wonderful friend) who believed in multiple formations, but like Phil Ottochian, was steadfast in his penchant to run the football.

As part of the season-opening football doubleheader at Ceppa Field, Sheehan High School would face Platt High School in the second game of the double-dip. Up first at 6:00 pm with the sun just beginning to set in the west, Lyman Hall faced a Maloney High School team with great running backs.

As we lined up for the opening kickoff, I stood next to Phil Ottochian as I often would over the next few decades, and he unsmilingly reminded me, "Stay in base, (meaning the Weak 4-3)".

Our guys were ready to roll with the new defense if, or whenever, I called it, but as this was my first game as defensive coordinator, I needed to be patient and avoid Phil's ire. I had watched Phil interact with previous defensive play-callers in Andy Borelli and Jim Lynch, but this was different. Any call I made other than "base" (Weak 4-3) was of a language only the team, and I fully understood. Despite the time I spent in front of the coaches at the blackboard, describing the defense, it often felt as though I was teaching Latin declensions. The thought of ticking off Phil made me more anxious than anything the Maloney offense might do, but I knew our relationship as Head Coach and defensive coordinator would take time to evolve. Act 1, Scene 1, ... curtain rising!

On defense, I did as Phil wanted me to do ... at least for the first quarter of football .... Before the game was half old, the defense would turn itself over to what would become the identity of '85, "a high pressure, blitzing defense," the like of which hadn't been seen before.

Lyman Hall gained the early lead as Guy Russo blocked a Victor Matias punt, giving the Trojans great field position. Fullback Matt Schmitt ran for 17 yards on first down. Five plays later, Vinnie Poggio scored the season's first touchdown from 2 yards out. As our <u>modus operandi</u> would be for kicking extra points most of the season, Greg Myerson missed the extra point attempt.

Playing that "base" defense on Maloney's next possession, tailback, Willie Dudley, broke into the Lyman Hall secondary but was hit on two sides by Guy Russo and Todd Barket, forcing a Dudley fumble as Matt Schmitt recovered. That was how the early going went with hard-hitting and Maloney having difficulty maintaining any long drives, despite Dudley's darting running.

With the Blue and White shifting into the "Vee-Formation," Vincent Poggio broke out for a long gain of 20 yards, down to the two-yard line. Schmitt powered in from two yards for the second Trojan TD. Quarterback Todd Barket engineered the bootleg, throwing to Schmitt for the two-point conversion, and Lyman Hall was up 14-0.

With Lyman Hall still playing the base 4-3 defense, the Spartan running game behind Willie Dudley began to gain significant chunks of yardage. Maloney scored its first touchdown on an 18-yard run by Matias, and Dudley ran in the two-point play, making the score 14-8.

As we took the field to play defense mid-way through the second quarter, I unveiled a blitz, signaling in the call "Bandit" to Guy Russo, who called the defenses in the huddle.

There was no settling-in period for the new attacking defense as Russo and Schmitt dropped Dudley for a loss. I never looked down the sideline at Coach Ottochian for approval or comment. I just kept calling our aggressive blitzing schemes that immediately resulted in havoc being played on the Maloney offense with multiple tackles of Maloney runners for losses. Maloney did score in the third quarter on a long run by Dudley, but that was the last time I called "Weak-3". From then on, I was committed to blitzing, virtually on every down, and the Spartans were unable to earn but a few first downs for the remainder of the contest.

On offense, Coach Ottochian began to milk the Ceppa Field clock with methodical runs by Poggio and Schmitt, but when Maloney got on offense, the possibility of a long touchdown was always a concern as the blitz required that we attack every gap, minimizing our team pursuit to the ball carrier. There was a demonstrable enthusiasm on defense whenever we hit a Maloney ball carrier in the backfield, and we were doing a lot of that.

In a critical sequence of the game in the fourth quarter, Maloney took possession on the Spartans 37-yard line. With the complete variety of blitzes coming at Maloney on every down, Lyman Hall linebackers Randy Pelletier and Guy Russo stopped Robinson for a two-yard loss on first down. On second down Matt Schmitt stopped Robinson for a one-yard loss. On 3rd & 13, Dudley was given the ball, looking to bounce the play outside, but Trojan defensive tackle Billy Goldstein drilled Dudley for a 2-yard loss, and the Spartans were forced to punt the ball away. That would be the last Maloney threat of the game.

Vincent Poggio carried the ball for 173 yards for Lyman Hall as the Trojans won their first game of the year, 21-14 over Maloney. However, the most compelling aspect of the game was the birth of the new Lyman Hall defense that would soon become known as "Blitz-O-Mania."

After our game, the first contest in the Meriden-Wallingford doubleheader, some of the coaches stuck around to scout Platt, our next opponent. Besides seeing a hard-hitting Platt team, what we witnessed was our first glimpse of Sheehan quarterback Brian Salisbury, who would come to occupy a lot of my time in the season ahead in film study and preparation. There was some surprise that Sheehan beat the Platt team of head coach Tom Ryan, but then again, there were plenty of surprised Wallingford folks that Lyman Hall was able to defeat a high-powered Maloney squad.

Chapter 74

Platt High School

– Second Game
September 21, 1985

Having seen the gold-helmeted Platt High School football team in person, the coaches acknowledged how imposing a team they were. We knew our offensive line would be facing a formidable defense, but this was just the next challenge for Klaverkamp, Myerson, Riley, Distante, and Goldstein.

In the Sunday coach's meeting after the Maloney game, we watched the game film, and although I was in the habit of writing copious notes at meetings, the coaches had little to say about the Maloney game, wanting to get on with the prep for Platt. Somewhere in the middle of the film review, Coach Ottochian spoke out, not calling me out by name, and stated, "Coach (meaning me), don't fall in love with the stunts (blitzes)."

On Saturday, September 21, 1985, a steamy hot day, a big powerful Platt High School football team arrived at Fitzgerald Field on the campus of LHHS in Wallingford for the game against the Trojans. Despite our win and Platt's loss in the opening game, the Waterbury Republican (newspaper) expected a Platt victory over the Trojans, the first of four times Lyman Hall would be predicted to come out on the short end of a game in 1985.

Coming off his big performance over Maloney in the first game of the season, Vincent Poggio would receive the lion-share of the attention from the Platt defense, who repeatedly called out his name to alert their defense where Poggio was aligned before most snaps. For the Meriden team, Todd McFadden was a superb tailback, possessing size, power, and speed. Quarterback Gavin Sheridan was a quality thrower for the Panthers who would challenge the attacking Trojan defense. Making matters worse for the Blue and White would be the return of 6-3, 245-pound tackle Carlos Pena, who missed the opener due to injury.

With the oppressive heat that reached 92 degrees, the Trojans opened the game with a successful drive of eight plays, highlighted by Poggio's 42-yard run. Quarterback Todd Barket bootlegged ("waggle" for those who remember the play calls) and threw to tight end Randy Pelletier for the touchdown for a 6-0 lead. Yes, Lyman Hall missed the extra point.

After the Maloney game, I put in a few more blitz variations and wasted little time with that "base" defense. Immediately, the blitz reaped rewards, penetrating the Platt offensive front, forcing Platt punts. However, Lyman Hall could not capitalize offensively, despite two successful screens to Poggio. Lyman Hall committed three key penalties and one huge dropped pass that kept the score at 6-0 at the half.

Platt came out of the locker room and imposed its power running game on the Trojans. The Panthers grinding running back, McFadden often seemed to be carrying Blue defenders on his back as he made runs of 11 and 26 yards in that first drive as Platt tied the score on a 3-yard run by the 6-1, 190 pound McFadden.

LHHS answered immediately on their next possession as Vincent (Poggio) broke off a run of 38 yards, resulting in a first down on the Platt 21-yard line. Poggio scored on a 15-yard run two downs later, giving the Trojans a 12-6 lead.

The game grinded on in the heat as Lyman Hall made many first downs, only to see potential drives stalled by mishandled handoffs and snaps from center. Platt began to feel the Blue and White defense's impact as Platt runners were caught behind the line of scrimmage five times, with defensive ends Greg Myerson and Ralph Riley doing much of the damage. By the end of the third quarter, the Trojan defense had sacked the Platt quarterback five times.

Platt had one more quality possession in the contest. After a long punt return, the Trojans almost got their 6th sack of the day, drilling Sheridan as he threw quickly to his left. The LHHS defense blitzed (this time with an "Express" call) as corner Scott Audet (#4) maintained great inside leverage, intercepting the pass and returning it for a 47-yard touchdown, the decisive play of the game.

Vince Poggio ran for 172 yards on 27 carries, and Matt Schmitt had 49 yards on 11 carries for the Blue & White. Platt's Todd McFadden had a good day himself, rushing for 112 yards on 23 carries. The most important statistic from the Platt game was that the Trojans were 2-0, heading into its traditional battle with Cheshire.

Chapter 75

Cheshire High School

– Third Game
September 30, 1985

There was a wonderful haze of good tidings as we prepared for our third game against Cheshire High School, but the last week of September in 1985, Hurricane Gloria moved into the region. In many towns across Connecticut, schools were closed, hurricane tape went up on windows throughout Wallingford as the entire region prepared for the worst tropical storm since Hurricane Donna in 1960.

The storm made landfall along Long Island on September 27, 1985, with a much weaker system than had been feared, but like most high schools, we lost practice time, just when we needed to tighten down the bolts of our defense. Gloria's strong winds wiped out power and telephone service in Wallingford for periods of time. Guy Russo (our middle linebacker), casting caution to the wind (literally), came to my home unannounced on Thursday evening, and we watched the Cheshire film and broke down the scouting charts until almost midnight.

I took him through my film breakdown process as I needed to get my work completed for the game. I thought he would get bored with my rather tedious film analysis procedures like most of our coaches did, but "Guy-Guy" (my nickname for him; his real name was Gaetano) was engaged every minute we were together in the cramped tiny room at the back of my garage. The sound of our voices was often blocked out by the sheets of hard rain banging on the sliding glass door.

Parenthetically, that little room with warped wood paneled walls and two lawn chairs and my portable projection screen would play a significant role in the events of 1985. During the Fall of 1985, other than my working hours in Hartford (as a member of the Connecticut State Department of Education) and my time on the practice field, I would usually spend four to ten hours a day in that room. I would often plug in an old Victrola (record player) and play one of the five long-playing records, over and over and over. The isolation of that room allowed me to concentrate and serve the school and team of my youthful dreams and of a love that comforted me in the lonely moments.

Cheshire employed a multiple formation offense that required an added layer of on-the-field communication. The team intelligence that always impressed me with the '85 gang came more into focus as the defense had to make several coverage checks. We had roughly two days to teach all of the checks and then apply those adjustments to each blitz I planned to call. The guys did a magnificent job of learning all this information with almost no appreciable practice time due to the hurricane.

After victories over difficult opponents, Maloney and Platt, in the opening two weeks of the 1985 season, our Lyman Hall team was feeling pretty good about itself, heading into game three against a pass-oriented Cheshire team that was scheduled for Saturday, September 28th. (Those were the days of Saturday football ... what the LHHS teams of today are missing.)

Then the heavy rains came on Friday night into Saturday morning, and the game was postponed until Monday. No one had artificial playing fields at that time, and the Cheshire field was deemed unplayable for Sunday. Despite the rains, the temperatures were in the high 80's and the humidity was brutal on that Monday afternoon.

The planning for facing Cheshire fit in well with our development as a defensive football team as the Rams gave us a lot of new formations that would test our communication that was critical to our success in this game and beyond. The defensive "Blue" played really well in this Housatonic League game, and we needed it because we kept turning the ball over on offense, five times to be exact.

In fact, Cheshire only crossed the LHHS 40 yard line ONCE in the entire game. The Ram quarterback was the victim of the Trojan blitzes, resulting in six sacks that limited the strong-armed Jeff DelRosso. The LHHS defense held Cheshire to a total of 42 yards rushing. In one memorable moment in the second quarter, the Cheshire QB opened up to his right, trying to set up to pass. A blitzing Guy Russo beat the block of the Ram right guard (no small thanks to the gap-slants of tackles Bill Goldstein and David Klaverkamp). The Cheshire passer seeing the lightning-quick Russo coming right down his throat, turned quickly to his left and was unceremoniously upended by Ralph Riley.

Lyman Hall scored late in the first quarter on a 5-yard pass from Todd Barket to Randy Pelletier that followed a 25 yard run by Vin Poggio. We were still living under the delusion that we could kick an extra point, so our kick failed, and we led 6-0.

With the Blue and White continuing to fumble away promising drives, that score remained the same until the 4th quarter. Despite once again racking up the yards, Vinnie got hit pretty hard in this game, fumbling a few times, and a rib injury forced him to leave the playing field. Vincent rushed for 135 yards on 19 carries and was coming close to breaking the career rushing mark of the legendary Rick Angelone.

With Poggio out of the game, Ed Charbonneau (#24) took over at tailback, and Al Ferreira (#7) became the cornerback. With Vince sidelined, there was immediate concern about his availability for the next week's game against state-ranked Derby.

Early in the 4th quarter, a Cheshire fumble recovered by free safety Todd Barket gave us reasonably good field position, and Coach "O" stayed on the ground with Matt Schmitt and Charbonneau carrying the ball. Matt scored from five yards out, and a pass from Barket to Pelletier for the two-point conversion gave us a 14-0 lead.

With the pressuring LHHS defense holding Cheshire without a first down for more than 10 minutes, late into the 4th quarter, Charbonneau broke away for a 22-yard touchdown that sealed the victory for the Trojans, 21-0. Oh ... by the way ... Greg Myerson successfully kicked the extra point. That hint of sarcasm is intended.

Fullback Matt Schmitt was a work-horse in this game, carrying 17 times for 59 yards. Those carries into the middle of the Cheshire defense was no small feat considering that Matt was our strong safety and never came out of the game.

My thoughts on the bus ride home were typically about the next opponent, making for an increasingly nervous stomach because the foe was Derby. Pre-season polls from the Waterbury Republican to the New Haven Register selected the Red Raiders to vie for the league championship with Shelton and end up in the Class S State Title game. I remember feeling very uneasy because we had a short week of preparation, having had to play Cheshire on that Monday.

As I left the locker room for home on that Monday after the Cheshire victory, I was surely not focused on my driving. Automotive operation was never my strong suit, so as I tugged and pulled on that steering wheel with (no power steering on that little Pinto), I turned down past Harrison Park towards North Colony Road to pick up a quick hamburger at McDonald's. I was not paying attention. My mind was squarely on Derby, not on the cars in front of me.

I ran headlong into the car in front of me, going down the hill. The accident was terrible as I creamed the front of the car and did some nasty damage to the vehicle in front of me. No one was hurt except for the bump on my forehead and nose. My first thought was, ... "is this going to screw up coaching this week"?

The first policeman on the scene asked me if I was all right and then inquired if I coached at Lyman Hall (since I had my pullover on). I remember he was more interested if we beat Cheshire than if I was well enough not to go to the hospital.

Chapter 76

Derby High School

Fourth Game
October 5, 1985

My chronicle entry of September 30, 1985, stated, "As I loaded the Derby film in my super-8 projector for the long night ahead of me to break down the Red Raiders, I wonder if this 3-0 start to the season would fizzle out. There is such little time to prepare our defense".

The day after the Cheshire game, the team was a little banged up at Tuesday's practice, especially Vincent (Poggio). This meant Al Ferreira got most of the reps (repetitions) at corner, but he still had to learn the coverage for the other three defensive back positions.

I am thankful for the guys on this team. Although they are apt to engage in some inside story references, giggling from time to time, they never lose a second of concentration at practice. We need every drop of prep time as Derby has an excellent veteran coaching staff, under third-year head coach Charlie DiCenso, a man of great integrity. Derby, with great personnel, was yet another offense with many formations and always possessing a handful of gadget plays ready to throw at you.

ANGRY WEATHER, AGAIN

WELI radio reported early cancellations of many of the New Haven area high school football games, but despite the magnitude of the 1985 Derby-Lyman Hall game, Phil Ottochian, ever the optimist, scarcely considered postponing the game. The combination of the Blue and White's early success is viewed as something of an apparition by the student body, and the threatening weather kept the crowd to under a few hundred spectators.

In the long 61-year history of the Housatonic League that began in 1924, the Lyman Hall-Derby football game (except for the period of football cancellation at LHHS from 1937-1949) would usually take place near season's end. In 1985 the league schedule was shaken up and flipped over, and the Red Raiders would play the Trojans early in the season.

Derby was 3-0 heading into the game, which meant instant recognition for the perennial football power in the state polls. LHHS was also 3-0 for the first time since 1977, but Lyman Hall football's lingering negative reputation, espoused by Connecticut sportswriters (the voters in the state polls), suggested that the Trojans would have to do a lot more work before receiving state ranking. Incidentally, as the first state high school football polls were taken in 1985, votes were given to LHHS opponents Shelton and Sheehan as Derby was ranked ninth in the state heading its October 5th game versus Lyman Hall. Although unbeaten to this point in the season, Lyman Hall received no votes from the 15 sportswriters who voted in the state polls.

Derby was loaded with talent, with a double-barreled threat at quarterback in Mark Searles and Cliff King. Derby led the league in scoring coming into the game, averaging 34 points per game, a remarkable achievement in those days, before the pass-happy high school game of the present day. Their 4-4 defense was a quality front with large defensive tackles.

The game was a mere few minutes old, and when the skies opened, and sheets of wind-swept rain crossed the playing field. We were all thoroughly drenched mid-way through the first quarter, and the dropping temperatures made the chills and body tremors of cold and rain an additional challenge for all … well, all except for Coach "O." The weather never seemed to impact him.

The weather notwithstanding, the defensive game plan was to blitz on every down. It seems bold to say, but that is precisely what we planned and what we did. We added a few new schemes for the Red Raiders, taking advantage of some emerging players on the defensive-unit.

The Cheshire game film revealed that the men on "D" were taking to the blitzing techniques. Most people, even coaches, view a blitz as a "run-to-this-gap." It is, in fact, a whole different mindset, based on timing and studying of your opponent, a finite analysis of the individual players in front of you. Any member of the '85 team will probably recall the hard copy scouting reports given out on Wednesday or Thursday of each week that included opponent statistics, photos of starters, and complete play charts. It was quite an instructional moment for the members of the team each week.

THE GAME BEGINS

We kicked off to Derby, and on their first series, they actually went backward, resulting in minus 4 yards on the first three running plays of the game. They punted on 4th down, and the Trojan offense came to life early. Derby was keying on Vincent Poggio (as all teams did), who was still banged up from the Cheshire game with rib and thumb injuries and stopped him without gain on first down. On second and ten, Coach Ottochian called a waggle (bootleg), and with Vinnie faking right, Todd Barket got on the left corner quickly with Kevin Distante blocking in front. Todd ran for a 43-yard touchdown. To be noted – Rick Poggio (Vin's dad and a mainstay on our sideline) loudly shouted, "I didn't think he could run that fast," … and Todd's father, Tony (standing with Rick as always) answered back, "Neither did I.")

No surprise after our difficulties kicking extra points ....
We missed the point after, but LHHS had the 6-0 lead.

The blitzing Trojan defense had our boys in the Derby
backfield on virtually every play. In this pivotal game, we
SACKED the Derby quarterbacks EIGHT TIMES with 12
tackles behind the line of scrimmage. Following our first
touchdown, Guy Russo (who had 4.5 sacks in this game)
drilled Derby tailback Jim Lewis as Randy Pelletier, also
blitzing on the play, recovered Lewis's fumble on the Derby
12 yard line. Coach Ottochian wasted no time coming back
to the "waggle" once again as Barket hit the tight end, Randy
Pelletier, for a touchdown. We went for two, were unsuccessful,
but we held an early 12-0 lead.

We had put in a punt block at the outset of the season,
but it always seemed that someone was out of place, failed to
push a blocker's shoulder, or didn't get off on the snap. Guy
Russo got a punt block in the Maloney game, but we had not
been consistent enough on the play since then. After we went
up 12-0, the team's enthusiasm was palatable; everyone was
pumped up on the field. Derby's next series was once again
held without a yard as the Derby QB was hit in the back by
Guy Russo before he took two steps from center. Some of
these hits were loud collisions, and early on, Derby's starting
quarterback Searles was taking a terrific beating. On 4th and
11, Derby punted from its own 26. Eddie Charbonneau broke
through the Derby punt protection's right side, blocked the
punt, and recovered on Red Raider 17-yard line.

Make no mistake, Derby was an outstanding team in 1985,
and their team's toughness and legacy of football achievement
that evolved over decades of highly successful teams reared
its masterful head after the punt block. The Red Raider
defense stiffened. Runs by Matt Schmitt and Vin Poggio were
minimal, but we were still moving forward. Unfortunately,
the physicality was taking its toll on Vince with the injuries
he sustained against Cheshire. Following a 5-yard waggle
from Barket to Schmitt, we were on the one-yard line. Coach
Ottochian lined the offense up in his vaunted "Vee formation,"
and Vinnie took it in for a touchdown. Poggio came out of the

game, and Ed Charbonneau took over at tailback for the two-point conversion try. Barket threw to Eddie for the two points, and the LHHS men were up 20-0.

This Derby game was a typical LHHS-Derby, hard-hitting clash, played in a ceaseless rainstorm where players on both sides were saying they could not see in the driving downpour. Immediately after the Blue and White went up 20-0, Derby ran back the ensuing kickoff. Rick Sheehy returned the ball 82 yards for the touchdown as the extra point kick failed.

With time running down in the first half and the rain now raking the field in thick sheets of water, you could hardly hear the person next to you. Despite the rain, the Trojans passed on their next possession, and Derby intercepted with the Red Raiders reaching the LHHS four-yard line. This was a critical time in the game, and Derby called time out to carefully call the next few plays that could cut the deficit to a one-touchdown game.

Derby closed their offensive line splits, attempting to negate the blitzing attack of Lyman Hall. Consequently, that shortened the corner for our outside blitzes to arrive a little sooner despite the mud inside the ten-yard line. A goal-line stand was required, and the "Blue and White" defense, more Blue & Mud colored now, answered the call. With Russo, Schmitt, Pelletier, and Charbonneau continuing the onslaught, Derby lost 2 yards on their four downs, and the half arrived with Lyman Hall ahead 20-6.

SECOND HALF – MUD AND GUTS

Out of the locker room at halftime, we looked at our Fitzgerald Field as a standing water, sloggy mud surface. Coach Charles DiCenzo of Derby, one of the most honorable men in the high school coaching ranks, told his team not to stretch on the ground. As his team stretched while standing, one of his players slipped so badly that his feet came right out from under him, a rather comical sight. To be sure, this second half would be played on a treacherous surface.

The third quarter wasn't much for offense, but the defensive hits kept coming. On a play that I thought would have put the game out of reach, Derby QB Searles tried to pass to his tight end. Todd Barket intercepted and ran it back 60 yards or so for a touchdown. The play was called back for roughing the passer as Guy Russo, and Ed Charbonneau upended the Searles after he had thrown the ball. A close call, but it would have sealed the game.

FOURTH QUARTER

Derby's first series of the 4th period resulted in two monster hits for sacks. The first one by Russo resulted in a 7-yard sack. On the very next play, Matt Schmitt hit Searles from one side, and Randy Pelletier got him higher on the other. Searles did not get up, at least for a while. Chris King came in to replace Searles. On a 3rd and 24, he burned us for a 95-yard touchdown pass. Dumb me …. Should have changed to cover 3. I knew better!

Now with the score 20-12, late in the 4th quarter, Derby had a shot to tie the game. Todd got intercepted, and Derby had the first down on our 23-yard line. On the next play, a Red Raider got caught for holding, taking Russo to the ground. The next play, Bill Goldstein and Randy Pelletier stopped the ball carrier, resulting in a fumble that Derby recovered.

CRITICAL PLAY: On third down, defensive tackle Dave Klaverkamp blew by the Derby guard and center for a 7-yard sack of King that left the Red Raiders with a 4th and 20. They elected to punt. That play by David stopped the last possible Derby scoring threat.

FOOTNOTES OF DERBY

Charles DiCenzo, Derby Head Coach, remembered the game, "When we arrived at Lyman Hall for the game, it was just drizzling, but by half time, it was a monsoon. We were told to stay in the locker room at halftime as there was lightning. We had a couple of big plays in the game, but neither team could do much offensively with that mud and rain".

For the game, the LHHS defense held Derby to 31 yards rushing and a total of four first downs in the game. Including that long 95-yard TD pass, Derby threw for 145 yards. The Trojans sacked the Derby QB's eight times. Matt Schmitt led Lyman Hall with 66 yards on 18 carries as Vin Poggio was limited to a season low of 39 yards.

Derby High School would finish the season with a 9-2 record, losing on Thanksgiving to Shelton, 10-7, while the Trojans shutout Sheehan 40-0, giving Lyman Hall sole possession of the 1985 Housatonic League Championship. Coach DiCenzo recalls the 1985 season this way, "There were so many good teams in the league that year. Almost any team could have won (the league championship)."

Chapter 77

Branford High School

Fifth Game
October 12, 1985

After the victory over Derby, there was considerable concern that our 1985 football team would not be as "up" as they needed to be against Branford. As most quality football coaches acknowledge, it is impossible for your team to be at the same level of emotional readiness for every game. That is why pre-game pep talks are over-rated. Sometimes, even when you feel your team or unit isn't as totally focused as you think they need to be, nothing you can say will change it. You only hope they have enough in the tank to overcome.

There was more churning than just our unbeaten, 5-0 team. Coach Ottochian was beginning to feel most disturbed at the lack of attention his team was receiving in the state polls. As a matter of fact, at this juncture of the season, three other Housatonic League schools were receiving votes, but despite the Derby win, Lyman Hall was still not on anyone's radar.

Going on the road to Branford on October 12, 1985, a team I had scouted twice, I was concerned about more than our team's psyche. As a psychometrician (an educator who practices the science of educational measurement), I was constantly analyzing the numbers within our game performances. In the last three games, we were blitzing on almost every down, and despite the use of the blitz to stop the pass, we were all but shutting down the running game of our opponents. Conversely, we were giving up big chunks of yardage on pass plays.

So in the roll-up to the Branford game, I was most concerned with the Branford quarterback, John Witkowski, a smooth passer and a physical runner in Richard Austin who was capable of big plays on the ground. Although being unbeaten this late in the season had not been accomplished since 1977, I had come to believe that the 1985 team wouldn't come out flat for Branford. Unfortunately, for every team in every sport, "distractions" are always a danger lurking to disrupt a team, whether it be a family issue, an argument with a girlfriend, or a misplaced pep rally.

We practiced well during the week on both sides of the ball. Coach Ottochian was determined to get a few more of our non-starters on the field on special teams or in certain circumstances.

On Saturday, October 12, 1985, it was a beautiful fall morning. This was one of those rare morning contests with the crisp breeze in Branford and the sparkling sunshine. Coach Ottochian kept the ball on the ground from the outset, as was his typical want with Vin Poggio and Matt Schmitt carrying the ball behind that amazing line of Greg Myerson, David Klaverkamp, Billy Goldstein, Kevin Distante, and Ralph Riley.

We scored on the opening drive of the game, a steady 72-yard drive, with the key play a 42-yard counter play from Vincent Poggio. Todd Barket scored from 4 yards out, but our attempted pass for the two-point conversion failed, and we were up quickly, 6-0. On Branford's first possession, we attacked the wide side of the field with blitzes, and the Hornets offense was true to form in their tendencies, fumbling the ball away on a TBL (tackle behind the line) as Randy Pelletier and Guy Russo drilled Branford running back, Richard Austin in the backfield as Greg Myerson recovered.

Our offense took over with an efficient 9-play drive, with Vincent scoring from 9-yards out. The essential play in that drive was a 16-yard pass play from Todd Barket to sophomore split end Al Ferreira. Glenn Root scored the 2-point conversion on a pass from Todd, and the Trojans were out in front 14-0.

The Blue and White defense was quick and relentless in the first half and stopped the Hornets cold again on their third possession without a first down, turning the ball over to LHHS at the Branford 44-yard line. Coach Ottochian opened up the offense just a tad, turning Barket loose as Todd threw a 21-yard bootleg pass (waggle) to fullback Matt Schmitt. Moments later, Todd passed to Al Ferreira for 22 yards down to the 3-yard line. I remember the pass to Al well, screaming, "get in Al," wanting to see No.7, a talented and tough sophomore, score on the lengthy pass. Vincent scored from 3 yards out, and Coach Ottochian elected to kick for the extra point as Greg Myerson kicked it true for a 21-0 halftime lead.

At halftime, the task was keeping our defensive focus as we knew Branford would begin in earnest to use their multiple formations, somewhat abandoning their wing-T buck sweep attack. In the second half, the proclaimed "Blitz-O-Mania" (originally coined by sportswriter Ron Piazza) defense hammered the Branford offense, recording six tackles behind the line of scrimmage and an additional six sacks for the game.

Coach Ottochian played everyone on the team on offense in the third and fourth quarters, but we were held without a third period score. In the fourth quarter, the LHHS offense ended the scoring on a second down and eight as Vincent ran 58 yards down to the Branford 15 yard line. A few plays later, Matt Schmitt banged it in from two yards away. Since we made the last extra point kick (sarcasm intended), we missed this one, and the scoring was complete, 27-0.

The men of the Blue & White defense were superb in this game, limiting Branford to only four first downs, a total of four yards rushing, and 49 yards passing (53 total yards). Cornerbacks Scott Audet and Vince Poggio each had an interception. Poggio had 175 yards rushing, and Matt Schmitt ran for 69 yards and 48 receiving.

Chapter 78

Running Out of Players ... Invent a Scout Team

The "Scout team" is a weekly group of players on the squad who are rapidly prepared to run the next opponent's offensive plays against our starting defense. I had previously run the "Scout team" for many years, one of my periphery responsibilities. Traditionally, the "Scout Team" is made up of non-starters on the varsity, and when backups to the starters received their repetitions, a varsity starter would jump in on scout team.

During the first five weeks of the season, we learned that we didn't have enough non-starters to run a competent scout team, so we mixed and matched every player at practice and added a few freshmen as we went along. This was exacting a heavy toll on our non-starters as the varsity defense, with its large, athletic and dedicated defense starters, brought their best efforts against the scout team. In other words, the varsity hammered the scout team every day.

Just before midway in the 1985 season, we were in desperate shape as far as the scout team was concerned. We hadn't enough non-starters to man the eleven positions on the scout team. We had previously tried half-line drills, a passing-skeleton period, and what Coach Ottochian would call a "chair drill," that was more a line up to opponent formations with no actual plays being run.

As most of our coaching staff were younger men who had played some college football, I approached Coach Bob

Corazzini and asked if he and the other coaches might be open to the idea of putting on the pads and helmet again and practice against our varsity. Not so surprising, they jumped at the notion of playing again. Coach Ottochian was skeptical about the idea but warmed up to it when he saw how it changed the tenor of team practices for the better.

The key coach/player in this invention of sorts was Scott Ottochian. Scott was a former quarterback, heady, and he was able to take my scouting report and direct the scout team to run the opponent plays exactly as they were drawn up. Scott was also a master of audibles. This meant that he would see how our varsity defense was aligned and, through a system of communication that only the scout team players knew, change the play at the line of scrimmage to try and catch our starting defense off-guard ... and he did it very well.

To ensure that all four assistant coaches, other than Coach Ottochian and diminutive me were available for this unique coaching duty, we always scheduled defensive team drills after the Freshmen team practice had concluded. This allowed us to commandeer a few freshmen players and their coaches, John Gawlak and John Wallace.

The "Scout team" had to be assembled on Tuesday, shown how the plays of our next opponent had to be run and then run those plays against our first defense. Our four coaches played the key opponent players of our next opponents, and they each did their level best to become that individual opponent player in deportment and in the scheme of the opponent's offensive plays. Coach Corazzini would usually play the top running back for our next foe. Coach Wallace would assume the role of our next opponent's tight end or their best lineman. Coach Gawlak would play fullback, and when Corazzini played the best receiver of the next adversary, Gawlak would play running back.

All of the coaches encouraged and involved every non-starter on the team, making participation on the "Scout Team" a matter of pride. Scout team standouts included Bill Sheridan, Bobby Lampo, Steve May, Glenn Root, Bill Corazzini, Sean Sheehan, Bret Barron, Tommy Berube, Jim Hannah, and the whirlwind of enthusiasm Ray (Ray-Ray) Cormier. The "Scout Team" was a component of 1985 that every member of the team remembers and would play an invaluable role in the weeks ahead. Said Tom Berube, "Scout Team was an all hands on deck thing, every week for everyone. When we won, every guy who played Scout Team had a piece of each win".

Chapter 79

North Haven High School

– Sixth Game
October 19, 1985

As we progressed from the very first session of double days, we realized the potential impact that just one injury could have on our football team. We had 24 players, and on most practice days, less than that. We could hardly field a scout squad at practice, and there were not automatic substitutions for every position on offense and defense. The common rhetorical, unanswerable question was, "What would we do when this one ... or that one ... got injured and was unable to play"?

The question was made manifest immediately following the Branford game when we learned that our captain, fullback, and strong safety, Matt Schmitt, had injured his back and would not play in our next game with North Haven.

Coach Ottochian made the decision right away and without any discussion with the coaches as to whom he would use to play fullback. In a move reminiscent of the one from 1926 when then coach Langdon Fernald moved his starting center, Charles Frauham, to the backfield, Ottochian moved center Greg Myerson to fullback to replace Schmitt. This would make sophomore Mark Wollen the starting center against North Haven.

As further evidence of the intelligence of the 1985 team, Greg, a linemen, picked up the offense almost immediately, his first foray in the offensive backfield. The entire offense was thrown at Greg on Monday and Tuesday, and Coach Ottochian felt no restrictions as to what he might call for plays in the game. Greg would remain at defensive end and handle the kicking duties as always, but now he was the backfield mate of Vin Poggio. Al Ferreira was inserted as strong safety with Matt Schmitt out of the upcoming game, but Al already knew the defense from the many practice repetitions he had gotten previously. Mark Wollen, now the center, was prepared as Dave Klaverkamp and Coach Corazzini made sure he knew his every assignment.

The often nasty rivalry with North Haven might evoke a new negativity level because of Greg's presence in the backfield. Greg was a vocational agriculture student at Lyman Hall High School from ... North Haven. Despite North Haven's rather antique offensive plays and play calling, they were very talented and statistically the second-best passing team in the league to this point, second only to Derby.

North Haven was talented at the skill positions. I scouted North Haven and watched their quarterback, Tony Fronte (#11), throw with great power and accuracy. Just for kickers, they had three rather talented, multiple sport receivers. Mike Kakalow was their flanker and tight ends, Rajesh Atluru (6-3) and Scott Johnson (6-1), all with ten or more receptions. The Indian tailback was the powerfully built, Angelo Annunziato one of the league's top rushers who had run for almost 400 yards coming into the game.

Additionally, North Haven had good size up front with tackle Joe Mikos (6-5, 247) and Greg Myerson's childhood friend, JOHN MAGOVENY (6-2, 215). My film review notes on Magoveny were most impressive. He had speed and was an outstanding tackler. Additionally, North Haven flip-flopped Magoveny to their opponent's tight end side every play, further illustrating how valuable he was to their defense.

As their play-calling was rather predictable, based on formations (and substitution patterns), I spoke with Guy Russo (our middle linebacker who called the defenses in the huddle) early in the week to explain that my defensive calls would come in late. Guy would give me the dirtiest looks

308

when I was tardy getting my calls in, but Guy and I had a great synergy, so he was extra patient with me. I waited till the very last second to call a defense against North Haven, looking for certain players to come into the game. This drove Guy crazy because he had to keep everyone in the huddle longer, meaning that our defense had minimal time to make their formation and coverage calls.

On October 19, 1985, we lined up for pre-game stretches at the North Haven High School (Vanacore) field. Immediately, members of the North Haven team were pointing at Greg, who obviously, was not wearing his #50 jersey and was taking snaps at fullback, wearing #38.

Coach Ottochian wasted no time in giving Greg the ball at the beginning of the game. I think we all were holding our collective breaths, not wanting an injury to befall a defensive mainstay. Vince Poggio, almost fully healed from rib and wrist injuries, suffered in the Cheshire game, scored on a 22-yard run in the first quarter.

Before Vinnie's touchdown run, Kevin Distante and Bill Goldstein pulled on our heavy counter play. Kevin's mission was to kick out the 9-technique end, and Billy led up through the hole with Vinnie following. The defensive end closed on the play as Kevin made initial contact, but there wasn't enough space for Goldstein to pull up through the gap, so Billy and Kevin wound up double teaming the end and got him off the ground flailing his arms and legs. It was a great play to watch on film on Sunday morning. Myerson kicked the extra point, and we were up 7-0.

As anticipated, North Haven came out throwing the football, primarily short range, run-action passes. Our preparations on defense were to play off their split end a little more than usual, respecting the arm strength of Fronte. Additionally, I thought we could get to him with our "bandit" and "express" blitzes, but they were wedge blocking on their passing plays, even the run-action passing plays. The Indians found a rhythm as quarterback Tony Fronte connected with Mike Kakalow six times in the first and second quarters, scoring their only touchdown of the game on a 5-yard pass.

In the second half, we adjusted the blitzes, closing quicker with our ends, Ralph Riley and Greg Myerson, and coming harder off the edge with Eddie Charbonneau (our Will linebacker) and Al Ferreira (playing in place of Matt Schmitt at strong safety) getting sacks.

We were a different team in the second half; we came at them with the full array of blitzes as the boys recorded seven sacks, 8 for the game, and five tackles behind the line of scrimmage.

Following the second-half kickoff, our fullback, Greg Myerson, carried for five yards on first down and then 6 yards on second down. After a few carries by Vinnie and a facemask penalty, Todd Barket executed a "waggle" and hit the tight end, Randy Pelletier, for a touchdown.

We kicked off to North Haven after the touchdown, and this next opponent's series against our "Blitz-O-Mania" defense was one I will always remember. It seemed that everyone in the front seven got into the act. Defensive tackles, David Klaverkamp and Bill Goldstein ripped through on their slant moves, and both got big pieces of Fronte as Ralph Riley finished the sack. That started it all. Three North Haven pass plays called and three consecutive sacks of Fronte.

Following the Indian punt and runs by Greg and Vinnie, we found ourselves with a 4th down and & 7 from the 20-yard line. Once again, Barket passed to Randy Pelletier for a 20-yard touchdown. The two-point play was one to remember. Vincent carried and was hit in the backfield. He escaped but was promptly belted by two North Haven defenders. Poggio refused to go down and muscled in for the two-point conversion.

The Trojan defense was quick, efficient, and seemed to anticipate every play North Haven ran.

Sacks, tackles for loss, interceptions, and North Haven was held to ONLY **one first down in the second half**.

A defining defensive moment was on a 4th down with North Haven trailing in the fourth period. Despite a long count to draw our blitzers off-side, Guy Russo sacked their quarterback, ending the last hope of an Indian score.

The Trojans took over on the 34-yard line as our QB Todd Barket ran for 10 yards on first down, followed by Vinnie's 11-yard run. Back to bootleg (waggle to you aficionados), as Todd passed to Randy Pelletier, who made a marvelous over-the-shoulder catch for his third TD pass reception of the game and a 27-6 victory.

So many of our players had exceptional games. Barket passed the ball six times, completing five, for 60 yards and three touchdowns, all to Pelletier. Greg Myerson, in his only start at fullback, carried the ball ten times for 54 yards. Vin Poggio, our cornerback (as well as our record-setting tailback), intercepted Fronte twice. Guy Russo had 13 tackles in the game, three sacks, and an interception.

For the fourth time in five games, the Trojan defense held the opposition to under 100 yards rushing. The Indians managed only 31 yards rushing, but NH did have 163 yards passing.

SPECIAL GAME NOTE: Vin Poggio continued to assault the record book. After this game, Vince had 858 yards rushing for the season and an average of 7 yards per carry. At this point of the season, Vince was only 600 yards from Hall of Famer, Mike Nesti's rushing record with five games to play, not including the yet to be added State Championship game.

Chapter 80

Shelton High School

To live ... and die a little inside
Seventh Game
October 26, 1985

Any discussion of the events preceding and following the Shelton-Lyman Hall game of 1985 is a matter of great personal reflection, remaining guilt and responsibility. No other single day in my life, especially relating to Lyman Hall High School, has required such rumination.

As the years have passed, I have come to see that "game" as a life-changing event of far more importance than that of simply a game. To state it clearly, this is not about a football game that we lost. To say that is to minimize the impact it had on me. As I have written daily since 1962, there are more than a few references to the events of the week of October 21, 1985.

Having made hundreds of speeches to organizations, conferences, churches for both student and adult groups in 27 of the continental United States, I have often included in my opening statements of the last 30 years, "God knew me before I knew God." That phase started a few days after the 1985 Shelton game. This event brought me to know my heart which is exactly what God had in mind.

Following the Cheshire victory, the magnitude of responsibility for this Lyman Hall High School football team increased almost daily. I had studied the history of my high school and now stood in a place that few others had or ever will stand. My thoughts were not of championships but of the many days and nights listening to or reading of the thoughts of former LHHS coaches before they would guide their teams into historic games. Never before had I known the level of intense preparation necessary for me to stand on the sideline as a decision-maker in a Housatonic League football game. There was no pause, no break, or even untethered sleep. It was all Lyman Hall High School. My nightly prayers were often of the same words, prayed in the same place, accompanied by tears, "God, let me be more than what I am. Let me not let these boys down".

The nights in that little room, studying the Shelton film over and over, with the same songs playing on the record player, were tedious. It was useless to attempt to do anything but my football preparation. I dared not think of what this could become in a week or a month from now. All of my being was focused on Shelton High School, and the coach I felt was the best in the league, Bob Riggio.

Yes, we were 6-0. I often allowed thoughts about Coach Ottochian, my friend, who was so deserving of a magical season. I felt terrible that he was annoyed in recent weeks by the newspaper stories coming out of the New Haven Register and Hartford Courant. Too many little sentences alluded to our "good fortune" and a "weak" schedule. In 1985 the Housatonic League had not a single opponent one could classify as a weak anything.

Was it too early to think about a berth in the state title game, first instituted in Connecticut in 1976? YES! We, as a team, did not need any distractions. We hadn't achieved a single thing. Not yet. I know I could not let anything or anyone pry my head away from preparation, and I took time away from my job to keep my head clear of anything but Shelton. Unfortunately, distractions were looming for the 1985 football team that negatively contributed to the events of October 26, 1985.

DISTRACTION 1 – STATE RANKINGS

For the first time since 1977, Lyman Hall cracked the top ten in the state polls. We were ranked No. 9. My chronicle of October 22 reads, "... why this week? They don't give us a stitch of credit when we knock off Derby, and now when we need to play without any pressure, they rank us this week."

DISTRACTION 2 – INTERRUPTING THE SCOUTING REPORT MEETING AFTER PRACTICE

The scouting reports always took time. There were no desktop computers then, so everything I did for those weekly documents took time. Each was done by hand and on a portable electric typewriter. All of that was worth it because each member of the team studied the materials and asked questions. The 1985 team never took anything for granted. Guy Russo was on every word of the scouting report and asked every question. He knew the defense like I wanted every one of my middle linebackers or those who declared the defensive call in the huddle to know the defense.

Tuesday was usually "scouting report" day when I handed out the copies of the reports to the members of the team. On those days, the boys didn't leave the locker room right after practice. They got directly to work with me with their scouting report study after Tuesday practice. On this day, as they sat at their lockers with me thundering on about this formation or that, a member of the cheerleaders comes to the locker room to ask to inspect the lockers for decorations for a pep-rally related activity. I tried to be nice, but it was just a minor distraction that we didn't need. Minutes later, a school administrator comes into the locker room to ask the team if they were "ready to go this week." We hadn't seen a member of the faculty come into the locker in years. Of course, the boys responded in kind, but this valuable time was being invaded by our people.

DISTRACTION 3 - TOO MUCH UNNECESSARY TALK

There was too much talk that week about decorating lockers and the pep rally, and Coach O and I were becoming more and more worried about its negative impact on the team. We had to stay consistent. We were all in unchartered waters ....
Undefeated ... League Title opportunity ... Sheehan was undefeated too ... and, for the first time in school history, a chance to play for a state title in football.

DISTRACTION 4 – WELL WISHERS

That week's practices were quality as the Scout Team did a good job simulating the Shelton offense. The weekly hitting that was always an indicator of the team's preparedness was of a high level. However, the practices had an inordinate number of well-wishers as former players, parents, well-meaning locals attending practice all week. Every one of the attendees wanted to get an up-close and personal look at the team. Coach Ottochian met every person with a handshake and a few words, but he would sometimes roll his eyes because we were trying to stay on task. Our coaching staff was short enough with every one of the coaches, except coach Ottochian and me, dressed for practice (pads/helmets). This was the only week that season this happened to this degree. Thank God, the week of the State Championship game, we didn't see anyone. Of course, most people, the press, and many of the student body didn't give us much of a chance in the state title game.

DISTRACTION 5 - THE PEP RALLY – THURSDAY

Why in the world did anyone think it necessary to hold a mid-season pep rally? Who could have thought this was a good idea? I learned many lessons about preparedness from my years around LHHS football teams, before and throughout

Coach Ottochian's tenure. I learned even more in my years at Norristown Area High School, where every sporting event was a sold-out crowd. This was just stupidity. Coach Ottochian would lecture his teams about keeping away from girlfriends and often repeated command, "Don't make plans for after the game. If you do, when the going gets tough in the game, you'll be thinking about the fun you'll have that night".

For me, I needed to be in front of my super-8mm projector at home watching Shelton on film. There was always "one more" piece of information you could learn. I didn't look at it as feeling pressure. I just wanted our team to be more prepared than our opponents. The communication element of defense is so critical to success, and spending a Thursday night at a standing room only pep rally was a total misuse of time. More importantly, instead of getting as much rest as possible, studying the scouting report, and just down-shifting the day, our team was being treated to the most raucous pep rally I had ever seen at Lyman Hall.

I tried not to think about all of that as I sat in the pep rally on Thursday evening. I remember Ralph Riley saying to me at the beginning of the event, and I have it in my chronicle, "do we really need this?"

SHELTON GAME DAY

There were so many former Trojans at the game. They lined the usually vacant pathway that led from our locker room to the fence's gate that encircled the Fitzgerald Field. It was all so odd ... a coming out party approach to a mid-season game. Granted, it was against an outstanding Shelton team that had played inconsistently for Coach Bob Riggio, the best coach in the Housatonic League. I got to know Bob rather well, became friends, and coached together for a season at Maloney with Bob Zito. He had a fascinating approach to the game, and we spent many hours talking defensive philosophy and tactics. Shelton was picked by the New Haven Register to win the Housatonic League title as they had so much talent, including quarterback Nick Verrichio, multi-talented Tom Oko, and the center of our defensive focus, Mike Bucci.

From the opening kickoff to the final second on the scoreboard, nothing went right. Despite what I saw in the Shelton offense, nothing I called seemed to stop the White and Orange Gaels' ability to move the ball. They were able to block down on most of our blitzes and run an off-tackle play that they used at least ten times in the game. In the 4th quarter, with eight minutes remaining with us down 26-6, I finally saw my strategy's error, confirmed by my talks many years later with Coach Riggio.

Although we did not score but a single touchdown in this game, in my heart, the entire weight of the loss was squarely at my feet. I had let my beloved Lyman Hall High School down in her greatest football hour to this point.

As we crossed the wind-swept field at the game's end to the locker room, I felt an emptiness that has never been equaled in any part of my life. The emotional pain was beyond anything I could ever have imagined. I actually felt pain in my back that made me walk with elbows in and head bowed.

Almost a lifetime of loving Lyman Hall, and I let her down in her biggest game to that point.

I went into the coach's locker room, not wanting to talk or even be seen. Coach Ottochian and I hardly made eye contact ...there was nothing to be said. We would talk, but not then. However, seated in the coach's room was a former coach, Gervais Barger. When I saw him sitting there in the corner, my eyes finally welled up, and I confessed, "I let them down, I let them down." He remembers that moment. After waiting for everyone to leave the locker room as it was beginning to grow dark outside, Gervais put his arm around me and said, "Coach, give it to God." At that moment, I had no idea what that meant. I told him that I was going to walk home that was Meriden at the time. I needed time to work this all out.

Gervais waited in the locker room with me until I stopped saying, "I let the school down." I know I said it for at least an hour. Gervais, with his arm around me ... prayed with me and asked me to hear his words. When I did get home, no one was there. I sat alone in the living room with game attire still on. I asked God to take this pain away. There was a sense that I just wanted to die. I had seen over 100 Lyman Hall football game losses in my life, but this one was MY FAULT, and I knew it.

I turned on the television, trying to find something to take my attention away from the Shelton game. We did not have cable at that time, just three basic stations. In the suddenness that is always God's love, I switched to a channel, and my favorite movie was on Rio Bravo. What I didn't realize was that we had been given one of those free weekends of cable television. Why then, why now? I sat on the floor and cried watching Rio Bravo.

At that moment, I prayed, really asked God to come into my life. I told Him what I had done and not done well. I never rationalized the game or sought to point a finger except at myself.

I fell asleep some hours later on the floor. When I awoke, I thanked God for helping me make it through the night. I needed to get to the coach's meeting. I wasn't sure how I could even look at the coaches in the face without apologizing, but as I drove into the parking lot of the high school that morning,

God had given me a sense of peace.

The sliver of a dream that floated in my head a week earlier that my Lyman Hall High School might play for a State Championship was lost with our defeat at the hands of Shelton. When I got into the locker room, before I could say a word, freshman coach John Wallace said to me, "Hoager" ... we are not out of it yet". He told me that we were still in position to get into the state title game if we win out. Then I did cry. I walked outside and thanked God for one more chance.

I would never let my boys or my Lyman Hall down again!

A SIDE STORY

My daughters, Maureen and Kathleen, were outstanding student-athletes at Lyman Hall (no thanks to me) and played hundreds of softball games in many summers, high school, and college, winning the 1998 state championship and No. 1 ranking. On the very rare occasion that they lost a softball game, we put on Rio Bravo. I wonder if they understand how that began.

Chapter 81

East Haven High School

– Eighth Game
Friday, November 1, 1985

After the Shelton game, the East Haven game could not get here fast enough. I think the entire team believed that. We all wanted to get the bitterness of the Shelton week behind us.

We were renewed in the belief that if we could win out, which was a pretty arrogant attitude for a Lyman Hall football team, we still might qualify for the state title game.

East Haven had beaten Shelton! Yes, they defeated Shelton. As we began preparations, we didn't mention this in our scouting report meeting of the week. Defensively, we focused on stopping All-Stater, Jody Longley whose speed and athleticism was worthy of our attention.

We recalibrated our blitzing schemes during the early week to avoid a "never again" reoccurrence of the option play, emanating from outside the tackle (known as outside veer) that Shelton used successfully against us. Eddie Charbonneau and Randy Pelletier were the focus of my attention, along with our defensive ends, Myerson and Riley. We were not going to get let anyone move the ball off-tackle again, not in 1985.

After the Shelton game, we dropped out of the state top ten polls and dropped down in the Class M Rankings. However, there was no drop in enthusiasm. The entire team and coaches knew we could get right back in the fight with some victories.

There would be no more pep rallies, glad-handers, or rah-rah offerings for the rest of the way.

We had four games left to the regular season with no soft touches. This was the HOUSATONIC LEAGUE, not the "popcorn" league as we now see across the state.

Guy Russo was so pumped up for this game. As my chronicle of November 2, 1985 states, "Guy-Guy was breathing fire before the game and had this way of heavy-breathing that made you feel he was short of breath and self-control and about to dominate."

I don't know if Guy even looked for my calls on the first defensive series. Whatever he called in the huddle, the boys destroyed East Haven quarterback Dom Acquaruolo on the first two plays, the second of which was a chest to chest sack by Guy.

After East Haven quickly turned the ball over on downs, Todd Barket ran 69 yards to the one-yard line on the bootleg (waggle), and we were off to the races, but we fumbled on the next play as the Yellowjackets took over.

When we didn't score, I felt this sense of we don't need any negative plays, not today. The defense was as smooth as silk on this night, and they kept coming at East Haven. We dropped them twice behind the line in their next offensive series with plays by Randy Pelletier and Matt Schmitt. They were forced to punt, and we blocked that punt and took over on their 23-yard.

The Easties tried to throw in the first quarter, and we sacked their quarterback four times in the period.

We seemed unable to get clean blocks on that next offensive series, but six plays later, Vincent Poggio scored from 7 yards out. We took care of their offense, stopping Don Hemstock, then Longley on consecutive plays on their next possession. As the second period opened, Vinnie picked up 71 yards, taking the ball to the one-yard line. Matt Schmitt banged it in from the one-yard line for the touchdown. Todd Barket passed to Scott Audet for the two-point conversion, and we were up 14-0.

This was when we got a little too loose. After the high

tension of Shelton, we played fast and loose against East Haven, but the Easties were a talented team, to be sure. We were up 14-0 in dominating fashion, but kicking off to Jody Longley was a dumb mistake. He was an outstanding returner with great speed. Taking our kick off on the ten-yard line, he raced 90 yards for a touchdown, breaking three tackle attempts. They went for two and got it, and it was 14-8.

Due mainly to the offensive line's punishing blocking, our offense drove the ball right down the field. The plays on this drive were spectacular. First, Todd Barket passed to Al Ferreira for a 28-yard gain. Matt Schmitt busted one up the middle for 19 yards, and Vincent out-raced the Yellowjackets around the right side for a 27-yard touchdown. The extra point kick by Ed Charbonneau was on target, and we were back in business.

East Haven tried to throw on first down, but Al Ferreira, "Mr. Versatility," intercepted Acquarulo as the first half was coming to a close. This was Al's day! Our offense began a quickly paced ten-play drive culminating in a Todd Barket pass to Ferreira on a 17-yard pass for a touchdown. We went into the locker room at Crisafi field with a 27-8 lead, and there was a moment to look at each other and breathe again.

You never knew what Coach Ottochian would do or say at halftime in any game. Whether we were up or down, Coach would do the unpredictable at halftime. At halftime in this game with a comfortable lead against East Haven, Coach Ottochian decides to assert himself as Al Ferreira remembers, "We're sitting there in the locker room at East Haven, and Coach Ottochian tells Greg Myerson to line up against him, and they fired-out head to head."

The second half was a defensive show for us as we kept knocking down their runners in the backfield. The Blue and White offense scored on a touchdown pass from Todd Barket to Randy Pelletier in the third period, and we closed out the scoring with a 38-yard run by Vincent for a touchdown.

"The Three Greatest"
Nesti, Poggio and Angelone

Vinnie had his best game thus far, ripping off 231 yards rushing, giving him 1,182 yards for the season, becoming the first Lyman Hall Trojan to have back-to-back 1,000 yard rushing seasons. Vincent was now just 278 yards from the all-time single-season rushing record of the immortal MICHAEL NESTI.

For his performance, Vincent Poggio was named New Haven Register, Player of the Week. The newspaper story stated that Vince was "concentrating on offense" and not playing defense, but there was no way we would go into our remaining games without our best defensive back.

The Trojan defense returned to their pre-Shelton game form, holding the Easties to 99 yards total offense, 67 of those yards coming on one play.

Whatever confidence we might have lost in the Shelton game was regained on this night, Friday, November 1, 1985.

Chapter 82

Seymour High School

Ninth Game
Saturday, November 9, 1985

Each season, the Valley teams of Derby, Shelton, and Seymour are loaded with top-flight talent, size, and toughness. This is why the Housatonic League was the toughness high school football league in Connecticut. There was never an easy touch, except some of the Lyman Hall teams of the 1950s and 1960s, all B.O. (before Ottochian). Once Coach Ottochian built the football program at Lyman Hall, we took our place at the Housatonic League table.

In 1985 Seymour had many outstanding players and was just a tick off from vying for the league crown. From my scouting work from 1984 and 1985, I believed that the most physical back in the Housatonic League in 1985 would be Jeff Hillman, a power back of speed and quickness, just a sensational inside runner. Although Hillman didn't have Vinnie Poggio's numbers, he was difficult to deal with in one-on-one tackling situations.

Seymour had an outstanding lineman in #77, K.C. Sirowich, and the film we had on him, especially on defense, was impressive. He may have been the best lineman we played against that year. The gem of the 1985 football team, yet to achieve stardom, was quarterback sophomore Joe Stochmal, who went on to break all the Seymour passing records.

We expected a difficult game and worked all week

tightening things up to avoid giving up any big plays to a team that often scored on Hillman's long runs and the bombs from Stochmal.

As the game started, we could hardly get a first down. Seymour had one of the better defenses in the league and was playing a stout defense against our offensive line. We were having a difficult time holding onto the football as the Trojans lost three fumbles. Seymour was concerned about our blitzing game and didn't come out throwing as they did in their previous three games. With Hillman carrying the ball on almost every down, we got some great hits on him in the backfield, but we were not always able to knock him down. Both teams were unable to score in the first quarter. Vinnie was taking some shots, even when he didn't carry the ball. Coach Ottochian called on Matt Schmitt to carry the ball more with all the attention that Vince was garnering, but we couldn't get much going.

Seymour finally broke through in the second quarter on a 1-yard run by Hillman. The Wildcats had one of the best, if not THE best kicker in the league, and I was concerned that their kicker might just be the difference in the game if it continued tight.

Truth be known, we were playing one of our best defensive games despite the pounding running of Hillman. Seymour was always in third and long situations, forcing them to throw the ball. Despite their elaborate pass schemes (way ahead of their time), we were causing a ton of incomplete passes and getting our sacks. Their best long yardage play were the counters to Hillman with Sirowich leading.

We entered the second half with vitality. The reality that the season was on the brink was enough to ignite this highly intelligent group of Trojans.

We immediately had our best drive of the game to open the second half. We drove the ball 56 yards for a touchdown, but the actual TD was one of the best runs I ever saw Matt Schmitt make. I'm not sure it was a Buck play, but it was right up the gut. Matt cleared the line of scrimmage but got hit multiple times on the second level. Matt tucking in low and spinning finally broke it for a 30-yard touchdown run. Our weakness on offense reared its ugly head again as we missed the extra point, and we trailed 7-6.

After stopping the Wildcats on their first possession of the half, it looked like we had lost some energy on defense. No excuses here; everyone was going both ways all season. Seymour ran Hillman on almost every play, and finally, their horse broke one for 29 yards and the touchdown. They kicked the extra point, and we were down 14-6 with 4:36 remaining in the third quarter.

Trojan lost fumbles, and four offensive penalties kept Seymour in control of the time of possession, and it was getting dangerously late in the game with us down by 8 points. Seymour had a 2nd down play on their 35-yard line or so. We had relied on blitzes to their open/split end side in the second half that was, more often than not, opposite the pulling Sirowich.

On this play, we drilled Hillman in the backfield, and Al Ferreira recovered Hillman's fumble, scooped it up, and brought it to the 30-yard line. We were in business with good field position. This maybe was the most protracted "drive" of the season. We had 30 yards to go to score. It took us 11 plays to get there, and we had burned all of our timeouts. On 4th down and goal from the two-yard line, with yet another "season on the brink" moment in this game, Matt Schmitt scored, making the score 14-12. Coach Ottochian decided to run Matt again for the two-point play. Matt was belted at the line of scrimmage, but he spun off the first tackler, bounced it outside, and outran the Seymour corner into the endzone. It was now 14-14. No breathing Yet!

Only precious few minutes remained in the contest as the sun began to set at Fitzgerald Field. The defense had played rather well all game, and in this next critical series, they were outstanding. We stopped their offense, giving up only two yards on first and second down, one of which was a bone-jarring hit by Bill Goldstein at the line of scrimmage. On third down, Guy Russo recorded a sack for a 7-yard loss on Stochmal, and the Wildcats were forced to punt.

We grabbed the momentum in the game, and on the next series, it looked like the offense was about to deliver. Matt and Vinnie alternated carrying the ball, and we had a first down on the Seymour 27 with two minutes to play. Todd Barket passed to Scott Audet for seven yards, and it all looked good for the Blue and White from the Seymour 20. Matt broke a tackle with a minute remaining and looked like he might break away for the go-ahead touchdown, but he was hit and lost the ball on a fumble.

This gave Seymour one more chance to break the 14-14 tie and upset our team with all the terrible consequences that would go along with it ... no Housatonic Title shot ... no State Title shot.

One first down, Stochmal was rushed to throw, that resulted in an incomplete pass. On that fateful second down, a play that will live on forever, Seymour called for a split end screen into the sideline that might, repeat, might have been a "hitch and pitch" play, a typical Seymour junk play.

According to the recollection of Greg Myerson of that play, "I was exhausted. This was the game I first hurt my shoulder. I saw their end widen his split, so I thought something was up. Instead of rushing the passer, which I was too tired to do at this point, I dropped into coverage, got a hand on it, and ran it in".

The final score was 20-14. We had seen our season saved by one of the most legendary plays in Lyman Hall High School history that would stand alongside Ernie Bercier's last seconds' basket in the 1953 championship game to beat East Haven and Mel Horowitz's last-second second shot to beat New Canaan in the 1961 State Tournament.

Chapter 83

Amity Regional High School

Tenth Game
Saturday, November 16, 1985

It was a cloudy, sun-splashed day at Fitzgerald Field for our last home game of the 1985 season. There were no omnipresent celebrations relative to a "senior day" per se. The collective coaching staff detested Senior Day, so after the distraction-filled Shelton week, Coach Ottochian made the pre-game with parents a quick and quiet walk-in. Yes, the parents and senior players were introduced, but it was kept low-key as it should, with the focus squarely on the game itself. On this day, it was conservatively orchestrated without a vestige of distraction.

The game began with lousy results as our kickoff team broke down yet again. We took the lead on our first possession as Vinnie Poggio scored from the one-yard line. Eddie Charbonneau kicked the extra point, and we were up 7-0.

After the quick touchdown, we kicked off, way down to the Amity goal line. Amity's Tom Forlano picked up the kickoff at the one-yard line and returned it 99 yards for a touchdown. Coach O almost lost his mind as our kickoff team arm tackled and failed to close. Their kicker missed the point after, LHHS 7 – Amity 6.

Our offense came right back with an efficient drive as Vinnie scored again from the one. Eddie missed the point after, and we still led by 13-6, but we were in for an uncomfortable first quarter.

On Amity's next possession, they ran a short trap up the middle by their fullback, Steve Vallie, akin to our buck play, and it went clean, 64 yards for a touchdown. All of a sudden, we were down 14-13. That one play served as quite a teaching point for the rest of our 1985 football life. We showed that play and talked about it over and over in the weeks ahead. Even though Sheehan did not run that specific play, I felt very sure that they would put it in their offense for us. There wasn't one scout team sequence in the weeks of preparation for Sheehan and Middletown that the "short trap" wasn't run against our defense. We had to seal the "A" gap on any blitz we ran, which led to a sideline timeout moments after that touchdown.

Candidly, that was the last bit of offense that Amity had the rest of the game.

Those two long touchdowns jolted all of us, and it seemed to awaken the giant as we dominated from that moment forward. We finally saw the "Blitz-O-Mania" we had come to know and love on the next defensive series. On first down, Matt Schmitt blitzing off the edge, drilled the Amity quarterback, Dave Chernovetz, for an 8-yard loss. An "express" blitz call resulted in Guy Russo through the "A" gap, and Eddie Charbonneau through the backside "B," and the Spartans had to punt again. Those schemes were opening so well because of our tackles Billy Goldstein and Dave Klaverkamp, who were beating the Amity guards off the ball.

That three and out by the defense led to our next possession when Vinnie Poggio ripped off a 62-yard TD run for a 26-13 lead. The awakened Trojans were rolling. Another minus yardage series by Amity led to another punt, and the offense wasted no time. Todd Barket ran one in from 13 yards out, and with a 2-point conversion run by Matt Schmitt, the rout was on, 34-14.

Time remained in the first half when we kicked off to Amity, but we stoned them cold and forced yet another punt. There were 23 seconds remaining in the half, up by 20 points, and what happened next caused the Amity coaches to walk toward us (coaches), yelling at us for "running up the score." We weren't calling timeouts, but with Vince and Matt running the ball right at Amity, we found ourselves right down near the goal line with those 23 seconds left. Matt banged the football over from the one-yard line for the touchdown and then ran for the 2-point play. We were now up 43-14 at the half. The Amity coaches felt we were running it up by going for 2 points, but if they cared to pay attention, they realized that we couldn't kick an extra point (all season), so we were compelled to go for two.

1985 was far from the scoring excesses of the spread offense in the new millennia when 50-point margins of victory and scoring parades are more the norm than the exception. The Housatonic League was a long-standing alignment of like-minded secondary schools that believed in respect for each other and competitive balance rather than domination without educational professionalism and integrity.

Coach Ottochian had no C.IA.C. or league rule to contend with, only his highly professional approach and sensitivity to the other team and the young men who played on the field opposite you. Coach Ottochian viewed every other coach as his friend, no matter the circumstances, and would never run up a score or take advantage of a school with a decisive disadvantage. This is why he was so widely respected.

Coming out of half-time, Coach Ottochian decided to play every man on the 24-member team (this included a few freshmen) on offense. He wanted no more scoring to take place on offense and told me so as we began the second half.

The third quarter of the Amity game saw no scoring. Our defense was shutting the Spartan offense down while keeping the clock moving. When we took over after a punt, we ran the ball with no deception, just buck, belly, and heavy. Phil (Ottochian) was content to win and move on to Thanksgiving.

In the 4th period, the Amity center snapped the ball over the head of the Spartan punter. The Amity punter scrambled to recover the ball in the endzone, and Vince Poggio tackled him for a safety. Vincent had discovered yet another way to score for the Trojans. The final touchdown was a 13-yard touchdown run by backup quarterback Glenn Root in the 4th quarter. Glenn never entered the game without this hunger to play his best and score. On this occasion, he bested the Amity first-teamers, who were still in the game till the end.

The final score of 52-14 was uncomfortable for Coach Ottochian as we walked across the wind-swept field at 3:42 pm. His teams never embarrassed an opponent, and he was almost apologetic when he shook the Amity head coach's hand.

The defense had played superbly ... limiting Amity to minus eight yards passing and 81 yards on 33 rushing attempts, incredible given that one play went for 64 yards. This meant that after that first quarter of play, the Lyman Hall defense limited Amity to 17 yards on 31 rushing carries. Guy Russo was the leader on defense yet again in his record-breaking season. Vincent Poggio had 196 yards on 19 carries, and Matt Schmitt had 71 yards on 12 rushing carries.

BACK STORIES OF AMITY WEEK ... SHEEHAN HIGH SCHOOL – FIRST WINNING SEASON

Despite the opponent, we had much football left to play with dual "pots of gold" out in front of the Blue and White. Sheehan, having defeated North Haven the week before, clinched a berth in the state Class SS Championship game. I was pleased for Sheehan's Head Coach, Andy Borelli, whom I had always thought the world of ... a kind man, who treated me with such kindness since I was a student at Dag Hammarskjold Junior High School. The reality was that his team had already qualified for the Class S State Championship game. Even with the Thanksgiving Day game with us on the horizon, Sheehan had their first winning season and would be "playing in December."

HEAD-SETS

Coach Ottochian, like other head coaches of that period, never liked wearing a headset during games, so I was the sideline coach on the headset. We had not invested in the better communication devices (headsets). Instead, we used a rather amateurish radio-shack headset of thin plastic with an antenna sticking out of the top. The coaches carried extra 9-volt batteries with them as the ones in the head-sets would usually crap out in an hour. I wore the headset, and one of the coaches in the press box (home games) or standing on a bus (away games) talked to me with the other unit. I was often told I looked like Ray Walston of the television show "My Favorite Martian" with the antennae attached to the top of my head.

We always kept the dialogue brief, and my standing rule for the coaches "up top" was tell me what I ask for or what I need to know. Never give me a play-by-play. Most importantly, don't get all emotional ... don't get excited no matter what happens on the field. For the first nine games of the season, the head-sets were of some value. John Wallace was usually the voice talking to me on the other end. I would tell the coaches what I needed to know for each game, against each opponent, and they did their best to comply.

Coach Ottochian had worked the week of the Amity game to insert some non-starters (younger team members) on the kickoff and kick return units to give our two-way starters a break during the game. In the first quarter of the Amity game, the Spartans scored on a long kickoff return, and Coach Ottochian lost his mind on the sideline. He screamed at me, "Give that head-set"! Coach Wallace seeing the seething Ottochian trying to put the head-set on correctly, decided to defuse what was about to happen. Once wearing the headset, Coach Ottochian screams into it, "Hey, you guys, what the hell is going on out there" (meaning on that kickoff return)? Whatever Wallace said to Phil, Coach Ottochian rips off the head-set, fires it into the ground, breaking into pieces, and shouts, "This damn thing doesn't work."

As the coaches came down from the press box at half-time,

I walked off the field with Coach Wallace, gave him the pieces of my broken headset, and asked him if he could repair it. "Wally," his nickname, put the pieces back together in short order. I then asked what he said to Coach Ottochian when he asked, "What was going out there"? Wally smiled and made a sound resembling static, "*chhhaaaaaaaaa*." Coach Wallace laughingly confessed, "There was no way I was going to listen to him screaming into the headset, so I faked it with the static noise.

CHRONICLE, SATURDAY, NOVEMBER 16, 1985

"It's just after 10:00 pm, and I need to pry away from the Sheehan film. Looking at Sheehan, particularly Salisbury, I know this will be no typical Thanksgiving Day. I keep thinking about our captains, Ralph, Matt, and Greg. What a perfect trio. They are always in a collective balance and so easy to like and admire. There have been so many football captains that I remember, but as a group, I can't help but place this group atop the rest. I guess I am too critical of the role of true leadership. Some individuals carried the title of captain at Lyman Hall so well, but these three are so special as a group. They deserve a crack at the state championship. Now, back to Sheehan … only on play 14".

1985 Captains
Myerson, Schmitt, Riley

AND NOW ... the stage was set ... the game that Wallingford could have only dreamed of was to be played. Lyman Hall High School would play crosstown Sheehan High School for the Housatonic League Championship ... with more at stake than anyone in the history of schoolboy sports could have ever imagined for a two-school town.

Chapter 84

The Unthinkable, The Unimaginable, ... and It Happened

If there was one day in the town's history when the "sports-minded" of Wallingford focused their hearts, minds, and eyes on one solitary event, it probably would have been Thursday, November 28, 1985. Indeed, back in the days of one high school, before 1971, the state basketball championship games galvanized the town, but this was different in so many ways.

The high school on Wallingford's westside, Sheehan, recorded its first winning football season in 1985. This same 1985 Sheehan team qualified for the Class S state title game before taking the field against Lyman Hall on Thanksgiving Day, and this same Sheehan team could win the Housatonic League championship with a win over Lyman Hall.

For Lyman Hall High School, the circumstances could not be more historically convoluted. Since the school's opening in 1917, one inconceivable inequitable effort after another was brought upon the sport of football to eliminate it from the school's landscape. This text has so articulated those actions and attempts. Now, in the 1985 season, after almost losing its coach to other coaching opportunities ... with the smallest roster in school history (24 players at season's end), with a record of 9-1, they must share the spotlight with the high school across town that also fashioned a 9-1 record.

While the Lyman Hall High School – Sheehan High School Thanksgiving football games since 1972 have had little luster, if any, with very little at stake in the annual outcome (except that one school or the other might have the childish "bragging rights" for a year), in the offering of the 1985 game the Housatonic League Championship rested in the outcome. With Sheehan already guaranteed a slot in the State Class S Championship game, Lyman Hall must win to edge out Bethel High School for a berth in the State Class M Championship game. Moreover, should Lyman Hall emerge victorious on Thanksgiving, whom would their opponent be? Why, none other than the State No.1 Ranked, and No. 24 Nationally Ranked, MIDDLETOWN HIGH SCHOOL team.

Against this backdrop, the state newspapers and television stations flocked to Wallingford for pre-game interviews. The distractions were many, and this time, they could not be avoided or dodged. Every football player on either school's roster knew what was at stake in this game. The athletic directors drooled at the financial windfall of the largest single game gate of any Wallingford athletic event in history.

November 28, 1985, was the 364th Thanksgiving Day since the European settlers came to our shores. Many of those Thanksgiving Days were marked by historical events such as Admiral Byrd's first flight to the South Pole in 1929, the Tehran meeting between Stalin, Churchill, and Roosevelt in 1943, and now, the Lyman Hall vs. Sheehan football game of 1985.

In the more than 35 years since this game was played, one fact remains self-evident. There was never a Town of Wallingford athletic event anything close to Thanksgiving, 1985 ... and there NEVER EVER will be again.

Chapter 85

The Prep Begins
for Sheehan

The routine that I had so locked myself into since the season's onset was only altered by the need for some additional preparations for the team. Players on each team knew of those on the opposition roster, and this added a bit to the manner in which names, positions, and statistics were printed in the weekly scouting reports.

With twelve days of preparation, every detail of the data was checked and double-checked. The most minuscule points were scrutinized, such as ... when running a specific play, what are the steps of each Sheehan lineman; ... which way did the center's head turn when he snapped the ball. It wasn't a matter of the plays Sheehan ran on offense, but "How" they ran each play, position by position. Each day and night was a study in incremental planning.

Each week of the season, the preparation of our Scouting Reports took time and a lot of trips to the professional printers to copy the report for each member of the team. When completed on the Thursday, November 21st, the Sheehan Scouting Report numbered 39 pages, the longest report of the season. After we handed out the reports to all team members and coaches, we held a slide presentation on Sheehan in the weight room that was a very serious combination of the banquet scene from the "Dirty Dozen" and the pledge class review scene from "Animal House."

After three days (Sunday-Tuesday) of non-stop breaking down of the Sheehan films, it was clear we had many significant tasks to complete, but nothing was more important than devising a plan to stop Sheehan's all-everything quarterback, Brian Salisbury. He could run, throw, and was a fearless competitor. So the first step was planning how to simulate Salisbury in our practices. For that, I turned to our offensive line coach, Bobby Corazzini.

EVERY STORY IN THE PAPERS

On November 20-21, 1985, there were seven newspaper articles in the Shoreline, New Haven Register, Record-Journal, Hartford Courant, and Middletown Press referencing the impending Lyman Hall – Sheehan football game scheduled for Thanksgiving Day.

In that same week, the Record-Journal started to run cartoons designed by their political cartoon writer on the game. They were most representative of the citizenry's feelings who looked forward to this one Thanksgiving Day football game.

THE SALISBURY SIM

One of the most significant challenges in preparing for Sheehan was simulating the trigger-man in the Sheehan offense, quarterback Brian Salisbury. It was more than a matter of his speed, as he was so quick to change directions. Coach Borelli had designed an offense that allowed Salisbury to optimize his many dazzling attributes.

During the course of the season, we faced some quality passers in Gavin Sheridan (Platt), Mark Searles (Derby), Jeff DelRosso (Cheshire), and others. We were able to simulate those quarterbacks with assistant coach Scott Ottochian donning the pads and quarterbacking the scout team. Salisbury presented a whole new scout team mosaic, and the only person who seemed to meet our need was assistant coach Bobby Corazzini. Bobby was fast, quick, and still had his college football mindset.

As we often did throughout the season with other weekly opponent defensive challenges, we took apart various pieces of Salisbury's play (the alignment of his feet under center; his first two steps on snap; his eye direction on snap; and his throwing motion.

Coach Corazzini was wonderfully adept at translating those scouting report elements and my cryptic, often verbose explanation of detail and sequence. On more than one occasion, as Bobby was trying to coach the offensive line during the offensive period, I would pull him away and say, "let's go through this again." I wanted Bobby prepared to "be-Salisbury" when we got to defensive period. Coach Ottochian would catch me talking defense with Bobby and ask me to "knock it off" in a more than flowery fashion.

As part of the "Salisbury Sim" from our film study, we would measure the depth of his drop or feet from the line of scrimmage as when Salisbury would sprint to the corner when Sheehan employed their "trips" formation.

Our "Scout Team" had done a masterful job in the second half of the season, led by coaches Scott Ottochian, John Wallace, John Gawlak, and Bobby Corazzini. In preparation for Sheehan, especially with a twelve-day layoff between our last game with Amity, we needed more from the "Scout Team." Heretofore, we began recruiting former players who were still in reasonably good shape to fill the Sheehan players' roles. One by one, we tried to find scout team players to approximate the skill-set of John MacKenzie, Bryan Cannata, John Santiago, and Marion Hanna, a powerful two-way performer.

Chapter 86

The Battle of Fitzgerald Field

This hybrid scout team was to be our opponent on the Saturday before Thanksgiving. Coach Ottochian agreed to let us run it as a game, using all the data I prepared, including down and distance tendencies, field location, and other interesting details that do not warrant this narrative.

Some of the recruited scout team players included center Jim Ryan, Brian Casey, and the "meilleur pour la fin" was quarterback Brian Hax. Brian was a former quarterback for us who decided to move over to soccer while at Lyman Hall. Brian was a splendid athlete with speed, power, and an outstanding arm. He was perfect to play Salisbury, leaving Corazzini free to play other critical positions. Coaches John Wallace, Scott Ottochian, and John Gawlak played the Sheehan skill players as they knew the data and characteristics of the Sheehan personnel.

Scripted down to the finest detail we could manage, the coaches on the scout team, using the reports, called the plays, and managed the down and distance with careful attention to Sheehan's pattern. From the first play to the last, the hitting was ferocious. Neither our varsity nor the scout team gave any quarter, nor did they except any. Brian was sharp with his passes and elusive sprinting the corner as Salisbury. Our defense hit him with some big shots, but Hax just trotted back to the huddle, and the next play was called. There were no time-outs and minimal stopping for corrective instruction. It was viewed as A GAME. John Gawlak played Marion Hanna at fullback and pounded the middle of our defense. He could tell you better than me how hard he was hit.

For 45 minutes, THE BATTLE OF FITZGERALD FIELD was waged. Although fathers Tony Barket and Rick Poggio were in attendance, there was BUT ONE PERSON in the stands.

This scrimmage turned out to be a no-holds-barred battle royale. The scout team was no less physical on defense than they were when on offense. After 45 minutes (at least) of non-stop football, Coach O said, "we've had enough."

All participants were covered in dirt. There weren't any grass stains because our football field had no grass at that late point in the season. There was a lot of hugging and compliments back and forth between our team members and the scout team. We collectively believed that this was a great pre-cursor for Sheehan. Our scout team was superb, particularly our non-starters like Kenny Priest, Billy Corazzini, Steve May, Glenn Root, Dave Canny, Bill Sheridan, Bobby Lampo, Steve May, Brett Baron, Tommy Berube, and Ray Cormier.

MIKE SHERMAN - FUTURE HEAD COACH, GREEN BAY PACKERS

As coach Ottochian talked to the "combatants" after the scrimmage, I saw a singular man sitting all by himself in the stands walking down the bleachers' stairs. As I usually trailed the team when coming off the field, the gentleman I did not know approached me. He introduced himself to me as Mike Sherman, offensive line coach of the College of the Holy Cross. He explained that he was there scouting, hoping to sign Ralph Riley. He told me that this was his first year at the College of the Holy Cross. Then he asked me if we practice like this all the time. I told him the circumstances by which we planned today's "practice."

Coach Sherman said, and I quote exactly, "THAT WAS THE HARDEST HITTING PRACTICE HE HAD EVER SEEN." Shaking his head, he told me he enjoyed every minute of it. "real football" ... he said ... "real football." The gentleman I was speaking with was, indeed, MIKE SHERMAN, future head coach of the Green Bay Packers from 2000-2005, who also served as head coach at Texas A & M.

Coach Sherman did, in fact, go on to coach Ralph Riley at the College of the Holy Cross.

LAST DAYS OF PRACTICE

By Monday, November 25, 1985, following the "Battle of Fitzgerald Field" on the previous Saturday, there was a quiet confidence about the Thanksgiving Day game with Sheehan. The offensive portion of our practices were crisp, with one extraordinary change in our lineup. After watching the North Haven game's film, Coach Ottochian liked what he saw of Mark Wollen at center. So much so that he made a bold move that most head coaches wouldn't have dared.

Ralph Riley was our best offensive lineman and probably the finest offensive tackle to ever play for Lyman Hall. He was a physical player, but Ralph was also an outstanding athlete. At the end of the 1985 season, he would be recognized as a consensus All-State tackle. With that in mind, Coach Ottochian decided to move Ralph Riley to tight end.

This meant that our regular tight end, Randy Pelletier, would move to the flanker/Vee-back position. Greg Myerson would slide over to guard with David Klaverkamp at tackle. Together, Myerson, Klaverkamp, and Riley were as imposing a trio of high school linemen as one could imagine.

Once again, we counted on our guys' intelligence to make all these positional changes this late in the season, and they did with ease.

The idea was to surprise Sheehan with this new alignment of personnel. Whatever Sheehan thought about this surprise element when we started the game, you'd have to ask them.

In practice, throughout the days of preparation for

Sheehan, you would never know that those guys were playing new positions. They were incredibly efficient. Ralph fit in so well at tight end you would think he had always played the position. Riley, Klaverkamp, and Myerson's blocking were so powerful and quick in practice, particularly on counter plays, that we thought Vinnie (Poggio) might have 250 yards on Thanksgiving. Naturally, Coach Borelli would be setting up his defense to stop Vincent.

What was intriguing about the personnel changes was how it might impact our limited passing game. About 15% of our offense was throwing the ball. Todd Barket, our quarterback, completed about 50% of his passes but heading into Thanksgiving, he only had thrown the ball 100 times. Matt Schmitt, our fullback led us in pass receptions; however, tight end Randy Pelletier was our scoring target. Randy had seven TD receptions as we approached the Sheehan game. So, the logical question was how would the move from tackle to tight end for Ralph Riley alter, if at all, our passing game? We would soon find out.

FINAL FEW DAYS OF DEFENSIVE PRACTICE

After twelve weeks of practice, installing a new defense, and then adjusting it in various ways to meet the strengths and weaknesses of our opponents' offense, we had several schemes in our defensive plan that we never utilized in a game. Admiring Andy Borelli as I did and do, coupled with the magnitude of the game, I anticipated that he and his coaching staff might add a wrinkle or two to his offense.

In our final week of practice, leading up to Thanksgiving Day, I inserted a group of blitzes we had yet to utilize, matching each with the in-game tendencies (primarily field position guided) that Sheehan might reveal. I had hoped not to need or call those blitzes that included "Lightning," a cornerback blitz with Vincent Poggio attacking the C-gap (between tackle and tight end); "Billy-Club," a *read-me* free safety blitz with

Todd Barket, reading the movement of the offensive tackle, with a fake "C-gap" blitz from our Sam Linebacker, Randy Pelletier; and "Hatchet," with Riley and Myerson, moving over from defensive ends to inside linebackers, attacking shoulder to shoulder through the "A-gap, (between center & guard) and B-gap, (between guard & tackle).

Following Saturday's scrimmage, we planned to back away from all "live" drills. We put so much time into situational defensive planning, but there was the aura of new wrinkles that Sheehan might throw against us. Subsequently, we prepared for a large variety of "maybes."

During this last week of practice for the Sheehan game, most of the assistant coaches wanted to talk about the real possibility that we would be facing top-ranked Middletown High School in a week, and we needed to start preparing. Some of our players went to see Middletown's last game, as did a few of our coaches, but I could not and would not discuss anything regarding Middletown. The sting of "distractions" was still reverberating inside me from the Shelton week, and I would not consider anything Middletown until we had beaten Sheehan. However, the coaches were not about to leave it alone.

THE TRADITIONAL LAST PRACTICE

Each practice, from Monday to Wednesday, practices seemed to become quieter. The normal byplay between players and the back-and-forth between the **"funkadelics"** (nickname of the linebackers and secondary) became increasingly mute. The boys in BLUE were ready. On the cold, overcast practice of Wednesday, November 27, 1985, we learned of the threat of SNOW the day before the game.

Nevertheless, after a crisp, quiet practice by a script, the seniors took their traditional final lap around the Fitzgerald Field. The underclassmen who numbered a few more than ten, counting freshmen, met the running seniors in the South endzone corner. There was little talk, just a huddle, the chant of "together, together, together," and then the walk to the locker room.

They had come such a long way from the last game of 1984 till now. As we watched them trot off the field, we hoped that this was not the last practice for Todd Barket, Ray Cormier, David Klaverkamp, Bob Lampo, Steve May, Greg Myerson, Vincent Poggio, Ralph Riley, Gaetano Russo, Matt Schmitt, and Bill Sheridan.

After the team hung up their gear and readied their individual lockers for tomorrow's early morning pre-game dress, they ate together as they did before each game, grinders from Rosa's Deli. We adjourned as a team to the tiered lecture hall, 14C, where each senior on the team addressed the team.

Always an emotional last night before the final game of each season, Ray Cormier was last to speak. Ray (#77) was the sideline cheerleader for the team. He insisted on playing every snap on scout team and was responsible for getting the extra point kicking tee into Greg Myerson after we scored a touchdown. With tears in his eyes, Ray candidly articulated his place and role on this team. He thanked Todd Barket for encouraging him to join the football team and never allowing him to quit. Of that night and that special season, Ray-Ray stated, "It was my duty and honor and place to be the voice on those sidelines, ... and a never quitting opponent on the Scout Team"!

As the team left the school that evening, some snow was beginning to fall. Coach Ottochian and I were, as always, the last to leave the school. Phil and I always talked together before we left the coaches' room. We always had things to share, concerns to be voiced. Our cars were parked close together. On this evening, we shared a hug before departing each other, and Coach O said, "Don't worry, coach, we're going to win."

Chapter 87

Snow Stalls the Biggest Football Game

Thanksgiving, November 28, 1985 ... the day that all of Wallingford had long awaited. The day when football was finally the only story in Wallingford. The day when Wallingford's two high schools would battle for more than just silly "local bragging rights." The day when championships were on the line and a seismic tremor of emotions riddled every Wallingford street and home.

The snow began to fall in earnest on November 27, shortly after the last practice of the Lyman Hall football team, as the last traditional lap was taken around Fitzgerald football field.

There were no more words to be spoken. There were no more preparations to be made, and the scouting reports were all committed to memory by the 24-members of the Blue and White football team.

It snowed and snowed, and it was evident that no "big game" would be played in Wallingford on Thanksgiving Day. The game was called, almost at dawn, on Thanksgiving Day, as the snow continued to fall. There were no artificial surfaces on either high school's field, and on this day, the snow rapidly covered the newly named Riccitelli Field at Sheehan High School, the site of the biggest game of any sport in Wallingford history.

Matt Schmitt recalls the shock of the decision not to play the Sheehan game due to snow, "I remember waking up early in the morning (Thanksgiving Day) at home, listening to the radio for a game update. The Stoddard Bowl (Thanksgiving Day game in neighboring Meriden) was played as scheduled. I vaguely remember making several calls to a phone number I thought might have information, but there was no answer. Having heard no news, I drove to Lyman Hall from home and pulled into the parking lot at the back of the school. It was a steady sheet of snow. When Coach Ottochian informed us that the game was postponed, I was beside myself. Of all the games we played, this was the one that I felt most ready for that day".

Only Mother Nature could have stalled the momentum of this game of all games. What we (the Lyman Hall coaches) worried about, and we said it to each other, ... "What if the delay of this game sapped our team of their fiery edge"? Once we knew that the game was postponed and despite the heavy snow falling, the Lyman Hall coaches met at the North Haven Holiday Inn on Thanksgiving morning. It was a serious, heartfelt meeting of the coaches.

As was his want, John Wallace was matter-of-fact in declaring that the snow and its subsequent delay would have no impact on our team's readiness to play. Coach Ottochian was not so strident as he remembered the previous snow-outs like the 1978 Shelton game when the Blue and White were playing well and fell to the Gaels.

We talked for over three hours. Bobby Corazzini thought that our senior leadership was such that there would be no letdown.

Then, although we agreed to NOT talk about Middletown, the conversation found its way to Middletown. Coach Ottochian was adamant that we should not talk about the recent scouting trips our assistant coaches made to see Middletown. Coach Wallace did not mince words. Between the mouthfuls of eggs and coffee, John (Wallace) characterized Middletown as the fastest high school team he had ever seen. Middletown (before our LHHS scouts) had played previously undefeated Wolcott and destroyed them 33-14 in a dazzling display of buck sweeps and long passes to Roosevelt James

(#22) and tight ends, Dean Wilborn (#10) and Chris Lipscomb (#11).

I kept asking that we not get engaged in this conversation but coaches Wallace, Gawlak, and Corazzini seemed to drift back to Middletown. No logic seemed acceptable to not open discourse on Middletown. If we don't defeat Sheehan ... there is no Middletown for which to be concerned.

As we spoke on Thanksgiving morning at the Holiday Inn, the snow continued to fall, and we all wondered if we would be able to get the game in on Friday morning. As it turned out, the amount of snow dictated that the town's public works could not prepare the field for a Friday game. Now the issue was gathering the team for practice on Friday. The snow just would not relent. Please, God, don't let our boys lose their edge.

Bobby Corazzini walked out with me from the restaurant to the parking lot. He was one of my earliest LHHS defensive backs, a splendid hard-working coach. He was matter-of-fact in rebuking me, "Coach, you can't wait to look at Middletown. You can't give them extra days to prepare for us. If we win, we have to practice and prepare for them on Sunday".

Bobby was right. I couldn't wait, but I did not want to be distracted from Sheehan. When we were once again snowed out on Friday, November 29th, we practiced, briefly, quietly with full attention to Sheehan.

After practice ... in the isolation of my film room (a little room off the garage), I began to study Middletown High School play charts that our coaches had written from their scouting of the Blue Dragons. Now, the challenge at hand ... focus on Sheehan!

Chapter 88

Wallingford's Greatest Athletic Game

Saturday, NOVEMBER 30, 1985

After an agonizing, two-day delay, the 1985 contest between Lyman Hall High School and Sheehan High School would be staged at the Hope Hill Road school (Sheehan). The morning was cold, and the snow still covered the ground around everyone's home. Mike Cassella and the Wallingford Public Works Department did a marvelous job of clearing and preparing the field. The PWD put "speedy dry" on most of the field, and as we stretched on the frozen mud at Riccitelli (Sheehan) Field, the surface felt like a sea of rabbit debris.

Both teams warmed up with hardly a sound being heard except the buzz of the overflow crowd. Speedy dry was on everyone's backside, and the coaches were continually wiping off our footballs if they hit the ground. You couldn't help notice the streams of people walking down the hill near the concession stand to enter the field. All around the upper rim of the field were wall-to-wall spectators. The bone-chilling temperatures would not be enough to keep the Town of Wallingford from watching what everyone thought would be an epic football battle ... or so people thought.

As we (the coaches) made the rounds, talking with our men as they warmed up, Guy Russo and I conversed. It was more a nervous talk from Guy as he often would in a big

349

moment or a big game. He wanted me to call "Express" on the first defensive down of the game. Guy liked that blitz as he would be shooting the "A" gap to the tight end side, Sheehan's offensive tendency on first down. Little did I know that Guy had additional things in mind on that first defensive play.

Only once before in the 13-year history of the Lyman Hall vs. Sheehan game was the contest postponed due to inclement weather, but this two-day delay was of particular concern relative to team psychological readiness. In my 35 years of coaching this great game, you never knew what negative impact it might have. Candidly, I never knew a weather delay to have a good effect unless the opponent responded with less focus than the teams I coached. The only other time a Sheehan vs. LHHS game had been postponed was 1975, and the Blue & White beat the west siders 21-7. Michael Nesti capped his senior season with a 204-yard effort against Sheehan that day, his 10th consecutive 100 yards plus game. Sheehan couldn't stop the Lyman Hall All-Time great!

IT IS FINALLY TIME ...

The 24 member Lyman Hall team, walked from the makeshift locker room in a Sheehan corridor as close to kickoff as possible. The crowd was such that we had to move people aside to walk as a team in a relatively straight line, two by two to the top of the hill, overlooking the newly named John Riccitelli Field.

The thunder of cheers erupted on the far side of the field as our Lyman Hall team, dressed in white with navy helmets, with white facemasks, and the orange "T" on both sides of our helmets, walked down the mud-soaked hill, leading to the field entrance.

Few teams in Lyman Hall football history ever made a more dramatic entrance. The only team that came close was the 1974 team. People on both sides of the aisle stood and watched the Lyman Hall team come on the field. It was a surreal beginning to a game for the ages.

We all wanted to play defense first ...

On Sheehan's first offensive possession, Guy Russo, who was so on fire he was talking to himself as he took the field, got what he wanted on my first defensive call. By nature, Sheehan's offensive cadence was long and protracted because they shifted their tailback on almost every play. Guy lined our defense up, and he immediately started talking to Sheehan quarterback Brian Salisbury. I saw him yapping but didn't know until later that he said, "Salisbury ... I'm coming to get you". The defense attacked with great effectiveness immediately, and Sheehan didn't move the ball but a few yards.

With both teams running the ball and subsequently keeping the clock running, Sheehan (Salisbury) set up to punt on fourth down late in the first quarter of a scoreless game. We worked hard on blocking punts, and we got five blocked before the Sheehan game. As our dominant tackles attacked inside, we came hard off the edge, drawing a lot of attention. Salisbury rushed his punt a little, as the Sheehan up-back absorbing our inside pressure backed up, and Salisbury punted the ball into the back of the up-back. We took over on the Sheehan 34-yard line.

We ran our offense, a mix of Matt Schmitt inside and Vin Poggio on counter plays. Six offensive plays of steady progress, and we were in a goal-to-go situation from the 4-yard line. Matt behind Myerson, Klaverkamp, and Riley banged it in for the touchdown. By this time in the season, we knew that our extra-point kicking was less than reliable. Coach Ottochian went for two on the conversion and, using his new weapon at tight end, Ralph Riley, we scored and led 8-0.

The defense was particularly emotional on this day. I had not seen this level of animation from our defense since the Derby game. An early Sheehan timeout brought me before a defensive unit who were eye-to-eye locked in on everything said. Greg Myerson said in the huddle, "call anything. We're killing them".

We penetrated quickly for a tackle for loss yardage on Sheehan's next offensive possession, leaving them in a 3rd and long. On the ensuing play, Ralph Riley closed quickly and hit

Salisbury, resulting in a fumble that Dave Klaverkamp, who had ripped deep into the Sheehan backfield, promptly fell on for a ten-yard loss.

We had a first and ten on the 39-yard line, and Coach Ottochian kept his ground attack moving steadily for ten plays that resulted in a two-yard touchdown run by Vinnie (Poggio). We didn't get the two-point play, but I noticed the light-blue-clad Middletown Blue Dragons assembled in the endzone for the first time. If I dared to care, I would have also been aware that the Montville football team and coaches were also packed into the endzone.

As the first half drew to a close, the assembled masses' roar was heard on almost every play as even the slightest success on either side was wildly celebrated. Near the end of the half, Ed Charbonneau caught Salisbury for a loss, and it seemed like the fans on our sideline (behind the ropes) were going to storm the field. The place was bedlam.

HALF TIME NOTES

When we walked up the hill, Bobby Corazzini got in my ear with a few things that he felt were hurting us defensively. Bobby had a keen eye for little things. One of those things was Sheehan's 3-wide formation, a conversation we previously held two weeks ago.

We went into the game with a plan to jump into a modified zone defense when Sheehan showed those 3-wide. We wanted to face Salisbury with the back of our defense as they were sprinting the corner with the option of Salisbury running or throwing the ball.

As soon as I got to our "back hall" locker room, we gathered the defensive unit and changed to a man scheme when Sheehan got into that 3x1 formation. Additionally, we widened up Ralph and Greg from their defensive end positions. This proved to open up our blitzes a little more in the second half.

If there was trepidation going into the second half, it was that Sheehan had great capabilities on offense and finished games very well. Sounds trite, but we could not allow Sheehan to get off to a positive start to begin the second half. We were only up 14-0 with so much on the line.

In the first half, we carefully charted Sheehan, and Sheehan stayed close to their season-long tendencies on offense, so the defensive calls were "on schedule." Sheehan was only down two touchdowns, and they weren't in "desperation mode" by any means, but if we got another score in before they were able to score, things could change. We wanted Sheehan to throw it.

SECOND HALF

Whatever adjustments Sheehan made or didn't make, our offensive line got it going in the second half. Vince broke off a modest six-yard run to our offensive right (Myerson, Klaverkamp, and Riley), and then Matt Schmitt, who would enjoy his single greatest individual day, broke a 50-yard touchdown run. A pass from Todd Barket to our new tight end, Ralph Riley, on the two-point play after touchdown, pushed the score to 22-0.

The Sheehan offense now settled into runs by Marion Hanna and Salisbury. The tailbacks hardly, if at all, touched the ball.

We stopped Sheehan on downs on their next possession, and the Blue offense went to work once again. Coach Ottochian was content to just hand the ball off to our fullback Matt Schmitt who carried the ball three consecutive plays. On his third carry, Matt bounced it outside to our left with Distante and Goldstein sealing the defensive front, and Schmitt (#35) dashed 32 yards for another touchdown.

With the score now 28-0, it might just be getting to THAT desperation time for the West Siders. To this point, both teams were running the ball, so the clock was moving along through the third quarter and into the fourth quarter. When Sheehan did attempt to pass, our defense was getting to their quarterback. The pressure of the blitz, coupled with excellent coverage on John MacKenzie (Sheehan's most explosive receiver) primarily by Todd Barket and Vin Poggio, minimized their passing game.

FOURTH QUARTER MADNESS

When we did turn the corner on the final period of play, you could feel the anticipation build among our most loyal fans, our players' fathers. I liked to isolate myself from others when we were on defense to make my calls without distraction. In the 4th period, I found myself sandwiched between Tony Barket and Rick Poggio, who were as giddy as little kids. Rick kept saying, "We're going to do it … we're going to do it." I was shaking my head with a smile, trying to escape these two, who were far more excited than anyone else.

With Sheehan forced to pass, our blitzes reached another level of effectiveness. The pressure on Brian Salisbury was coming on every down as Myerson, Riley, Schmitt, and Charbonneau combined for sacks. On third and long, Sheehan ran a draw to Hanna as Bill Goldstein, and David Klaverkamp flooded the A-gaps on our "Zulu" blitz to stuff the play.

With seven minutes remaining, some smiles were starting to show on our players' faces. Todd Barket, our quarterback and free safety who never came out of the game, ran to the near hash and yelled something at me. I didn't quite hear him. I raised my hands to show that I did not hear him, so Todd did something he was not supposed to do. He crossed the hash mark to get closer to me, yelling at me …. "CALL BILLY CLUB. " "Billy Club" was one of the blitzes we worked on for the Sheehan game if game circumstances were such that it was warranted. We hadn't used that blitz. We hadn't needed to use that blitz.

Running back to the defensive huddle, still looking back at me, imploring me to call "Billy-Club," it occurred to me that if I call it and Todd gets hurt, I might have to walk home after the game. Taking a deep breath, hoping that our starting quarterback doesn't get clobbered, I signaled in "18" to Guy Russo, the designation of the never-before-called "Billy Club" blitz. Todd, our Free Safety, who was most often aligned in man coverage on the tight end, started in his normal alignment. As Salisbury (Sheehan's QB) started his cadence, our strong safety, Matt Schmitt, moved inside to cover the tight end and our free safety; Todd blitzed the "C" gap. IF the offensive tackle bites on Randy's C to B blitz, Todd goes clean to the quarterback.

It was an obvious pass situation with Sheehan way behind on the scoreboard. Matt was matched with the much taller MacKenzie. I was watching the Sheehan tackle. If he steps down, we got it. Sure as shooting, the tackle is eyeing Randy. Todd goes straight through and sacks Salisbury for an eight-yard loss. With that, I get it from two sides. Coach Ottochian quickly runs down the sideline to me, yelling at me, "What are you doing? That's our quarterback." Todd, without celebration, trots over to me and says, "...call it again". Guy in echo mode yells out, "Coach, 18 again"? No, I didn't call it again, but it did stay in the package for Middletown. Final sidebar on this moment ... Tony Barket, Todd's father, who was right near me, comes over and whispers, "... you could have done that all year".

MINUTES TO GO ...

One of the consequences of having only 24 members on a football team (including freshmen) that is prolific on both offense and defense is that everyone is playing the entire game. You can't look down the sideline and put in the Junior Varsity team because we didn't have one. As the clock wound down, we were compelled to keep most of the starters in the game, substituting on offense and making sure everyone on the team played.

With approximately five minutes remaining and Matt Schmitt exhausted, having carried 17 times of hard inside running, not missing a down on defense or special teams, Coach called on our quarterback, Todd (Barket), to run the option and keep the ball in bounds. By this time, I'm sure Sheehan had to be feeling the situation in frustration and fatigue. We were content to punt the ball back to Sheehan rather than risk plays that might stop the clock. However, Todd broke away on a 39-yard run for a touchdown, and the score reached 34-0. We lined up for an extra point kick, but in seasonal fashion, it was missed.

Now, we made sure that everyone on our roster played, especially on offense. Coach Ottochian yells out to no one in particular, "No more scoring. We are done scoring." The fact that we were on defense when he said those words did not escape my meretricious middle linebacker, Guy Russo, who happened to be standing next to me for the first call of the Sheehan offensive series. Guy looked at me with that "face" he sometimes gave me and said, "Tell Coach, if we get a fumble, we'll just fall on it."

Despite the score and less than a minute remaining, we turned Sheehan over deep in their territory. Glenn Root was inserted into the lineup at quarterback. With 17 seconds left, Coach Ottochian calls "38 option". He didn't say take a knee. I leaned into him and asked, "Why don't you tell Glenn to take a knee"? Coach Ottochian said, "We won't score."

Glenn did what the play called for and ran the option, ... kept it ... and sailed into the endzone.

In the instant of the signal for a touchdown, Coach went ballistic. Daring not to write what was actually said, Coach Ottochian imparted to Glenn that Andy Borelli is his friend and did not want to run up the score. Glenn was surely taken aback as he just ran the play he was told.

So, the final score was a shocking 40-0. No one could have expected this outcome, but then again, no one in the living world could have predicted that both Wallingford (a non-traditional football town) high schools would play for the now and sorely missed Housatonic League championship. Everything about this season was astounding. There was no normal.

AFTERMATH – WALLINGFORD'S GREATEST FOOTBALL GAME

The scene at the trophy presentation was relatively quiet from both teams' demeanor. There were no crazy jumping up and down and celebrating that characterizes the simplest of high school victories these days. Both teams knew how to comport themselves. The conduct of both teams should be a training tape for high school athletic teams. There were smiles, tears, and some applause, but there was compassion and appreciation for what had just happened in this game.

Derby's loss to Housatonic League foe, Shelton, that day left Lyman Hall in sole possession of the Housatonic League Title, the last league championship LHHS would ever win.

Matt Schmitt was the game's Most Valuable Player. Mathew carried the ball 17 times for 182 yards with three touchdowns. He played every down on defense. Vinnie Poggio, who was the apple of the Sheehan defense's eye, ran for 61 yards on 18 carries, and quarterback Todd Barket ran for 51 yards on five carries.

BLITZ-0-MANIA ROLLED

The Lyman Hall defense continued to rack up the sacks and tackles for loss. The Sheehan quarterback was sacked six times in the contest, and there were seven tackles for loss on running plays. Sheehan was limited to 95 yards rushing on 41 attempts as Marion Hanna led Sheehan with 69 yards on 20 carries, and Brian Salisbury had 16 yards on 17 carries. Sheehan completed five passes for 61 yards. Guy Russo was the defensive player of the game for Lyman Hall.

WE PLAY IN DECEMBER ...

As we left Riccitelli Field, there were some well-wishers on the top of the hill where our bus waited for us, but by and large, the crowd was left stunned by the final score and the "head-shaking" reality that both teams would play for a State Championship.

Now, there was no more stopping our coaches from discussing Middletown. Coach John Wallace had the most memorable comment when I asked him about Middletown. To quote John, "Hoager (his unflattering nickname for me) ... WHOAAAAAAAAAAAA". Not one coach on our staff offered anything but total admiration for Middletown. The newspapers and media outlets gave us <u>NO CHANCE</u> against the nationally-ranked Middletown Blue Dragons.

THE BUS RIDE HOME & THE QUIET TIME

If the mud-soaked members of the 1985 football team wanted to celebrate on the crosstown trip back to Lyman Hall, they struggled to show it. The physical and emotional build-up and the game itself had all but zapped the team. There were smiles throughout the steamy and sweat-soaked bus, but not a lot of talk. Whatever the team was feeling after their victory, it was visually tempered. There was now ... one more battle left to fight.

Coach wasted no time in announcing something he had set up before the Sheehan game. Before we left Sheehan, he told the team that we would practice TOMORROW, Sunday, December 1, 1985, at the fieldhouse on the campus of Choate School. There were no gripes nor groans, but Coach and I talked about how little (physically and emotionally) these guys would have tomorrow to practice with after a long season and the physical and highly emotional event of today.

"GET TO WORK"

Our locker room slowly emptied after arriving back from the Sheehan game. There was little talk, other than our coaches' room where Coach Ottochian offered a handshake to every coach and Coach Ottochian's charge to me of ... "Coach, GET TO WORK." This was his way of saying he knew what I had to do to prepare for Middletown, and ... there was no time to waste.

The coaches walked out of the building together, but I was the last person actually to get in my car. I stood there looking through the bare trees at our football field, thanking God for this moment and the moment yet to come. The French say it best, ... a cet instant et le moment à venir.

Now, onto to Middletown.

Lyman Hall had just won the Housatonic League Championship with a 10-1 record. It was Saturday evening, November 30, 1985, the night after the two-day delayed Thanksgiving Day game and a 40-0 victory over Sheehan.

No one was in celebration mode. There wasn't time to celebrate. Six days from today, December 7, 1985, we would face the unbeatable foe, Middletown High School, in the Class M State Championship game at Memorial Field (now torn down) on the campus of the University Connecticut.

From the moment I arrived home, it was down to that little room, off the garage, to focus in earnest on nothing but Middletown High School. About halfway through Middletown's play charts against Wolcott High School that coach John Wallace had prepared, I realized how little time I had to design a defensive plan. As usual, when "Wally" scouted a game, he would write a lot of peripheral comments. If I take all of his remarks with the spice of his profanity that he wrote in the margins to heart, it might convince me that we have little chance to defeat Middletown. The game (Sheehan) was over only five hours ago, but it feels like six weeks ago.

We have our first practice tomorrow for Middletown, and I have to have the defensive scout team sheets ready. I must have spliced this first film on Middletown together five times before midnight. My super 8 projector has just about had it. I don't have time to scotch tape this film all night. I played the same record album over and over as I have since the Derby game as I worked on the charts, film study, and trying to get the plan together.

Good thing I didn't get tired of this Purple Rain album. I've scratched the record many times from picking up and putting down the worn-out needle on the record, but I will probably burn it after the Middletown game. There is one song, "Take Me with You" (second band, first side), on the record that helps me relax and think of someone incredibly special to me. I am so thankful to God, overwhelmed that this team allowed me to tag along on this glorious season. Now back to Middletown. It's 9:15 pm, and we practice at Choate tomorrow".

Chapter 89

All About Middletown High School

SUNDAY, CHOATE SCHOOL PRACTICE

The day after the Sheehan game was a Sunday, December 1, 1985. For our team, there was no holiday respite, no day off from the football work week. As they entered the indoor Choate facility, there were some sore, bruised, and emotionally drained Lyman Hall football players. I don't know if any of our team, particularly our nine two-way starters, were feeling all that well. Matt Schmitt looked particularly tired. The Sheehan game took its temporary toll on the entire team, both physically and emotionally. This was a significant advantage for Middletown as they hadn't played a game since Saturday, November 23rd.

We tried to approach the Choate practice like any other, first reviewing the opposition's defense against our offensive sets. The coaches could only smile and watch our limping, stiff players as they tried in earnest to line up in formations and run our base plays against the 4-4 of Middletown. Try as they might, the boys were just plain exhausted. Coach Ottochian talked only quietly to the effort the team tried to make.

After 30 minutes or so, coach lined up the team to run or, as he said, "Let's get the kinks out." We ran, but it was a "move as fast as you could" back and forth. Finally, in a little less than an hour together, Coach Ottochian brought the team up and talked with them very briefly. As the team left, I showed some of the results of the film study to Coach Ottochian. Phil didn't have a lot to say in response, but we did agree that we could not hit in practice as we were used to doing in the last 11 weeks. We needed to be as healed and rested as we could for an opponent that was as different from any other team we had faced this season, or for that matter, any other season. He told me to "keep working." It was clear Phil needed some down hours as well.

Monday (tomorrow) would begin the real "heavy lifting" for us, not in the physical sense, but in the mental preparedness necessary to meet and defeat an outstanding juggernaut of an opponent.

I might add that an onslaught of the state's sports press corps was about to descend on us. We had never known this added distraction or pressure.

NO TIME FOR NEW THINGS, BUT NEW THINGS WERE ADDED

We learned quickly that you have little time to prepare for your opponent when you play in a state tournament or state championship game. Your hours of practice are less than usual, and the distraction and excitement of the upcoming game tugs at the team's concentration. Consistent with the years of challenges that faced Lyman Hall High School football's very survival, we were coming off a highly intensified game against Sheehan. Yes, we soundly defeated Sheehan for the league crown, but the weeks of anticipation and the game itself had to have taken something out of the team. Now, in the wake of the thunderous victory over Sheehan, we faced a team who most "experts" believed was one of the best Connecticut high school teams in schoolboy history. In retrospect, it was only fitting that historically hapless Lyman Hall would face the unconquerable adversary.

The final five days of practice were tranquil. There was

little of the customary byplay. The light-hearted kidding about was absent. It was all single-minded field preparation. The scouting report was completed and distributed on Wednesday with a longer than normal question-answer period.

Coach Ottochian called me at my office in Hartford early on Monday, December 2, 1985, and asked me to meet him at the school earlier than usual. There was an urgency today with so few days remaining, so I put in my paperwork for more vacation time and met him in the faculty room at Lyman Hall at 11:15 am or so. Coach Ottochian was talking it up with the "good ole boys" (other LHHS teachers). We immediately headed to his office for something he said, "You have to see."

When we got to his office, he proceeded to illustrate on a yellow legal pad a new shift for the offense. I asked him if he intended to use this against Middletown, and he never hesitated in saying that he would "put it in today."

Over the years, Coach Ottochian had taught me that an offense must force the defense to play balanced. This was another example of that teaching. He showed me four shifts, some we had already employed and some we hadn't as yet. We had only a few days until the State Championship game, but he was not done planning for Middletown.

The shift he wanted to show me was a VEE Right formation where "Vee-back" Randy Pelletier (our regular tight end until the Sheehan game) should shift to either the left or right tight end position and current tight end, Ralph Riley would either trade to the opposite tight end position or stay where he is. The result of which was a two-tight end I- formation. It was basic, but it forced Middletown to stay in a balanced 4-4 (four down linemen, four linebackers) alignment.

The beauty of this shift was that IF Middletown should kick down or move their defensive front over to the shift side, it would leave them vulnerable to the side away from the shift.

They observed us against Sheehan, and if they followed our pattern of that game, they would kick down to the shift side and leave themselves with one less man to one side.

Now, this shift put us in a two-tight end formation, putting their outside linebackers on the "proverbial island." Forgive me for talking "football-jargon." In the 4-4 defense of Middletown, the outside linebacker should align in the "C" gap to the tight end side. If there are two tight ends, both outside linebackers would be aligned in the "C" gap, placing the cornerback in a position to cover the tight end and protect the edge. It was a quality idea from Coach Ottochian, even though we had only two days to put it into the offensive plan.

As it turned out, Coach Ottochian not only put this two-tight end shift in days before the State Championship game against Middletown, but he opened the contest with it, and as you will see or did see, we gashed the racehorse fast Middletown defense with it in the first quarter.

FULLBACK COUNTER

With the new two tight end alignment Coach Ottochian installed for Middletown and our exceptional offensive line, he knew that our line could execute our tailback counter, known as Heavy Counter, with great precision. However, as we experienced throughout the season, every defense was primed to stop Vince Poggio, and Middletown would be no exception.

Coach Ottochian needed a play to keep the Middletown defense honest if they did overplay Vincent. This play was ... fullback counter! The critical element was the logical attention that Middletown's "fast-flow" 4-4 defense would pay to Vincent. Not to get into the actual game just yet, but Coach Ottochian could not have designed a more perfect play for Middletown.

DEFENSE VS. MIDDLETOWN FIREPOWER

When the coaches came back from scouting Middletown's last game, they were figuratively frothing at the mouth to tell me all about this Blue Dragon team. Once we had beaten Sheehan, they could not be contained. We hadn't even gotten on the bus after the Sheehan game to return to Lyman Hall when they bombarded me with anecdotes of the Middletown speed and athleticism.

That Saturday night, I committed myself to a complete inculcation of the Middletown offense, founded in the most thorough study of their game films possible.

At first review, I was amazed at how many break-away threats the Blue Dragons had on their offense. Their running backs were faster than any team we had faced this season, where just one broken or missed tackle results in a very long touchdown. Their prolific running game began with fullback Tony Rankins (#31), who averaged 10.4 yards a carry with fifteen touchdowns and 1,186 yards rushing. That data alone mandated that specific blitzes be used so we wouldn't fall victim to that quick trap up the middle. Now the problem ..., when will they run the fullback, the ole' "down and distance" data.

The most lethal weapon in the Middletown offense was All-State quarterback Dennis Wade (#12), the best all-around athlete of any quarterback Lyman Hall had ever faced.

As Middletown scored fast in every one of their games, they never trailed in a single game and were rarely, if ever, forced to throw the ball. Wade had an incredible arm, but his leg speed made him especially dangerous throwing on the run. In their run-first Wing-T offense, Wade threw for 1,223 yards and 23 touchdowns. His pass completions averaged 28.2 yards per completion. With the possible exception of Vincent Poggio, all the Middletown receivers were faster than us.

Middletown had never trailed in a game this season and were the owners of the longest active winning streak in Connecticut. They averaged 39.9 points per game while allowing an average of 5.9 points on defense. Conversely, we scored on an average of 26.5 points per game while giving up an average of 9.6 points per game. With that level of point differential, it can be deduced that the Middletown starters did not have to play in the fourth quarter of many (if any) of their games. To be sure, this was a great football team, but one that had not had to play their starters for four full quarters of football.

COWBOY COVERAGE

From all this information and analysis, it was clear to me that we needed a pass coverage designed explicitly for Middletown. The Blue Dragons could put four or five receivers in the pattern with blazing speed, making our man coverages bordering on high-risk. Late on the Sunday evening after the Sheehan game (we played on Saturday), I called an old friend and confidant, Tony Marotta, who was coaching at Wagner College. The subject was Middletown's airpower attack. Tony and I had discussed some coverage possibilities a month earlier, but now against an explosive Middletown passing game, I knew we needed an additional coverage to limit a possible all-out air assault if it came to that in our game.

We talked for quite some time, and after getting off the phone with Tony, I fine-tuned a coverage that became known as COWBOY. The coverage placed David Klaverkamp at nose-tackle with Ralph Riley and Greg Myerson at "loose" defensive ends. In this coverage, we played man coverage with our linebackers, on their two halfbacks and fullback. Guy Russo drew the responsibility of covering Tony Rankin. Bill Goldstein came out on Cowboy, replaced by Al Ferreira, an additional defensive back. We covered their tight end and split receiver with tight man coverage and then placed Todd Barket, Matt Schmitt, and Vince Poggio in a three-deep zone alignment behind the man coverage. The defense's two basic principles were to keep the quarterback from running out of bounds to stop the clock and, second, double cover the receiver to Wade's roll or eyes.

We practiced many repetitions on this coverage against every conceivable pass play in practice the last four days, and I hoped we would never need to use it. As it turned out, "Cowboy" played a significant part of the 4th quarter of the 1985 State Championship game.

ANTICIPATING TACKLE TRAP PASS

After looking at so many hours of Middletown super-8 film, it became like learning commercials or song lyrics by just hearing them. I felt as assured as possible with the learning of a new opponent, the sequences of the plays, and the down & distance tendencies of John Skubel (the Middletown head coach) from the film and scouting charts of our coaches.

Scott Ottochian, Bobby Corazzini, John Gawlak, and John Wallace worked so hard scouting Middletown. They brought back every piece of minutia I had asked for and more.

Middletown had a lot of extra time to prepare for us. They had played their last regular-season game the Saturday before Thanksgiving.

We played our last game the Saturday after Thanksgiving. So, they had a full week more to prepare for us! Their entire team and coaching staff had the luxury to see us in person against Sheehan.

Our scouts and the hours of film study were in harmony that Middletown had the capability of not only running a great play called Tackle Trap, but the manner in which they ran their Tackle Trap play would set up a pass play off that run action. (Sorry for the football jargon.) We ran the Tackle Trap and Tackle Trap Pass at Tuesday's practice, and both plays were successful against our defense. Coach John Wallace played the pulling tackle and did a great job simulating the pulling tackle's depth and quickness.

I felt that this play presented a real threat for us because of the way our two defensive ends played their technique. By the nature of our defense, our defensive ends confined (closed down) the "C" gap (the relative gap between offensive tackle and tight end), as we taught them to check flare and screen to their side.

It is one thing to defend one of your opponent's plays in practice. It is quite another to recognize it in the game. We worked on those two plays facetiously on Tuesday, and it got the point that Ralph and Greg saw it coming. Now, if I could anticipate when Middletown would run the play, I would call our ZULU blitz that shot our strong safety, Matt Schmitt, through the C-gap to the tight end side. This would disrupt the back-side pulling tackle as Eddie Charbonneau, our Will linebacker, would blitz the corner to the split end side, subsequently nailing the "jab-stepping" ball carrier at the point of the actual handoff.

Chapter 90

The Media Parade

- waiting for the Middletown Coronation

Each day during that week of practice before the Middletown game, members of the media showed up at practice to interview Coach Ottochian and members of the team. Bob Picozzi of Channel 8 television came to the practice field on a drizzly day that week. He interviewed Coach Ottochian and Todd Barket. We tried to continue the practice, but Mr. Picozzi's interview was a must-watch.

We completed preparations on December 5th, 1985, for the Middletown team that every newspaper and radio host, including the legendary Arnold Dean (The Dean of Sports) of WTIC, picked to win their second straight state championship.

Mr. Dean, on his nightly radio show, went through every class title game matchup and saved ours for last. When he got to the Class M game, he first complimented the team from Wallingford for ... as he put it .... "Getting this far." He cited the fact (and I am paraphrasing) that Lyman Hall has not seen a team with the athleticism of Middletown.

Each morning of that week, Connecticut's state newspapers included stories and predictions of Lyman Hall High School's demise and a large margin of defeat. It was the consensus that the Blue and White would fall victim to one of the worst mismatches since the Connecticut State Championships were initiated in 1976.

For a multitude of reasons, every Connecticut newspaper

covered the State Class M State Championship game. The consensus of writers was that they all wanted to be at the coronation of the 1985 Middletown High School football team. If Middletown had won, stated New Haven Register sportswriter Steve Wilson, "Middletown would have been acknowledged as one of the greatest high school football teams, if not THE greatest" in the history of Connecticut."

The state's newspapers were all over this game, some at the exclusion of the other class state games. Not one newspaper gave Lyman Hall much of a chance to defeat the nationally-ranked Blue Dragons. The Waterbury Republican that picked the scores of many high school games predicted the score:

Middletown 27 – Lyman Hall 6.
The New Haven Register prediction:
Middletown 28 - Lyman Hall 8

The Middletown Press:
(Please reference the misspelling of our players' names in these exact excerpts.) "The Blue Dragons have so many weapons in the arsenal, including running back, Tony Rankins (1,186 yards on 113 carries), and Jay Robinson (740 yards on 74 carries). The two have accounted for 30 touchdowns. Middletown has a pair of sure-handed receivers in Chris Lipscomb (18 receptions for 463 yards) and Roosevelt James (18 receptions for 435 yards and seven TD's). The big weapon is quarterback Dennis Wade, a senior who has thrown for 1,223 yards and 23 touchdowns while completing 50% of his passes. The Trojan backfield highlights Vinnie Poggi, who has 1,500 yards. The Blue Dragons finished the regular season 11-0 while outscoring their opponents 439-65. Middletown is first in Connecticut in points scored and 4th in points allowed".

Shoreline Post: HAL LEVY
One of the great Connecticut high school sportswriters was Hal Levy, a talented spinner of the language. At a chance meeting when Coach Ottochian and I were scouting Sheehan

late in the season, Mr. Levy asked us whom we might play if we defeated Sheehan on Thanksgiving. Coach Ottochian retorted, Middletown, to which Hal Levy rolled his eyes and remarked, …. "Forget it; no one is beating that team." Phil (Ottochian) was taken aback at the frankness of the comment. Mr. Levy went on to say, "If you have to play Middletown, pray for another hurricane."

THE BAND VOTES NO!

In notion and historically documented fact, when it came to football at Lyman Hall High School, there had been a litany of contemptuous events and people who made the events of December 7, 1985, nothing short of a miracle. There was one more event that demonstrated the disregard shown to LHHS football.

On Wednesday, December 4, 1985, before going out to practice, we learned that the Lyman Hall High School marching band had VOTED not to attend the State Championship football game. Coach Ottochian was more than stunned. We all were! Trying not to get aggravated or distracted, Phil felt that this was right in sync with the many people and their actions over the years, that neither cared about football at Lyman Hall nor had an appreciation for what this team had accomplished in just getting to the most significant game in school history.

We found out some hours later that the reason for the band members' vote was their concern that their band uniforms might get wet with the possibility of snow in the forecast. We didn't have time to worry about the band and its lack of leadership. On Thursday, December 5, 1985, Dale Wilson, our principal, exerted some pressure on the *musical vestment mavens* and the band, minus some members traveled to Storrs after all.

THE LAST LAST LAP

During the Phil Ottochian years, 1968-1999, the night before the Thanksgiving Day game (our traditional last game of the season), was a quiet practice, followed by grinders or pizza in the cafeteria, and then the seniors, one by one, would stand before their teammates and speak some final words before their final game.

The season's final practice was usually a light run-through of our offense, special teams' in & outs, and defensive formation checks and adjustments. Every last practice of the season was scripted, short and sweet, ... that is except for one year, 1999. At the end of each year's final practice, the seniors would take a last lap together, a casual run as a final goodbye to the field that the seniors would always remember as their football home.

The underclassmen would form a gauntlet in the endzone at the end of the lap. The underclassmen would offer some modest applause and well wishes to the seniors as each passed through. The night before the 1985 Thanksgiving Day game (snowed out until the following Saturday), there was a last lap, but after having beaten Sheehan, there was one more "last lap" to be taken before the State Championship game. After the run-through, last practice on our worn-out, grassless game field (Fitzgerald Field) that we finished earlier than usual, there was one more task to perform.

On December 6, 1985, the night before the bus ride to the University of Connecticut in Storrs, Connecticut, for the state title game, the seniors of the class of 1986 ran one more FINAL LAP.

LAST LAP STORY IN CONTRAST

In what turned out to be Coach Ottochian's last season (1999), that last practice was brutally bad. For whatever reason, the offense couldn't run a play without a mistake. Coach Ottochian was never one to end practice on a negative note, but this final practice of the 1999 season went on long after we should have been off the field. It was pitiful. Coach Ottochian, as was his wont, kept invoking the words, "One More Play," a phrase that still makes LHHS Hall of Fame linebacker Mike Tyrrell instantly ill. Tom Brockett, our defensive line coach at that time (now the Ansonia High School Head Coach), stood next to me during that practice and stated, "We're going to get killed tomorrow (against Sheehan)."

That last practice was so error-filled, taking twice as much time (almost 90 minutes) as was scheduled for offense, that when the offense was finally done and Coach Ottochian turned to me as defensive coordinator and said, "OK, you got 'em," meaning that it was "defensive period" ... I looked at Tommy and told coach, "I'm all set." Consequently, it was better we ended that last practice. We didn't run a defensive practice the day before the Sheehan game in 1999. Parenthetically, we defeated the heavily favored Sheehan team.

BACK TO THE PRESENT ...

In 1985 with snow remaining on the field from Thanksgiving week, our last practice was over and done in a shade over 45 minutes. There was hardly a sound except for Todd Barket's cadence and our defensive secondary calling their coverage checks. We all wanted to believe that the team was "ready." From my chronicle notes from that night, I wrote, "Asked Bobby (Corazzini) if he thought we were ready. Bobby responded with his accustomed quick giggle, "They better be." We left the final practice of 1985 with one assurance. The team had done everything it could do to prepare for this game.

Middletown, with their enormous talent and succession of blow-out victories, Coach John Skubel had extra time to experiment and add additional wrinkles to their offense if he so chose.

Our defensive unit was communicating on every play in every practice as they had done throughout the season. Coach Ottochian was keen on asking me. "What if they do this ... what if they do that?" When you coached with Phil Ottochian, you had to keep your football powder dry.

FINAL BRIEFING OF THE TEAM

Playing in a State Title game was all new for all of us. Coach told the team to dress in jackets and ties for the approximate one hour-fifteen-minute bus trip to the University of Connecticut in Storrs. The team was to carry their gear with them. The school permitted our team to travel in a coach bus, a far cry from the yellow school bus we ordinarily rode in for away games. Further, he told the team to bring "sneakers" with them in the event that the field was frozen. Not a soul on the team failed to appreciate the game's enormity and the moment yet to come. We were all more than a little nervous, but there was a unity of purpose. That night before leaving the locker room, I finished affixing a slogan on everyone's helmet, the sticker, "Team of Destiny." It indeed felt that way, but to get there, we had to slay Goliath, Middletown.

When the team exited from our final meeting, there were a lot of handshakes, some hugs, and a lot of fragmented sentences with the sentiments ..." we'll beat them ... don't worry coach ... we're ready ... and a lot of "I LOVE YOU'S."

The coaches congregated in the coaches' office for a short

time. Coach Ottochian evoked one of his time-honored quips, "Let's blow this garage." That was always our cue to leave. Coach Ottochian and I walked out together. We looked at each other in the parking lot, and for the first time in a long time, there was nothing left to say. I looked at him, wishing I could just give him this one victory, something he had spent the last 18 years of his life building.

CHRONICLE ENTRY
DECEMBER 6, 1985
(11:00 PM)

"It was difficult saying goodbye to Coach Ottochian after practice tonight. I had known him since he came to Wallingford before he coached even a single game at Lyman Hall. I know what this game means to me, but for Phil ... he has worked so hard for so many years and almost left Lyman Hall. No man ever deserved a crowning moment more than Phil Ottochian. God, please don't let me let him down tomorrow".

Chapter 91

Game Day – Before
the First Hit

DEPARTING FOR THE 1985 CLASS
M STATE CHAMPIONSHIP GAME

The morning was crisp, chilly and snow was on the ground
as we arrived at Lyman Hall High School to load the coach
bus that would take us to the University of Connecticut, the
Class M State Championship game site.

As it was a coach bus, the side storage compartments were
used to transport the pads, helmets, cleats, and uniforms for
each team member. We would dress 25 players for the game,
so there was plenty of room, and no one was stuffed into seats
or forced to sit in the middle aisle as we were used to with
those yellow school buses. I don't think any member of the
team put any thought into the ambiance of the coach. They
each were filled with the anxiety and anticipation of the day
that was about to unfold.

We learned that snow had fallen onto storied Memorial
Field at the University of Connecticut, where we would play.
The temperatures in the high 20's and low 30's would persist
until mid-day, so we anticipated a frozen field.

The ride up I-91 was reasonably quiet except for a few brief
conversations about the game. The demeanor of this team was

consistent on bus trips to and from away games. This was not a team that did much celebrating before, during, or after games. There was a calm efficiency about the young men on the '85 Trojans.

Pulling into the University of Connecticut, our players' eyes began to turn to the sight of Memorial Field. It was the largest venue our young men had ever played in, and the emptiness of the stadium made it look that much more imposing.

WALKING MEMORIAL FIELD

We arrived earlier than expected and decided to walk the field. As soon as we dropped our gear off in the locker room near the scoreboard, the team, still attired in jackets and ties, walked around the snow-covered Memorial Field. I watched many of our guys looking up at the tall expanse of the stadium.

Coach Ottochian and I hadn't walked 20 yards when we felt the ground frozen beneath our shoes. Coach Ottochian and the coaches discussed the possible consequences of our players' cleats not providing any traction on the frozen turf.

Coach Ottochian immediately circulated through the team, walking the field, and recommended that they wear the sneakers they had brought with them, but sneakers would not necessarily provide firmer footing. What we probably needed were turf shoes. I had worn a pair of black Riddell coaching shoes that I brought in 1976. I wore them only for games, but they were special to me, and I polished them to a spit shine almost weekly. Anyone who knows me will acknowledge my vanity, reflective in my attire.

On that morning, asking around the team, I discovered that Al Ferreira (our split end, kick returner, and defensive back) and I wore the same size shoe. I offered to let him wear my shoes. At first, Al declined, not wishing to deny me the opportunity to wear those classic (not made anymore) shoes. I insisted. On that historic day, I was honored that Al Ferreira wore my shoes. I still have them, and I still polish them regularly. I have told the story many times ... I was denied the honor and opportunity to play for Lyman Hall as a student, but I can say that Al Ferreira wore my shoes in the biggest game in Lyman Hall history.

Coach Ottochian fearing a footing disaster on the icy field encouraged the members of the team to change their foot attire from cleats to sneakers. At least that was the initial plan. Except for a few members of the team, most of the guys decided to stay with cleats.

The team was anxious to dress and get this game going. When we started back to the locker room after we walked around the field, we saw that Middletown had not arrived as yet. They did a better job of scheduling the arrival time than we did. The old UCONN locker room was an old throwback to the 1950s with wooden benches, no place to meet with units of the team, and a small shower area, but not as tiny as our Lyman Hall showers. The main double doors to the locker room faced the South goalposts. When the door was opened, a hearty wind seemed to pour through the locker room, and it was a cold wind.

MIDDLETOWN ARRIVES WITH FANFARE!

When our team was almost dressed for the game in our white jerseys, the racket from the Middletown High School team's arrival startled most of us. Where our team was serenely quiet when we arrived at UCONN, the Middletown team was cheering and hollering with all the bravado possible. In the Housatonic League, such actions, coming or going, just didn't happen. The Blue Dragons came off their buses dressed in their game gear except for their shoulder pads. Yes, there was more to our contrasts than speed vs. size.

TIME TO STRETCH

Dressed and helmeted, we lined up outside the UCONN locker room door to stretch for the game.

Two-by-two, the 25 members of the team trotted onto the field for stretching and warm-ups. Already on the field was Middletown quarterback Dennis Wade (#12) with a few of their skill players. My eyes were immediately trained on Wade. His steps before each warm-up throw were precise and quick.

Each pass was a perfect spiral, and not a pass was dropped. To put a fine point on it, he didn't miss a target. After five minutes of two-step throws to his receivers, he began to execute a five-step drop, a belly pass drop, and the waggle (bootleg) steps. Wade's every throw was a "pea." Coach Bobby Corazzini was standing alongside me and commented, ..." I told you he was good." I told Bobby, "...yes, you all told me."

The Blue Dragon team came on the field for their stretches and warm-up, HIGH-STEPPING and (we're No.1) FINGER WAVING. The Middletown band played almost throughout their warm-up. This team was fully supported by their school. There were cheers from the Middletown cheerleaders and student body, calling out each player by name or number. It was loud and sustained. For us, our 25 guys remained focused on our regular stretches and regular pre-game warm-up.

COACH OTTOCHIAN & ME

Of all the photos taken of the game. In fact, of all the photos related to Lyman Hall High School football, the one that still touches my heart was the shot of Coach Ottochian and me standing together on the sideline in front of our bench before the kickoff of the state championship game. At the moment that picture was snapped, Coach Ottochian leaned into me and offered these words, **"Coach, don't get conservative"**!

With those words, he finally expressed confidence in me. It took eleven games that season to get to that point, but it meant the world to me.

INTRODUCTION OF THE TEAMS

Another illustration of the two teams' differences came just before the Middletown Band played the national anthem. The two teams were introduced. We were not aware ... nor accustomed, nor informed by anyone, that the members of our offense would be introduced and would be expected to run out to the numbers. Middletown had been through this before and came through a sizeable paper-covered hoop held by the cheerleaders. Our team hovered around each other while the Blue Dragons high-stepped and high-fived during the introductions.

Coach Ottochian wanted the ball to start the second half, but he felt confident in our defense. As it turned out, a problem that plagued us throughout the season reared its ugly head again to start the game.

The press box was filled with sports reporters from every Connecticut newspaper. These sports reporters were familiar with each other and were more than comfortable speaking candidly about their predictions as to the game's outcome and point spread. Some of them were making bets before the game as to the margin of victory for Middletown over Lyman Hall. Not one sportswriter wanted any bet of fewer than 14 points. Then the game started with a play that turned the entire press box into a laugh fest.

Chapter 92

Kicking Off ... Lyman Hall Vs. Middletown

~1985 Class MM State Championship Game~
Memorial Stadium
University of Connecticut
December 7, 1985
1:00 pm

Greg Myerson kicked off to Middletown. Coach Ottochian was hoping that Greg might kick it into the endzone to give us good field position to start the game. Jay Robinson (#40), one of Middletown's speed merchants, positioned himself to field Greg's kickoff, but it bounced off his chest. As the shape of the football is so fashioned for odd bounces, it jumped right back into Robinson's arms. A few of our younger kickoff team players came out of their lanes, and Robinson raced 87 yards for a touchdown. All-State kicker Sal Morello of Middletown missed the extra point, and the Blue Dragons were in front, 6-0 before a single offensive play was run.

This set off a plethora of laughter and head-shaking in the press box, whereupon noted reporter Hal Levy yells out, "Who will give me Lyman Hall and 40 points". For those of you not in the sports betting frame of reference, this meant that Lyman Hall could be given 40 points to start the game, and Middletown still wins.

Of that opening kickoff for a touchdown, Tri-Captain Ralph Riley stated, "That kickoff return haunts me to this day. As the contain man on the right side of the kickoff team, I was obsessed with not letting returns go outside. Middletown's return called for a double team on me, and this created a gap large enough for a speedy return player to get through. I dove at and made contact with his legs. However, it had no impact on his stride. That was a wake-up call as to this team's (Middletown) ability and speed. No arm tackles were going to stop them".

The late great sportswriter, Bo Kolinsky, told me years later that any other high school team faced with such an opponent and having just given away an easy touchdown probably would have crumbled, but not the '85 Lyman Hall team.

THE LYMAN HALL OFFENSE TAKES OVER

After the Middletown touchdown, the 1985 team hardly grumbled as they came up the field to receive the kickoff from Middletown's Morello. Billy Goldstein, one of our defensive tackles, fielded one of his two kickoff returns in the game (I told you how versatile we were.), and we set up for our first offensive series on our side of the field.

On first down, Coach Ottochian wasted no time in shifting to his two-tight end formation from the VEE. Fullback Matt Schmitt broke the first play (fullback counter) in the opposite direction of the shift and raced 44 yards to the Middletown 22. Vincent Poggio was next to carry the ball, rambling for 11 more yards.

Coach Ottochian was in one of his "alternating ball carriers" play-calling modes. Matt carried the ball next for three yards and then Vincent again for seven, bringing the ball down to the Middletown one-yard line. This set up the kind of circumstance that Coach Ottochian had in mind when he moved Ralph Riley to tight end with David Klaverkamp to tackle and Greg Myerson to guard. On the next play, Dave,

Greg, and Ralph buried the right side of the Middletown defense, and Matt quasi-vaulted in for the tying touchdown.

We set up for an apparent extra-point kick as Middletown covered every game with two defenders at the edges. Todd Barket took a knee, positioning the extra point tee to hold for the point after attempt, and called the next shift we planned, throwing the kicking block out of the way. Lining up in our base offense, Todd executed our version of the Waggle (bootleg with the fullback running a pattern in the flat), he threw to Matt in the endzone, but the pass wasn't on target. However, Matt made a leaping catch for the two-point conversion, and ... FOR THE FIRST TIME in the 1985 season, Middletown was behind in a football game. That's a fact! ... Middletown had not been behind in a football game since the Daniel Hand game in 1984 when Hand scored the first TD of their game in week four of 1984.

There was no cheap self-aggrandizing celebration. The touchdown just was a precursor to the defense's first opportunity to unleash "Blitz-O'Mania" on Middletown when the Blue Dragons took over on offense. Guy Russo and Randy Pelletier penetrated on first down as the Blue Dragons ran their vaunted Buck Sweep. The blitz didn't allow Middletown to run the play off-tackle as it was designed as the LHHS defense stopped the Middletown offense for little gain.

The same result occurred on second down, setting up a 3rd and long. As the charts indicated, Middletown would waggle (bootleg) early on 3rd & long. They tried the bootleg to our defensive left, but Guy's blitz forced Dennis Wade deeper, and Ralph Riley overpowered the pulling Middletown guards as Wade was sacked for an 18-yard loss.

After a short Middletown punt, the Blue and White offense took over. On first down, the quick Blue Dragon defense was no match for Vincent (#33), who ran 45 yards through the left side of their defense for a touchdown. Once again, we shifted from an extra point alignment to the I-formation for a two-point play. Todd Barket (#5) looked left and threw right to Ralph Riley, who had reached far back for the pass that was way off target. Ralph was all but laying on his side in the end zone and caught the ball for the two-point play. Ralph's catch was more remarkable given the fact that it was only his second game at tight end.

LHHS BLITZ OVERWHELMS MIDDLETOWN

It was still in the first quarter, and the Lyman Hall defense was laying the wood to the crowned Middletown offense. The Blue Dragons led the state in scoring offense, but the Trojans kept the pressure on with their onslaught of blitzes. Middletown got the ball back on their own 36 after the kickoff. Middletown tried to run that vaunted short-trap (buck), but the Trojan blitz stuffed the fullback, leading rusher Tony Rankins on first down.

On second down, fleet halfback Jay Robinson (#40), averaging over 10 yards a carry coming into this game, was drilled by Greg Myerson (#50) as the ball was knocked loose. Will linebacker Eddie Charbonneau (#24) pounced on the fumble, and Lyman Hall had the ball again, this time on the Middletown 17-yard line.

The offense was over-powering early in the game, made possible by our offensive line of Mark Wollen (#67), David Klaverkamp (#53), Greg Myerson, Bill Goldstein (#55), and Kevin Distante (#58), who were knocking the Middletown defensive linemen backward.

On first down, Vincent Poggio bolted for all 17 yards to paydirt, giving Lyman Hall a 22-6 lead.

On the fourth possession of the Blue Dragons, starting on their own 20-yard line, Middletown got into a slot formation and tried to run a double-out with their two wide receivers to our defensive left. Our cornerback, Scott Audet (#4), had man coverage on their split end, Roosevelt James (#22). Scottie noticed that James had shortened his split (from the tackle). We ran an "Express" blitz as Ed Charbonneau (#24) came clean to their quarterback as Wade was forced to throw it earlier than he would have liked. Scottie made a diving interception.

Late in the second quarter, with temperatures beginning to drop, Lyman Hall held a 22-6 advantage, a lead that no one on either side of the field could have imagined. The Lyman Hall defense was keeping the Middletown offense in check, and the Trojan offense was doing just enough to avoid turnovers while maintaining field position. Middletown altered their offense and began to attack us with screens and different formations. Taking over on its own 20-yard line, Wade passed to his tight end for a first down as Todd Barket made a touchdown-saving tackle. Shortly thereafter, Wade hit Mark Spicer in the endzone for a 22-year touchdown pass, and the lead was cut to 22-12.

A MOMENT OF DREAD

With just minutes remaining in the first half in an "all-of-sudden moment," a Lyman Hall offensive play resulted in a one-yard gain, and left one Trojan player lying on the frozen ground, Greg Myerson (#50).

As Coach Ottochian and I trotted out to see Greg, there was a collective groan from the Lyman Hall fandom when they realized who was on the ground. As I walked out and the fact that it was Greg, I never thought for a second he wouldn't just jump right up, provide a whimsical "Myerson-ism" and we would proceed with the game, but he didn't get up.

Unlike most other players we had coached, Greg never acknowledged pain, suffering, or anxiety.

Greg waved off an ambulance that wasted no time coming on the field when Greg went down.

Greg walked off the field holding his arm, and the trainer told us it was a separated shoulder. I could not believe that he wouldn't be all right in a few minutes, and Greg's few words were, "I'll be OK." We were able to finish that offensive series with Guy Russo at guard playing in place of Greg. With seconds remaining in the first half of play, we inserted Ken Priest (#76), a sophomore, into the game to play defensive end.

Priest remembers the moment, "When I was sent in for Greg, I was scared. I said to myself, I hope that Middletown doesn't run the ball at me, but they did. I didn't make a tackle, but Middletown came right at me".

What happened next are the makings of one of the greatest legends in the 100-year history of Lyman Hall High School.

With the first half over and LHHS ahead, 22-12, Greg had already gone into the locker room to see the head UCONN athletic doctor. Phil and I walked together, quietly talking as to who on the team could play each of the positions now vacated by Greg's injury.

One of the coaches who were in the booth at the top of the stadium, who talked with me on the headsets during the game, rushed to my side in the locker room and said, "*Myerson is done. You should have seen the hit he took. He's through.*"

Chapter 93

Halftime

As we entered the locker room at halftime, coaches Corazzini, Wallace, and Gawlak were asked the same question by me, "How will they (Middletown) come out of the locker room"? However, all any of them wanted to talk about was related to Greg Myerson.

I could not believe that he wouldn't be all right in a few minutes, and Greg's few words were, "I'll be OK."

To the immediate problem, the game ... without Greg, we lost a guard, defensive end, our kicker, and punter.

What happened next are the makings of one of the greatest legends in the 100-year history of Lyman Hall High School.

Greg had already gone into the locker room to see the head UCONN athletic doctor. Phil and I walked together, talking quietly as to whom on the team could play each of the positions now vacant if Greg could not return. One of the coaches who was in the booth at the top of the stadium, who talked with me on the headsets, rushed to my side and said, *"Myerson is done. You should have seen the hit he took. He's through."*

My routine was always to gather the defense together immediately upon getting into the locker room and review the card with my hand-written notes of the first half, making the adjustments necessary. My comments of that specific halftime (I still have the card.) were made more difficult because the guys on the team were reacting to the probable loss of Greg.

Besides coaching up Brett Baron and Kenny Priest, the two defensive end options to play in Greg's defensive end spot, I discussed with the unit the possibility of flip-flopping our other incredible defensive end, Ralph Riley, from one end to the other, should Middletown attack Greg's replacement. To be sure, there were other concerns that we had to address, specifically in our pass defense where Middletown had a decisive speed advantage.

As soon as I finished my 15-minute session with the defense, I moved across the locker room where the UCONN doctor had just confirmed and told Coach Ottochian that Greg had a Grade 3 dislocation. With Greg standing stripped to the waist as the doctor is pointing to this part of his shoulder and that, as if Greg was a teaching cadaver, he looks at Phil and says, "This boy is through for the game!"

Greg candidly, in a clear articulation of his point of view, ... "Bullshit, I'm playing." Phil and I are standing there and not saying anything. It was a moment of total helplessness, and lest we forget ... we had a half to play, and we had to be on the field in five minutes. Now, the doctor starts to turn pediatrician (child doctor) and tries to calmly tell Greg that he could do serious damage to his shoulder if he were to play. Greg is having none of this talk and tells the players and coaches, "GET MY PADS."

The doctor now turns to Phil and says, "I will not allow this boy to play.

He is out for the game". Greg is as steely-eyed focused as I ever saw him, shouting at the doctor and trainer, "I'm fine. Tape me up. Strap me up.

I'm playing."

Greg was not in any manner flipping out or hurling profanities.

That was not Greg. Now, the doctor tells Phil of the legal outcomes if Greg is allowed to play. The doctor was becoming agitated because everyone in that locker room wanted to help Greg put on his pads and jersey.

The doctor is right in front of Phil, telling him, "If you do

NOT follow my instructions and you allow this boy to play, YOU will be held liable ...".

During these heated moments, I was looking right into Greg's face. To my untrained eye, there was no doubt that he was in a lot of pain. Greg's lips were pursed together, and his stare was straight ahead. As the UCONN doctor was finger-wagging, laying into Coach Ottochian, members of the team were helping Greg with his shoulder pads with his arm pressed against his chest, trying not to have any movement of his shoulder. As he was helped to put on his #50 jersey, he had to move the arm. The doctor was watching Greg re-assemble, but Greg gave no sign or facial expression. Finally, he was dressed for the second half, but the doctor was not done with Coach Ottochian.

The field site coordinator came to the door of the locker room and yelled, "Time to go, Lyman Hall." We heard the Middletown team screaming, leaving their locker room, but our team was subdued as we lined up to leave the locker room and start the second half of football.

In one of the most seminal moments of my life, the scene that followed shall remain with me and everyone present that day, December 7, 1985.

Greg put on his helmet with one hand. He moved to the front of the line with fellow, Tri-Captains, Ralph Riley, and Matt Schmitt. Phil and I walked out first with the doctor, who was still chirping away at Phil that letting Greg even dress was a mistake and that he must be taken to a hospital immediately.

Phil and I walked to the team's front left side, trying to exorcise ourselves from the doctor, but the UCONN medicine man would not relent.

I turned back and watched Greg at the front of the line. Just then, the afternoon sun broke through the clouds and gleamed. No, that is not entirely accurate ... it (the sun) reflected off the front portion of Greg Myerson's helmet. The hundred or so Lyman Hall faithful that had gathered outside our locker room door began to clamor and yell, over and over,

"It's Myerson!" "He's going to play." "Greg is dressed." Mixed in were a few, "Oh My God, Myerson is going to play."

Then the cheering grew louder as the team walked into the endzone to run to the sideline.

Once the team was in the endzone, every eye was on Myerson. As I stood and watched this surreal scene, standing near the 20-yard line, I could almost hear the deep pipe organ at Yale University playing a piece by Miklos Rozsa, the "El Cid" theme.

Greg and the team ran to our sideline with the blinding reflection of the sun on Greg's navy blue helmet with the orange "T."

Tony Barket, the father of our quarterback, stood near me at that moment and said pointedly, "Coach did you see that"? When I turned to Tony to ask him what I should have seen, Tony touched the top of his head with his hand and said, "Myerson."

Just before the kickoff of the second half, the doctor insisted on looking at Greg again.

The doctor was adamant. He was <u>not</u> going to let Greg play. Phil wanted to do the right thing and would have relented if Greg demonstrated in word or body language the slightest waffle toward not playing.

Finally, Greg reached an end. As the doctor was spouting medical and legal consequences once more, telling Greg, "I will NOT ALLOW YOU ON THE FIELD," Greg looked him right in the eye and said .... **<u>If I don't play, I'll kill you.</u>**

The doctor quickly departed down our sideline and out of our lives.

Greg was back at guard on offense, and he manned his defensive end position to start the second half. Middletown wasted no time attacking him, running outside plays to his side. Blue Dragon pulling linemen came after Greg as he kept his arm tucked tight to his chest and side, protecting his separated shoulder from the impact of their blocks. Despite his obvious pain, Greg never failed to execute his responsibilities.

On one play late in the third quarter, the Middletown quarterback sprinted the corner, bringing two backs to block

Greg so that the much-harassed quarterback, Dennis Wade, could throw one of his classic 40-yard passes. Greg lowered his good shoulder, low enough to protect his injured shoulder, but so low that when he engaged the first blocker, he head-butted him, de-cleating the Middletown blocker to the ground. The result was that Wade was pulled up, denied the edge of our defense, throwing another incomplete pass.

Greg played the entire second half on defense in intense pain with one arm. Middletown had narrowed the margin to 22-18 in the third quarter on a 29-yard touchdown pass to Roosevelt James. The Blue & White had played heroically, but during the second half, we were hard-pressed to make first downs on offense, so the defense was forced to defend a relentless Middletown aerial attack. Becoming a game of punting, we needed to make it into the fourth quarter with the lead. By this time, Middletown knew Lyman Hall had no intention to throw the football as we had only attempted four passes. They crowded the line of scrimmage, daring our offense to throw, but we continued to run the football.

Our coaches in the press box were alerting me to a multitude of Middletown passing formations as we turned into the fourth quarter. Conversely, the Middletown coaches were imploring their head coach, John Skubel, to call specific pass plays, such as "Y-seam" and stop running "buck sweep."

Chapter 94

End of Game Strategy

On a critical third down, Middletown called time out. I came out to call the next defense a change in tactics/coverage. I felt it was time to call "**Cowboy.**" This was the coverage I put in just for this game, and now, it was time to see if there was wisdom in the scheme. "Cowboy" put a ton of pressure on our three best defensive linemen, Myerson, Ralph Riley, and David Klaverkamp. Each of these three young men had played the entire game, blocking and getting hit on every day.

They were nothing less than heroic. Their assignment (in Cowboy) was to keep the Middletown quarterback, Dennis Wade, from running out of bounds, thereby stopping the clock. At the back end of the defense, we played man coverage on every eligible receiver with a three-deep zone behind them.

I was worried about Greg in this coverage as he was assigned to run with Wade if he came to his side, and this would surely aggravate the shoulder with the arm movements necessary to run. Before I called the coverage in the huddle, I looked at Greg and asked if he would be ok if we go to Cowboy coverage. Greg knew what this would entail, but he didn't hesitate in his answer,

"I'll run him down, coach. CALL IT!"

If one were to watch this game's film, one would see the one-armed Myerson compensating with every other body part to make plays. When we went to Cowboy, Greg found yet another level of play.

Running as if he had no injury, he, David, and Ralph

ran with the speedy Dennis Wade to the boundary. On one occasion, the Middletown quarterback, trying to buy time to launch yet another long pass, was chased out of bounds by Riley and ended up in the hedgerow behind our bench.

With two minutes remaining in the game, I switched back to our blitzing defense. With Middletown out of timeouts, if we could get Wade tackled in bounds one more time, we could run the clock down to seconds.

Heretofore, I called the blitz "Express," designed to come with outside pressure from Greg's side with our outside linebacker, Eddie Charbonneau, and inside pressure from Guy Russo and Randy Pelletier. Not realizing that we had returned to our pressure defense, the Blue Dragons did not pass protect to Greg's side, and Eddie Charbonneau (#24) came clean, jack-knifing Wade as he wound up to throw. The ball was jarred from Wade's grasp as he was hit, whereupon Ralph Riley scooped it up and scored from 34 yards out, making the score 28-18.

THE GAME IS OVER ... BUT IT WASN'T ... YET

Lyman Hall kicked off to Middletown for what turned out to be their last possession of the state title game. With 1:19 remaining in the game, Middletown attempted a halfback option pass with the Trojans back in their "Cowboy" defense.

Todd Barket intercepted the halfback pass.

With less than a minute in the 1985 state championship game at the University of Connecticut's Memorial Stadium, Todd Barket (#5) made the quarterback privileged gesture of moving his arms up and down, signaling the Wallingford audience to quell their noise so that he could call his cadence. Todd would tell me later that he always wanted to be in a position to make that gesture. There would be no more bucks, counters, and Vee-shifts as Barket took a knee and ran the clock dry of time.

In an instant, the game was over. A shiver.

This was a moment that transcended all emotional and physical feeling. Now, at this moment, a lifetime of love for my Lyman Hall stood still in my heart. Suddenly all of the games, the losses, wins, the passion, and collections of memories since the 1950s came together.

I watched from my spot on the sideline as the team hugged and tried to communicate with each other. I wanted to see everything all at once and remember it all. I was aware of the moment's seminal importance and did not want to alter it in any way.

Coach Ottochian was hugged by his brother, Frankie, who was our guest on the sideline. Tony Barket and Rick Poggio ran onto the field to find their sons who had played so brilliantly. The group "Together" hug of the players was so beautiful to observe. Understandably, most didn't know exactly quite what to say or do as this was so totally NEW. In character, there was no brash demonstration of celebration as most high school, college, and professional athletes are so engaged after a big victory. All was happening so rapidly.

Covered in mud, sweat, and so drained of energy, individual team members found each other for hugs and words that were so limited in verbiage and so filled with meaning. The CIAC game officials sought out Coach Ottochian to present him with the Championship plaque as members of the Connecticut sports press corps pressed in around Coach Ottochian, not knowing exactly what to ask him after the Lyman Hall super upset.

Before even the most trivial question was asked, the Lyman Hall team of white uniforms, stained in mud, sweat, and some blood, raised Coach Phil Ottochian on their shoulders.

With my eyes trained on the Middletown coaches trying to console their own players yards in front of us, I found myself hoisted first by Guy Russo, Ed Charbonneau, Ralph Riley, and then other members of the team. I instantly felt, "what, why me," but I was blessed to receive my own little "shoulder raising" by the young men who gave me more than I could ever have given them. It was the singular honor of my life, and I still feel that way.

The members of the press corps swarmed Coach Ottochian. As Coach Ottochian was overwhelmed in exhalation, he didn't answer their questions, deferring to speaking about the things that flooded his thoughts to his mouth.

He defended his play-calling in the game when no one asked him about his choices of plays. The reporters only wanted to know, "How do you explain what happened"?

An emotional, straight from the heart man, Phil had done many interviews since 1968 but was in a new undiscovered place in his life. He was the head football coach of the best football team in Connecticut, and that was just starting to settle in his consciousness.

Chapter 95

The Victory Won – State Champions

WALKING OFF MEMORIAL STADIUM

As the sun was setting at Memorial Stadium on the University of Connecticut campus, we were all trying to get to the locker room. We all needed to be together. As I crossed the 40-yard, heading to the locker room, I kneeled and grabbed a fist full of chewed-up field dirt and pushed it deep into my tan slacks. I still have it, kept in a small bottle.

The multitude of the estimated 2,500 persons who sat and stood at Memorial Stadium that December afternoon witnessed the consummate "David and Goliath" mismatch. The shocking outcome of the contest left many lingering questions on the lips of those who came to see Middletown win their 23rd straight game, "How could this have happened? Was the team over-confident? Did we take Lyman Hall too lightly"?

For many of the people who traveled to Storrs to see the Lyman Hall High School football team, few would have proudly proclaimed that the Trojans would definitively vanquish the Middletown team before kickoff. For others, the game, while a can't be missed event, was a curiosity, "Could the Trojans "hang in there" against the state's finest team"?

If you weren't a parent or relative, made blind by family ties, the game's end brought a wash of disbelief that this had happened. A team of a tad over two dozen, looking like fewer standing on the broad sideline of Memorial Stadium, even with the presence of a few fathers, a few sportswriters, and the requisite hangers-on.

The Middletown band that played the school fight song non-stop throughout the pre-game, and much of the game was silent now. The champion Trojans, mud-covered and exhausted, walked to the locker room, some with family members and girlfriends. Many former football players from bygone eras stood near the endzone where the Connecticut-shaped scoreboard still showed the final score, 28-18. They smiled, patted the '85 Trojans on their shoulder pads as they passed by, and shared in the achievement that no one thought possible.

THE LOCKER ROOM AFTER THE GAME

Most people who ask about the game and the subsequent scene in our locker room have the impression that there must have been a crazy jubilation after the contest. There were smiles and hugs and some kisses for the team members and their coaches, but as the team members entered the locker room, there was exhaustion, an enervation from preparing and playing the game without substitution or the acknowledgment of injury and pain. They hung the shingle of "Together" before every huddle and practice. It was more than a word. "Together" was the manner in which all was possible and no obstacle was insurmountable.

As the boys pulled off their sweat and blood-soaked white jerseys and mud-caked pants, strained to share their own stylized congratulatory words, they struggled to find a groove of celebration. The often-highbrow kidding of members of the team, referencing current movie jargon from the movies, the Karate Kid and Back to Future, was absent, and some of the team seemed to be working hard to eek a laugh as Matt Schmitt, Guy Russo, and Todd Barket usually did in the wake of practices and games.

Greg Myerson was hurting but did not speak of his pain.

He was quieter than I had seen him in previous post-game moments as his eyes were three-quarter open at times, nodding his head in response to questions or comments about the game from team members and coaches.

FRUSTRATION

In a not-so-good post-game event, some of the Middletown players lost their composure immediately after the final seconds ticked off the clock. A Middletown Press photographer, who had covered the Middletown football juggernaut all season, tried to capture the disappointment and frustration as it became clear that Lyman Hall would defeat the nationally-ranked Blue Dragons.

In contrast to the classic yet profoundly meaningful photo of Sheehan's Ricky Allen following the Thanksgiving Day game, a few Middletown football program members took matters into their own hands when the photographer prepared to take his photos.

To quote the account of the actual moment by the Middletown Press of December 9, 1985, "When the photographer attempted to shoot reaction photos of the Dragons, he was covered by student managers who stood in front of his camera so he couldn't take the photos.

One lineman then stuck his hand in the photographer's face in an attempt to move him away from the bench. Then a star back grabbed the photographer and pulled him away from the field where he wanted to shoot the photos. It could have been an uglier scene had not the athletic director and some of the coaches pulled the players away from the photographer".

AFTER GAME

On the other side of the field and locker, things weren't going so well. The Middletown players were reacting with shock, disbelief, and frustration immediately after the game, so overwhelmingly confident as they entered the state title game. Coach John Skubel, who sensed that his players were not responding in the best of manners, told his coaches to round up all team members and get them to their locker room. Coach Skubel told the reporters that he needed to speak with his team for a while. First, Coach Skubel wanted to meet with our team in our locker room and talk to us with Coach Ottochian's permission.

With members of the Lyman Hall team standing in the shower stall and others sitting on the UCONN locker room's benches, Head Coach John Skubel of the just vanquished Middletown High School team appeared in our locker room. He was gracious to Coach Ottochian and me, requesting to take a moment and address our team.

We gathered the team to the middle of the locker room, dressed, half-dressed, and still in-game attire. Coach Skubel showed no symptoms of the hurt that he must have clenched within his heart for his team after what he later described as the most disappointing and lingering loss of his coaching career. He spoke quietly and eloquently, directing platitudes of meticulously worded compliments to the individual team members and the Lyman Hall team as a whole. He let no emotion enter into his words to us. Coach Skubel was kind, and his few words to me as he exited our locker room were repeated many years later as we began to know each other after he retired from coaching as he battled cancer, passing away in 2014.

COACH SKUBEL'S WORDS ...

Here is an excerpt of Coach John Skubel's **exact** words (taken by a recording of a sportswriter) to the Lyman Hall team from his brief talk in our victorious team locker room:

"I didn't come in here to get up on a soapbox and say how great you are because I think it's a nice thing to do. I just want to congratulate each of you on the great job you did today. We were here last year, and it's a great feeling. Today is your day. Enjoy it. I know your coaching staff

is proud of you, and you should be proud of yourselves. Congratulations, men."

Few coaches, if any, before our since, were so amiable. Only after this speech did Coach John Skubel walk to his locker room and quietly talk to each team member one by one. As he later told me, it was the most difficult locker room time he ever went through as he spoke to each of his players, some of whom were inconsolable.

As the years passed, I became a friend of Middletown Head Coach, John Skubel, a wonderful man who was open with me about the events of that day in December. Coach Skubel told me that when Myerson went off with a separated shoulder, their coaches felt that they would just run the ball at whomever we put in Myerson's place.

When Myerson came out dressed for the second half, he didn't think Greg would play. In Coach Skubel's words, "That injury to any mere mortal would sideline him for two or three weeks." He never understood how Greg withstood the intense pain.

BUS RIDE HOME

We loaded the coach bus for our long ride back to Wallingford. The events of the days had rendered the team all but drained. There were no cheers or songs of exultation, just the two dozen young men and six coaches scattered through the seats of the bus.

Upon taking my traditional seat next to Coach Ottochian (we sat next to each other on every away bus ride for over 20 years), we both mentioned how quiet the bus was. There were conversations and a sprinkle of laughter, particularly that of Matt Schmitt, who had a most distinctive laugh.

Every so often, one of the team would yell out, "State Champions" ... "No. 1", but although it was met with a response of applause and cheers, it all was somewhat muted. It had not sunk into anyone's mind yet, the miracle that had just occurred.

Things changed in tenor and emotion as we neared the Cromwell/Meriden town lines on I-91. A police car escort had formed around us, accented by the cars of some parents. As soon as we hit the Wallingford Town line near the route 68 exit, the police unit sirens and horns started to blare, and they didn't cease until we entered the school parking lot. Cars were waiting for us in the parking lot, but certainly not the numbers of vehicles that I thought would be there waiting for us. Having possessed photos of the return home from the 1953 State Championship basketball game at the Payne Whitney Gymnasium, I hoped that the town would have turned out as they did for the '53 title team. In the end, I was thankful for the cars that were waiting for us when we returned.

BACK HOME – ONE MORE GOODBYE

When we arrived back at the Lyman Hall High School locker room, we dragged tons of mud with us from the state title game and left a lot of it on the floor. Without much banter, the state champions left one by one. I stood at the exit door, near the coaches' locker room, and tried to say goodbye to each member of the team as all the coaches did.

When the hugs and warm thoughts, expressed in few words, had come to a close for tonight, it had come time to depart the school, my Lyman Hall High School. The last of the team walked slowly out of the cramped confines of our locker room, the remnants of their last game strewn everywhere. Caked mud, ripped athletic tape, discarded tee-shirts, and socks attacked the visual, and the scent of sweat filled my nostrils. Ordinarily, that locker room scene would lead to recriminations, requiring that the members of the team be ordered to clean the locker room, but not tonight.

The boys had done it.

I was a little part of this season ... this team.

I was overcome by the sheer munificence of the day. Coach Ottochian called out to me ... "coach, time to blow this garage." I smiled at the many times he said that to me over the years. As usual, we were the two last to leave. The parking lot that was half-filled with well-wishers with car horns blowing loudly just an hour ago was now empty, that is except for three cars, Coach Ottochian's, my Ford Pinto, and one other that was cast in the shadows.

The coach was anxious to get home and celebrate with his family. We shared one final hug, and he told me that he would see me later that evening at the Schmitt's (Matt Schmitt's post-game get-together). As Coach pulled out of the parking lot, I looked back at my high school. My feelings were hard to discern, but great loneliness enveloped me. I didn't want to leave. I wanted the feeling of this day in victory to last longer.

The 1985 football Trojans of Lyman Hall High School had emerged as if from a darkened land, a gallant vanguard of losing seasons past, having survived the efforts of people and environs to end the sport or at the very least to marginalize the sport. For the men who once donned the blue & white from the earliest days of the "Orangemen" forward, a cut of the victory now found a resting place in their hearts.

ONE MORE POIGNANT MOMENT

As I stood there on the edge of the parking lot where the light post illuminated the locker room door, now locked for the weekend, there was a serene silence. For me, the intensity of the last four months came to an abrupt halt. As with every night sitting alone in that little room behind my garage, there was a great loneliness. Each night I would reach into my heart for the memory of someone so very special to me.

Now, standing by my car with the lights of the school turned dark and the emptiness of the parking lot, except for my car and one other, I felt one of the most alone feelings I had ever experienced. The exhilaration of the State Championship game was gone now, and all I could feel was the void left by a dream now realized, gone by without the semblance of a sustained feeling. I had experienced similar moments in my life, but this was so eerily solitary. I felt I had no place to go, no location to rekindle the joys of today.

From out of the darkness, a perfect voice pierced the blanket of silence. "Stephen," ... softly called out the voice. At first, I saw no one, and then with the most pristine smile, this voice that had captured the essence of my heart so many years ago summoned my attention again ..." Stephen?".

Through the shadow, she was there. Her hair glimmered against the beam of floodlighting from the parking lot stanchions. Her velvet eyes found mine then as they did now, and my emotions, already drained, were undone with the love of past days and decades pouring over me. How perfect she was to me and always will be.

Walking but a few yards to me out of the darkness, all at once, I was standing alone with the most beautiful girl I had ever seen. At first, I could not speak. Almost in a whisper, she told me she had heard the game on the radio, and she had to seek me out. I could not take my eyes from her as tears now dripped on my cheeks. With the gentleness of a summer breeze at dusk, she took me in her arms, expressing that she was proud of me. If the day had not had enough passion and emotion, December 7, 1985, had now overflowed its banks.

She stood with me as we held each other. No words seemed worthy of the voice except "I love you" that we traded in sound and a single kiss.

She left almost as quickly as she appeared, entering her car and driving away.

God had brought her to me that night. She changed the direction of my life way back in 1974, and now, she changed forever how I looked at December 7, 1985. I needed no game ball or other form of recognition to recall this day. She was all the honor any man could receive and not deserve.

Epilogue

Having served as the chairman of the Lyman Hall High School Hall of Fame for almost 40 years, I have had the privilege of meeting hundreds of alumni and former coaches that together brought the school many victories and great honors.

Having coached football at Lyman Hall High School longer than any assistant coach in any sport, I have a deep appreciation for the arrangement of circumstances and the necessary individual athletic talent required to win consistently.

Few, if any, former LHHS football players were blessed to stand with a team that had achieved a championship, but the 1985 team was of such fabric of humility and style that every young man who ever pulled on the Lyman Hall jersey, whether those of the Orangemen or Trojans, owned a little piece of the 1985 State Title.

Only ONE LHHS team has ever won a state football championship, and should a LHHS team ever approach a state title again; I hope they will not have to face the obstacles that the 1985 team met and were required to overcome.

That team of two dozen young men faced tremendous challenges before 1985 and during the 1985 season. They were bonded "together" by forces unknown by most student-athletes who aspire to team greatness. Their goal of continuous improvement drove them to practice each day with a unity of purpose. They moved from victory to victory, never looking beyond the next snap of the football against any opponent.

As evidenced in this book, they were of high intelligence and character, refraining from falling victim to the hyperbole and nonsense that most high school athletic teams do so willingly embrace. They enjoyed a private joke, laughed at themselves, and loved every fellow member of the team.

Their team meetings were laboratories for football study and opponent preparation. They did not seek self-aggrandizement despite the many records that they individually and collectively set and shattered.

The 1985 Lyman Hall Football team was to be loved, not because they won, rather because they dared to make a miracle come true. They didn't talk about wins or championships. It would have embarrassed them.

As adults, loving parents, professionals, and contributing citizens, they are scattered across the country. Some have died, and the 1985 football team will never be physically all "together" again. The spirit of the 1985 football team will always be with those who love Wallingford and Lyman Hall High School.

This book is a methodical walk through every era, especially concerning basketball as the backdrop with the exploits of those that shall never be equaled. In the reading of those times long past, culminating with the 1985 State Class M football championship, let us remember them all ... from Frauham, to Inguaggiato, to Combs, to Bercier, to Potter, to Horowitz, to Chrisman, to Stupakevich, to Angelone, to Nesti, and every member of the 1985 State Championship team.

Let us remember them ... BEFORE THE PICTURE FADES!

APPENDIX A

1985
LYMAN HALL HIGH SCHOOL
Football Roster

No.	Name	Height	Weight	Year
4	Scott Audet	5-9	150	junior
5	Todd Barket	6-1	170	senior
7	Alfred Ferreira	5-8	150	sophomore
15	Glenn Root	6-2	180	junior
16	Sean Sheehan	5-6	155	sophomore
21	Robert Vasquez	5-9	160	freshman
23	Anthony Angueira	5-8	165	junior
24	Edward Charbonneau	6-0	175	junior
33	Vincent Poggio	5-11	165	senior
35	Mathew Schmitt	5-9	170	senior
40	Randy Pelletier	6-0	185	junior
50	Gregory Myerson	6-3	240	senior
51	William Sheridan	6-1	200	senior
53	David Klaverkamp	6-2	215	senior
54	Ralph Riley	6-3	240	senior
55	William Goldstein	5-11	220	junior
56	Gaetano Russo	5-10	180	senior

58	Kevin Distante	5-9	180	junior
59	Steven May	5-8	180	senior
61	David Canny	5-11	170	freshman
66	William Corazzini	5-6	170	junior
67	Mark Wollen	5-11	185	sophomore
71	Robert Lampo	5-10	220	senior
76	Kenneth Priest	6-0	205	sophomore
77	Raymond Cormier	5-11	230	senior
85	Brett Baron	6-0	190	sophomore
86	James Hannah	6-1	170	junior
88	Thomas Berube	6-1	175	junior

Phil Ottochian, Head Coach
Stephen W. Hoag, Defensive Coordinator
Robert Corazzini, Line Coach
Scott Ottochian, Defensive End/Receiver Coach
John Gawlak, Freshmen Coach
John Wallace, Freshman Coach

APPENDIX B

STINGING STATE RANKINGS

Immediately following the title game, the questions swirled regarding Lyman Hall's worthiness to ranked No.1 in the Final Poll. Here are the three major arguments, espoused by sportswriters and some state coaches who cared to chime into the discourse:

1. Since the polls were taken for the first time, a team (Lyman Hall) had defeated three teams who would figure in the TOP 10, Sheehan, Derby, and Middletown.

1. The total wins of Lyman Hall opponents were 68. The total wins of Hillhouse opponents were 30.

1. Hillhouse played two weak out-of-state teams on their schedule and did not defeat a ranked opponent.

Yes, Hillhouse turned out to be the only undefeated team of 1985, but that alone did not warrant them being voted No.1. The facts are the facts and their record against a schedule full of marginal teams, including two out-of-state teams, should not have earned them the No.1 ranking.

The 1985 Lyman Hall Trojans were No.2 in the Final State Polls in Connecticut and the No. 6th Ranked team in New England.

TOM YANTZ OF THE HARTFORD COURANT

"Lyman Hall of Wallingford should be the No.1 scholastic football team in Connecticut. The Trojans defeated the Class S champion Derby and Class SS champion Sheehan teams during the regular season and Middletown for the Class M title. And beating Middletown, the No. 1 team before the class finals should have sealed the No. 1 decision for Lyman Hall".

JEFF OTTERBEIN OF THE HARTFORD COURANT

"The slight that was accorded to Lyman Hall has two probable sources. First, the Academics (Hillhouse) finished with an undefeated record and that had to impress 10 coaches who gave them first-place votes in The Courant's final poll. Two coaches voted for Lyman Hall. Second and more relevant to the Jackson Newspapers, Hillhouse was a sentimental favorite. There is a strong downstate flavor to this voting, making New Haven-based Hillhouse an emotional preference. The lessons are clear. Polls make for good conversation, but not much else. And, as The Courant voting reminds us, coaches are just as unbalanced and subjective in their choices as the media. None of us has a monopoly on making mistakes".

APPENDIX C

STATISTICS of THE MIDDLETOWN Game

POGGIO & SCHMITT

The New Haven Register had a team of writers at the game, and unlike most of the newspapers, their writers interviewed our players. Like many people, especially Middletown's team, the writers were all surprised that Lyman Hall could run the ball so efficiently against the speed-driven Dragon defense.

Our tailback, Vinnie Poggio, was the object of their attention, running for 150 yards on 21 carries. However, fullback Matt Schmitt also ran for 100 yards with 137 yards on 23 carries. After the game, Matt was interview by John Antonini of the Register. Matt was asked why the Trojans ran so well against the Blue Dragons as they had NOT given up a hundred-yard rusher day in two seasons.

Matt stated, "I don't know why we ran so well against them. I guess they got faked out. I'd be running and see a big hole; then I would bounce outside. That counterplay (that set up the first touchdown) was put in just a few days ago".

KUDOS FOR RUSSO

An interesting quote from Coach Skubel was, "They were blitzing and anticipating our snap count."

In 2006 I talked with Coach Skubel, and he expanded on this quote that I entered in my chronicle of Friday, October

27, 2006. <u>Coach Skubel</u> told me, "We were trying to draw you (LHHS) offsides with our snap count.

Your linebacker, that number 56 (Guy Russo) he didn't flinch. He seemed to know every snap count, and he kept beating us on the blitz before some of our men could get out of their stances. He seemed to be in on every tackle".

DATA EXTRACT

TEAM STATS:
Middletown Turnovers: 5
Lyman Hall Turnovers: 0

MIDDLETOWN SEASON vs. TITLE GAME

Middletown regular-season average yards rushing a game: 287
Middletown yards rushing against LHHS: 13
Middletown regular-season completion percentage: 50%
Middletown pass completion percentage against LHHS: 35%
Middletown fullback season average yards per game: 107 yards
Middletown Fullback yards versus LHHS: 53 yards

APPENDIX D

1985
END OF SEASON
STATISTICS

Rushing

Name	carries	yards	TD's	av. yds. car.
Poggio	255	1653	16	6.482
Schmitt	161	891	11	5.534
Barket	67	264	5	3.940
Charbonneau	31	151	1	4.870
Myerson	10	54	0	5.400
Root	5	12	2	2.400
Sheehan	6	9	0	1.500
Engelhardt	4	4	0	1.000
Vasquez	2	3	0	2.000
Pelletier	1	4	0	4.000

Passing

Name	atts	comp	yards	TD	int
Barket	116	664	640	8	6
Poggio	1	0	0	0	1

Receiving

Name	recep	yards	TD
Schmitt	20	203	0
Pelletier	16	203	7
Ferreira	10	138	1
Poggio	5	35	0
Riley	3	12	0
Audet	3	16	0
Root	2	18	0
Myerson	2	9	0
Charbonneau	2	6	0

1985 INDIVIDUAL DEFENSIVE STATISTICS

Name	solo	1st hit	assists	Total	TBL	yds	sacks	yds	int
Russo	25	48	68	141	36	-161	20	-109	1
Riley	22	24	39	85	21	-122	14	-84	0
Myerson	30	23	27	80	17	-96	10	-69	1
Pelletier	7	31	42	80	10	-47	6.5	-39	4
Schmitt	24	19	32	75	19.5	-105	8.5	-58	1
Klaverkamp	8	32	33	73	6.5	-26	3.5	-18	0
Charbonneau	16	23	31	70	17.5	-103	9.5	-63	0
Barket	20	13	24	57	2	-13	1	-8	4
Goldstein	4	20	32	56	4.5	-19	2	-9	0
Audet	10	13	15	38					3
Ferreira	8	7	22	37	4	-22	2	-13	1
Poggio	9	9	10	28					4
Corazzini	0	5	14	19					
Sheehan	3	3	9	15	2	-13	1	-7	
May	1	3	9	13					
Distanti	2	4	4	10	1	-5	1	-5	
Priest	1	3	2	6					
Wollen	0	2	3	5					
Sheridan	0	0	3	3					
Root	0	0	2	2					

Cormier	0	0	1	1
Lampo	0	0	1	1
Canny	0	0	1	1
Padilla	0	0	1	1

TEAM SACKS: 79
Yards lost sacks: 482
Sacks per game: 6.58

Leading Sack Leaders:
Guy Russo 20 sacks
Ralph Riley 14 sacks
Greg Myerson 10 sacks
Ed Charbonneau 9.5 sacks
Matt Schmitt 8.5 sacks
Randy Pelletier 6.5 sacks
Dave Klaverkamp 3.5 sacks
Goldstein 2 sacks

Team Tackles for Minus Yards:
Team tackles for minus yardage: 141
Team yards lost from caught behind the line tackles: 732
Average per game tackles for minus yardage: 11.75

Team Turnovers: 49
32 fumbles recovered
17 interceptions
LHHS offensive turnovers: 22

ALL-HOUSATONIC LEAGUE HONORS
Ralph Riley, First Team-Offense, Tackle
Gregory Myerson, First Team-Offense, Guard
Vincent Poggio, First Team-Offense, Running Back
Mathew Schmitt, First Team-Defense, Defensive Back
Todd Barket, Second Team-Offense, Quarterback
David Klaverkamp, Second Team-Defense, Defensive Tackle
Guy Russo, Second Team Defense, Linebacker
Bill Goldstein, Honorable Mention, Defensive Tackle
Gregory Myerson, Honorable Mention, Defensive End

ALL-STATE HONORS

Gregory Myerson, First Team-Defense
  New Haven Register, Defensive End
Gregory Myerson, Honorable Mention-Offense
  New Haven Register, Guard
Vincent Poggio, Second Team-Offense
  Hartford Courant-Coaches All-State, Running Back
Vincent Poggio, First Team-Offense
New Haven Register, Running Back
Ralph Riley, First Team-Offense,
  Hartford Courant-Coaches All-State, Tackle
Ralph Riley, First Team-Offense,
  New Haven Register All-State, Tackle

ALL-AMERICAN HONORS

Gregory Myerson, Honorable Mention, USA Today-Defensive End
Vincent Poggio, Honorable Mention, USA Today-Running Back

AUTHOR PAGE

An innovative, passionate educator, football coach, and mentor, Dr. Hoag was a Connecticut State Department of Education member for over 35 years. An accomplished speaker, he has entertained and thrilled audiences throughout his lifetime with his anecdotes and philosophy on teaching, parenthood, athletic coaching, and leadership. Dr. Hoag has received state and national recognition for teaching, coaching, education assessment, and community service. Of the many awards, Dr. Hoag was the recipient of the national 2008 C. Thomas Olivio Award, presented to one person annually for leadership and creativity in student assessment by the National Occupational Competency Testing Institute. In 2013 Dr. Hoag was honored with the Silver Eagle Award of the Connecticut Council of Deliberation for "sterling service to uplift humanity"; and the 2016 Outstanding Community Service Award by the Urban League of Greater Hartford. Dr. Hoag created and directed the groundbreaking Developing Tomorrow's Professionals (DTP)

program for Black and Hispanic young men. Stephen Hoag is the author of "A Son's Handbook, Bringing Up Mom with Alzheimer's/Dementia," a stirring personal account of his ten years caring for his mother with this dreaded disease. In 2018, Dr. Hoag's romantic novel, "Whisper of a Kiss," was released with the emotional moving book "Vows" in 2020, winning acclaim for its inspirational acumen and encouraging approach to understanding one person's impact on another.